The Essence of Reality

A Defense of Philosophical Sufism

Letter from the General Editor

The Library of Arabic Literature makes available Arabic editions and English translations of significant works of Arabic literature, with an emphasis on the seventh to nineteenth centuries. The Library of Arabic Literature thus includes texts from the pre-Islamic era to the cusp of the modern period, and encompasses a wide range of genres, including poetry, poetics, fiction, religion, philosophy, law, science, travel writing, history, and historiography.

Books in the series are edited and translated by internationally recognized scholars. They are published as hardcovers in parallel-text format with Arabic and English on facing pages, as English-only paperbacks, and as downloadable Arabic editions. For some texts, the series also publishes separate scholarly editions with full critical apparatus.

The Library encourages scholars to produce authoritative Arabic editions, accompanied by modern, lucid English translations, with the ultimate goal of introducing Arabic's rich literary heritage to a general audience of readers as well as to scholars and students.

The publications of the Library of Arabic Literature are generously supported by Tamkeen under the NYU Abu Dhabi Research Institute Award G1003 and are published by NYU Press.

Philip F. Kennedy
General Editor, Library of Arabic Literature

زبدة الحقائق

عين القضاة

LIBRARY OF
المكتبة
ARABIC
العربية
LITERATURE

The Essence of Reality

A Defense of Philosophical Sufism

ʿAyn al-Quḍāt

Edited and translated by
Mohammed Rustom

Volume editor
Bilal Orfali

NEW YORK UNIVERSITY PRESS
New York

NEW YORK UNIVERSITY PRESS
New York

Library of Congress Cataloging-in-Publication Data

Names: ʿAyn al-Quḍāh al-Hamadhānī, ʿAbd Allāh ibn Muḥammad, -1131, author. | Rustom, Mohammed, editor, translator. | ʿAyn al-Quḍāh al-Hamadhānī, ʿAbd Allāh ibn Muḥammad, -1131. Zubdat al-ḥaqāʾiq.
Title: The essence of reality : a defense of philosophical Sufism = Zubdat al-ḥaqāʾiq / ʿAyn al-Quḍāt ; edited and translated by Mohammed Rustom.
Other titles: Zubdat al-ḥaqāʾiq. English | Zubdat al-ḥaqāʾiq
Description: New York : New York University Press, 2022. | Includes bibliographical references and index. | In English and Arabic; translated from Arabic. | Summary: "The Essence of Reality consists of one hundred brief chapters interspersed with Qurʾanic verses, prophetic sayings, Sufi maxims, and poetry. The book takes readers on a philosophical journey, with expositions of questions including the problem of the eternity of the world; the nature of God's essence and attributes; the concepts of "before" and "after"; and the soul's relationship to the body"-- Provided by publisher.
Identifiers: LCCN 2021056520 | ISBN 9781479816590 (cloth) | ISBN 9781479816613 (ebook) | ISBN 9781479816620 (ebook)
Subjects: LCSH: Sufism--Early works to 1800. | God (Islam)--Early works to 1800.
Classification: LCC BP188.9 .A92513 2022 | DDC 297.401--dc23/eng/20211208
LC record available at https://lccn.loc.gov/2021056520

New York University Press books are printed on acid-free paper, and their binding materials are chosen for strength and durability.

Series design by Titus Nemeth.

Typeset in Tasmeem, using DecoType Naskh and Emiri.

Typesetting and digitization by Stuart Brown.

Manufactured in the United States of America
c10 9 8 7 6 5 4 3 2 1

Table of Contents

In memory of Richard Blackburn, my first Arabic teacher

Acknowledgments

Working on and publishing a bilingual edition of *The Essence of Reality* has long been a dream of mine. This dream is now actualized thanks to several fellowships administered by the Library of Arabic Literature (LAL) and Humanities Research Fellowship programs at the New York University Abu Dhabi Institute, where I had the good fortune of spending several years immersed in ʿAyn al-Quḍāt's writings. No less important was the support of many fine colleagues, particularly Philip Kennedy, James Montgomery, Shawkat Toorawa, Bilal Orfali, Chip Rossetti, Lucie Taylor, Amani Alzoubi, Reindert Falkenburg, Martin Klimke, Taneli Kukkonen, Alexandra Sandu, and Raya Lakova.

A special note of thanks goes to this volume's project editor, my dear friend Bilal Orfali, who assisted me in innumerable ways. I am also grateful to LAL's external reviewers for their comments on my translation, as well as LAL's executive reviewer, who helped loosen it up in masterful fashion.

William Chittick generously shared his unparalleled knowledge of Sufi texts with me, and important references and essential resources were provided by Shuaib Ally, Hassan Arif, Amir Hossein Asghari, Ahab Bdaiwi, Youssef Berrada, Jeremy Farrell, Muhammad Faruque, Hany Ibrahim, Salimeh Maghsoudlou, Abdel Baki Meftah, Maurice Pomerantz, Reza Pourjavady, Joel Richmond, and Ayman Shihadeh. Yousef Casewit, Muhammad Faruque, and Cyrus Zargar made useful comments and suggestions on early drafts of the translation, as did Stuart Brown and Keith Miller on the entire volume.

My wife, Nosheen, and our children, Isa, Suhayla, and Sophia, always fondly smile when I speak about ʿAyn al-Quḍāt. They have no doubt benefited from his timely teachings as much as I have, if not more. They have always made sacrifices for my research, but this time they did so amid a pandemic, a global move, and a makeshift homeschooling endeavor.

Reflecting on my journey in the world of Arabic literature, I vividly recall my first day of undergraduate studies at the University of Toronto. As a trepid teenager, I asked the erudite professor of Arabic Richard Blackburn a rather naïve question after he had finished his first Introduction to Arabic lesson: "Sir, if I complete this course, will I be able to read the Qur'an *with understanding*?" He answered in the affirmative, and I never looked back. Professor

Blackburn opened up the world of Arabic (and English!) grammar to me, and I will forever be in his debt. With profound gratitude, this book is dedicated to his memory.

Introduction

The *Zubdat al-ḥaqāʾiq*, or *The Essence of Reality*, was dictated over the course of three days in 1120 by a twenty-four-year-old premodern scholar. This edition and translation was completed over the course of three years in 2020 by a contemporary scholar after twenty-four years of academic preparation. The text, like its author, is remarkable for many reasons—it is in all likelihood the earliest philosophical exposition of mysticism in the Islamic intellectual tradition, and was thus quite influential upon the developed forms of classical Islamic philosophy (*falsafah*) and philosophical mysticism (*ḥikmah*).

ʿAyn al-Quḍāt: Life and Work

Muḥammad ibn Abī Bakr was the given name of the mystic philosopher and jurist known as ʿAyn al-Quḍāt ("the most eminent judge"). He was born into a scholarly family in 490/1097 in Hamadān in western Iran. The young ʿAyn al-Quḍāt was distinctively precocious, particularly in the Islamic intellectual sciences, Shāfiʿī law, mathematics, and Arabic literature. As a teenager, he became popular in both literary and philosophical-theological circles, and was eventually appointed as the main judge of Hamadān, perhaps in his late teens.[1]

ʿAyn al-Quḍāt was a master of both Arabic and his native Persian, and works of his in both languages have survived. The earliest of these writings is an Arabic poem of one thousand lines written at the age of sixteen under the title *Nuzhat al-ʿushshāq wa-nuhzat al-mushtāq* (*The Lovers' Excursion and the Beloved's Chance*).[2] This work, unlike his other books, is concerned with human love and beauty, and its author would later indicate that this excursion of his was an effective bridge to divine love, the main focus of his mystical theology. But before diving into the ocean of divine love, ʿAyn al-Quḍāt had to first walk along its shores, which is where he would place the sciences of philosophy and rational theology (*kalām*).

ʿAyn al-Quḍāt had mastered rational theology by the time he was twenty-one. We know this because he wrote a book in the discipline, although it has not survived. Thankfully, the one book that has survived, and that clearly demonstrates his high level of proficiency in the Islamic rational sciences, is the *Essence*. This is not an ordinary work of philosophy or theology. In fact, according to

ʿAyn al-Quḍāt's testimony in the *Essence* itself, it represents the culmination of his immersion in, and even departure from, these modes of knowledge. As already stated, he dictated this work in 514/1120 at the age of twenty-four, and in a matter of three days. We can confidently assert the length of time it took him to complete it, not on account of what he says in the *Essence* (where he remarks he had finished the work in a "few" days), but on the basis of another text in which he specifies that these few days were in fact "two or three."[3]

ʿAyn al-Quḍāt would also attribute the rapid completion and intellectual and spiritual achievement of this title to a factor that is often overlooked in the secondary literature—namely, its having been written in the presence of one of his earliest spiritual teachers, the great master Barakah Hamadānī (d. 520/1126). ʿAyn al-Quḍāt had a particularly strong attachment to Shaykh Barakah, and extolled his virtues and spiritual feats in his writings.[4]

Before this master's influence upon the composition of the *Essence*, two other important factors led ʿAyn al-Quḍāt to take up the pen, both of which he recounts in the *Essence*. The first was a crisis of certainty he encountered in 506/1112 at the age of sixteen, as had the great Abū Ḥāmid al-Ghazālī, who had passed away the year before (505/1111). A careful study of al-Ghazālī's writings over the course of nearly four years helped ʿAyn al-Quḍāt to recover from this crisis and regain his spiritual bearings.

Then came ʿAyn al-Quḍāt's meeting at the age of twenty-three with another al-Ghazālī—that is, Shaykh Aḥmad (d. 520/1126), the younger brother of Abū Ḥāmid.[5] Aḥmad al-Ghazālī was a well-known and highly revered spiritual master in Persian Sufi circles. It was during one of his visits to Hamadān that ʿAyn al-Quḍāt formally became his disciple. According to the account in the *Essence* of their time together, this discipleship was the main catalyst for ʿAyn al-Quḍāt's spiritual awakening. When ʿAyn al-Quḍāt began to dictate the *Essence*, therefore, he was already intellectually and spiritually accomplished and wanted to share the fruits of his spiritual knowledge with his audience, but in a manner that would be both clear and intelligible.

Six years after ʿAyn al-Quḍāt completed the *Essence*, Aḥmad al-Ghazālī passed away and appointed him as his spiritual successor. Thus, alongside his existing role as a teacher of the Islamic sciences who would give multiple public lessons in Hamadān each day,[6] ʿAyn al-Quḍāt now had the added responsibility of being a spiritual guide. His function as a Sufi master and visionary extraordinaire comes out best in his magnum opus in Persian, the *Tamhīdāt* (*Paving the Path*), which was completed in 521/1127.

Paving the Path is a unique text in the history of Sufism and Islamic philosophy.[7] Its style impresses itself immediately upon the reader and defies classification not only because of the extemporaneous nature of the prose and the lofty Persian verse interspersed throughout the work, but because it tackles a variety of issues in metaphysics, aesthetics, epistemology, cosmology, theology, psychology, love theory, Satanology, scriptural hermeneutics, and Hadith commentary from multiple vantage points and perspectives. Reading this work is akin to walking in a maze that constantly refigures itself even as one tries to escape. The best one can do is to enjoy the exhilarating journey and let the maze and its perpetual reconfigurations become one's guides. This is not to say that there is no logical structure to *Paving the Path*. Indeed there is, but it only reveals itself after one comes to terms with its author's genius and allows him to say what he wants to say in the way that he wants to say it.

Reading *Paving the Path* is a rewarding experience, which explains why it was so well received in Persianate Sufism, particularly in Indian Sufi circles well into the eleventh/seventeenth century.[8] In many ways, *Paving the Path* takes the insights that we find in the *Essence* and brings them to an entirely new level. It is grounded in the worldview of the *Essence* but manages to apply its teachings largely in the language of myth, symbolism, love, and beauty.

Since many of ʿAyn al-Quḍāt's disciples were not only aspiring scholars but also dignitaries and state officials who were peripatetic in western Iran, one way in which he offered guidance to them was through written correspondence, as his own master had done with him.[9] We are fortunate in that these letters by ʿAyn al-Quḍāt, which date from 520/1126 to 525/1131, are extant under the Persian title *Nāmah-hā* (*Letters*).[10]

Written almost entirely in Persian, this extensive collection of letters reveals ʿAyn al-Quḍāt in all his glory—as a spiritual advisor, philosopher, theologian, legal scholar, autobiographer, love theorist, hagiologist, historian, Qur'anic exegete, and master stylist of Persian prose writing. The *Letters* also reveal a dimension of their author's personality that cannot be found in any of his other writings but that is especially relevant to his biography: ʿAyn al-Quḍāt as a vociferous critic of the Seljuq government and its corrupt financial practices, which oppressed the poor and the less fortunate.

It had been a widely held belief that ʿAyn al-Quḍāt was put to death by the Seljuqs on account of his "unorthodox" views, such as his robust vindication of the Devil as a fallen lover of God.[11] His execution is also cited by some as being linked to his supposed claim to be God in some fashion, the same accusation leveled against al-Ḥallāj (d. 309/922), whom he deeply admired. Thanks to recent scholarship, we now know the precise reasons behind ʿAyn al-Quḍāt's execution.[12] For the most part,[13] they had to do with certain statements he made—not pertaining to religious dogma, but to the Seljuqs. These criticisms are enshrined in the *Letters*, and were also voiced by ʿAyn al-Quḍāt from his pulpit in Hamadān, an office of high visibility.

The *Letters* reveal that ʿAyn al-Quḍāt was particularly concerned with social justice and the feeding of the needy. Thus, he castigated a number of his own students who were employees of the corrupt Seljuq state, as well as every other Seljuq, including Sultan Maḥmūd II (d. 525/1131).[14] The gist of ʿAyn al-Quḍāt's argument was that service at the court of unjust rulers was incompatible with a religious and spiritual life.

An opportunity to execute ʿAyn al-Quḍāt presented itself to the ruthless Seljuq vizier Qawwām al-Dīn Abū l-Qāsim Dargazīnī (d. 527/1133) when he entered into a feud with one of ʿAyn al-Quḍāt's students who worked for the Seljuqs. Dargazīnī reasoned that by accusing ʿAyn al-Quḍāt of heresy, he would be ridding the Seljuqs of their problem. He would also be ridding himself of his problem, since ʿAyn al-Quḍāt's death meant that his student, an enemy of Dargazīnī, would be left without his influential supporter.[15]

The charge of heresy, made in 522/1128, had to do with some of his positions in the *Essence*. One of these is ʿAyn al-Quḍāt's reference to God as the "source" (*maṣdar*) of existence. The Seljuqs were bitter ideological enemies of the Ismailis, and, at first blush, speaking of God as the source of existence would seem to imply acquiescence to the Ismaili doctrine that God is beyond being.[16] The other view that is cited from the *Essence* is ʿAyn al-Quḍāt's alleged belief that the Friends of God (*awliyāʾ*) are higher than the Prophets sent by God.

The evidence that the charge of heresy against ʿAyn al-Quḍāt was put together opportunistically lies in the fact that it was only statements in the *Essence* that were used to label him a heretic. However, the text of the *Essence* shows these charges to be problematic, both because ʿAyn al-Quḍāt's actual views are to the contrary and because many of them are derived from well-established theological positions that were defended by the likes of al-Ghazālī, who enjoyed the patronage of the Seljuqs. This is in fact a point that ʿAyn al-Quḍāt made when the Seljuqs presented him with an "opportunity" to defend himself. He did so in a small Arabic treatise entitled *Shakwā l-gharīb* (*The Exile's Complaint*), which he wrote while imprisoned in Baghdad in 523/1129.[17] *The Exile's Complaint* is the only contemporaneous Arabic record that documents the accusations against ʿAyn al-Quḍāt; by the same token, it is the only text we have that directly addresses these accusations.

The Seljuqs only allowed ʿAyn al-Quḍāt to write *The Exile's Complaint* because of the potential public backlash if the author, beloved to so many, was put to death without having had the chance to defend himself. And it is clear from the somber tone of this text that ʿAyn al-Quḍāt saw through this Seljuq smokescreen.

At the order of Sultan Maḥmūd II, ʿAyn al-Quḍāt was publicly executed in Hamadān in 525/1131 at the age of thirty-five. A shrine was erected in his honor by as late as the eighth/fourteenth century, but it did not survive the vicissitudes of time. In today's Hamadān, ʿAyn al-Quḍāt is regarded as a regional icon, and there are streets, buildings, and a cultural center dedicated to his name.[18]

The Essence of Reality in Context

Unlike the Seljuqs, who had used the *Essence* to undermine its author and eventually present a case for his unjust execution, the later Islamic intellectual tradition welcomed it with open arms. The *Essence* traveled from Hamadān to Marāghah, which is some 280 miles northwest of Hamadān, in a relatively short period of time. We know this because the *Essence* is one of the texts that have been preserved in what is known as the Marāghah Codex, a document that dates to 596/1199 or 597/1200, some eighty years after the composition of the *Essence*. The Marāghah Codex formed the standard teaching curriculum of the Madrasah Mujāhidiyyah, an important center of learning that operated in Marāghah well into the seventh/thirteenth century.[19]

The Marāghah Codex bears witness to a unique moment in the historical transmission and teaching of Islamic philosophy, philosophical theology, and philosophical mysticism in western Iran. Along with the *Essence*, it includes major works in these disciplines by such illustrious authors as al-Fārābī (d. 339/950), Avicenna (d. 428/1037), al-Ghazālī, and ʿUmar ibn Sahlān al-Sāwī (d. after 537/1143). This reading list gives us considerable insight into how the worldview of Sufi metaphysics, in which rational discourse is wedded to mystical insight and higher modes of nondiscursive knowledge, was disseminated at the Mujāhidiyyah in the sixth/twelfth century. At the same time, its presence gives us a unique window into how texts like the *Essence* would have been received and naturalized into the post-Avicennan Islamic intellectual tradition. Some of the most important figures in this later phase of Islamic thought had studied at the Madrasah Mujāhidiyyah and would have read the *Essence*. Among them were Shihāb al-Dīn al-Suhrawardī (d. 587/1191) and Fakhr al-Dīn al-Rāzī (d. 606/1210).

We also know that, under the auspices of Hülegü Khan in Marāghah, the celebrated philosopher and scientist Naṣīr al-Dīn al-Ṭūsī (d. 672/1274) translated the *Essence* into Persian, but the translation is no longer extant.[20] The *Essence* was still being read six centuries later. This is evidenced by its use in a treatise in defense of philosophical Sufism by Faḍl-i Ḥaqq Khayrābādī (d. 1277/1861), an important thinker who witnessed the rise of the British Raj.[21] Outside of Persianate intellectual and spiritual circles, the *Essence* was also popular in what were predominantly Arabic zones of the Muslim world. This is particularly evident in the work of the great Arab theologian and mystic ʿAbd al-Ghanī al-Nābulusī (d. 1143/1731), who praises the book's ability to locate the "problem" of reason when one is in search of God.[22] Indeed, the *Essence* is likely the first fully developed, mystically informed rational case concerning the limitations of the intellect in the Islamic tradition, and in this regard it goes far beyond works like al-Ghazālī's *Mishkāt al-anwār* (*The Niche of Lights*).[23]

But the *Essence* is not simply an argument against the use of the intellect, nor is it anti-rational. As we have seen, ʿAyn al-Quḍāt was well trained in rational theology and did not see it as an impediment in the search for knowledge. It only became problematic for him when he was unable to unlock the mystery of existence through its discursive methods. Having discovered a different mode of knowing that better accords with the nondiscursive nature of these mysteries, ʿAyn al-Quḍāt sought to share these insights in the *Essence*. At the same time, he tackles a variety of problems that seem out of place in a work on mysticism. There is, for example, an extended presentation of the problem of causality and of the nature of God's priority before the world. How these discussions lend support to ʿAyn al-Quḍāt's arguments is not always clear at first, but as one moves through the text the author's intentions and the lines of influence on his own thinking become more and more apparent.

This later dimension of ʿAyn al-Quḍāt's worldview has been brought out particularly well by Salimeh Maghsoudlou in her study of ʿAyn al-Quḍāt's philosophical and theological doctrines.[24] For example, she shows how, in the final analysis, ʿAyn al-Quḍāt forged his own way between the two intellectual giants to whose views he was heir and to whom he was in many ways responding: Avicenna and al-Ghazālī. Yet, as ʿAyn al-Quḍāt makes abundantly clear, he was not trying to chart a new philosophical way, much less a novel method for philosophical theology. He employed these methods insofar as they allowed him to show his readers their utility and also their limitations. By clearing the ground like this on a number of fronts, ʿAyn al-Quḍāt was then able to put forward some of his main theses.

His entire perspective in the book is premised on his own lived experience of God, which is why he intersperses accounts of his "spiritual experiences" throughout. The key factor to understanding what are higher modes of knowing is not more rational argumentation that demonstrates the presence of this knowledge. Rather, it is a straightforward kind of knowing akin to our affective and sensory experiences, particularly that of taste. This is why, following al-Ghazālī,[25] ʿAyn al-Quḍāt places throughout the *Essence* a premium on the notion of tasting (*dhawq*).[26] Moving beyond the confines of rational thought and cognitive modes of knowledge, tasting is the exclusive claim of the recognizer (*ʿārif*)—namely, the person who recognizes God in all things, and especially within his own soul. Tasting breaks down the barrier between subject and object, and in fact points the way to the unity between them. After all, when we taste a thing we know something about it that is much more real and palpable than if we were to try to discursively wrap our minds around it, describe it, and trap it in some kind of conceptual grid.

ʿAyn al-Quḍāt states that a number of the doctrines he discusses in the *Essence* are themselves the result of tasting and can best be understood through this enhanced epistemic mode. Chief among these is the vision he attempts to communicate in which the cosmos is in a perpetual state of renewal (*tajdīd al-khalq*). This position is informed by ʿAyn al-Quḍāt's view, perfectly in line with al-Ghazālī before him and the likes of Ibn al-ʿArabī (d. 638/1240) after him, to the effect that there is no reality but the divine reality, and hence that there is nothing in existence but God.[27] For the recognizer, all things are therefore like evanescent images in the mirror of existence. Such a view takes ʿAyn al-Quḍāt to a unique exposition of what he calls "withness" (*maʿiyyah*), by which he seeks to explain how God is "with" His creatures but they are in no wise "with" Him. The "borrowed" nature of our individual existence is fully felt by someone who can access this reality, which, again, can only be obtained by way of tasting.

ʿAyn al-Quḍāt's arguments are supported by many interesting examples, which seek to highlight the fact that we cannot entirely rely on our senses or even our intelligence to know the true nature of things. In the manner of al-Ghazālī, he explains how the planets in the sky look like little gold coins, or how the sun looks like a little plate, whereas in truth they are much larger than meets the eye. This allows ʿAyn al-Quḍāt to drive home an essential teaching: our discursive reasoning is helpful for knowing what can be known—that is, for knowing things that fall within its purview and remit. But when it comes to knowing God, the knowledge in question is quite deceptive. We can, after all, have knowledge *of* something, but that does not mean we understand it, or that we know its true nature. This is also a point that Ibn al-ʿArabī sought to drive home in his famous letter to Fakhr al-Dīn al-Rāzī, which has some parallels with cognate points in the *Essence*: there is a fundamental difference between knowledge *of* God's existence and actually knowing God.[28]

If ʿAyn al-Quḍāt were alive today, he would undoubtedly have many interesting examples to draw on from the physical world and our sensory and rational perception of it. For example, in contemporary physics we know that the behavior of the constituent stuff of the physical universe is incredibly diverse, dynamic, and, at a subatomic level, even unpredictable. Our senses and indeed our reason tell us, for instance, that light is a particular kind of thing and that it behaves in a specific way. But at the quantum level, light shows itself to have a dual nature—that of a wave and that of a particle.[29]

Discursive knowledge, the linchpin of rational theology and philosophy, has a hard time squaring this kind of a circle because it is solely concerned with either/or propositions, and not with this/that propositions. For ʿAyn al-Quḍāt, the latter are much more indicative of the true nature of reality. Nowhere is this more evident to him than when he takes up the question of the ontological status of God's names and attributes. Following Avicenna, he sees them as relations (*nisab*) and thus not somehow superadded to or inhering in God's essence.[30] This position would be influential in the later Sufi tradition, particularly from the time of Ibn al-ʿArabī onward.[31] Yet, since the divine names do positively characterize God, they can also be said to not not be God—this latter view accords more with the Ashʿarī tradition in which ʿAyn al-Quḍāt was trained.

If the intellect has its limitations in knowing the reality of God, then it is also limited in understanding other aspects of religion, particularly prophecy (*nubuwwah*) and eschatology (*maʿād*). One has to taste these, too, but how is that possible? In the *Essence*, ʿAyn al-Quḍāt does not chart a method of how to access these higher levels of knowledge as such. This is because the work is almost entirely a theoretical exposition of the subject matter and goals of mysticism insofar as language and the human mind can conceive of them in coherent terms.

What tasting will do is bring a person to complete conviction in something that ʿAyn al-Quḍāt calls the "stage beyond the intellect" (*al-ṭawr warāʾ al-ʿaql*).

Although he borrows this term from al-Ghazālī,[32] he develops it in a manner that is entirely unique and very much in line with his project in the *Essence*. This stage beyond the intellect cannot be simply spoken about or thought of, since that would implicate the knowing subject within the very intellect that he is supposed to transcend. This again is where tasting is extremely helpful as an epistemic "tool." One of the things to be tasted at this exalted stage is the true meaning of love. Before one transcends the intellect, love is a mere concept; but after going beyond one's sense of self as an individual lover who has an object of love somewhere "out there," love, lover, and beloved are one, and this is because seeking, the seeker, and the sought are one.

Only by tasting the stage beyond the intellect, by coming to know it firsthand, can one walk away with a clear understanding of what it is ultimately about. Since the reality of God and eschatological events transcend time and space, to know them one must have access to a kind of knowledge that itself transcends time and space. This is precisely what the stage beyond the intellect is intended to do. And since there is not just one dimension beyond this realm of ours, ʿAyn al-Quḍāt also makes it clear that there is not just one stage beyond the intellect, but many stages. Friendship with God (*walāyah*), for example, corresponds to one of these stages (and it itself has many sub-stages), and beyond that stage there is the reality of prophecy itself.

Throughout the *Essence*, ʿAyn al-Quḍāt drives home the fact that what is needed in order to access these higher modes of knowing and to taste them is spiritual companionship, a Sufi guide, and a heart free of blameworthy character traits and worldly attachments. By being unfettered to the cage of phenomenal existence and the desire to know everything on one's own terms, the heart longs for the presence of God. It is then ready to receive His light, which will open up the way to higher stages of knowing. ʿAyn al-Quḍāt puts it best in the following climactic passage in the *Essence*:

> When your heart is expanded for faith in the unseen, God will cause a light to pour into your inner self, the likes of which you have not witnessed before. This is one of the traces of that stage that appears after the stage of the intellect. So intensify your search, for that alone is what you need in order to attain awareness![33]

Note on the Text

Arabic edition

In order to produce my Arabic edition of *The Essence of Reality*, I applied a rather straightforward principle: to stick as closely as possible to the source manuscript of this work (*aṣl*) as it is to be found in the Marāghah Codex (number 1 below). I have only deviated from this principle in instances when the reading offered in the *aṣl* is absolutely incorrect, or when the text is illegible. In such cases, I have had recourse to the readings in two other manuscripts (numbers 2 and 3) and the printed edition of the text (4), indicating on such occasions which reading I have chosen to adopt. I have only drawn attention to the variant readings, additions, and omissions to be found in these two manuscripts and the printed edition when they significantly alter or sufficiently problematize the reading given in the *aṣl*.

1. Marāghah Codex (aṣl) = أ

Dated 596/1199 or 597/1200. At some point in the early twentieth century, the family of the famed Iranian bibliophile Asghar Mahdavi obtained a copy of أ and housed it in their library. Thereafter, the University of Tehran Library obtained permission from Mahdavi to microfilm a number of the manuscripts from his family's collection, one of which was أ. In the mid-1950s, the editor of ʿAyn al-Quḍāt's writings, ʿAfīf ʿUsayrān, obtained a copy of the relevant microfilm and used the manuscript of the *Essence* contained therein as one of the four manuscripts he used to establish his edition of the text (see number 4 below). Manuscript أ became better known some twenty years ago, when it was obtained by the great scholar of Sufi texts Nasrollah Pourjavady from the Mahdavi family library and published as a facsimile edition.[34]

I have selected the text of the *Essence* as enshrined in أ as the basis for my Arabic edition primarily because it can be dated to some eighty years from the time it was completed by the author (514/1120). Given the relative geographic proximity between Hamadān and Marāghah, it is possible that the *Essence* traveled to Marāghah at some point during ʿAyn al-Quḍāt's short life. At any rate, the eighty-year gap between the actual writing of this work and its appearance in أ leaves little room for any serious errors to have crept into it.

It is indeed surprising to read ʿUsayrān's pronouncement on this manuscript. He says that he made spare use of it because the manuscript's copyist had a weak command of Arabic, which caused him to introduce many errors into the text when it was being dictated to him.[35] Quite the contrary: there are few real conceptual "errors" in this manuscript, although the scribe's rather sloppy style lends itself to many unnecessary but clearly detectable transcription slips. He also ignores diacritical marks (a scribal custom) and has a particularly bad habit of not featuring parity between feminine nouns and verbs.

In a number of cases where the readings in ʿUsayrān's edition and the other two manuscripts are unclear or incorrect, more felicitous readings can be found in أ. This is to say that many of the readings that seem to have been ironed out by copyists of the later manuscripts arguably appear in أ in their raw and natural form. This would explain why close study of this manuscript reveals it to be quite consistent with the content, tone, and style of ʿAyn al-Quḍāt's other writings.

2. *Carullah 2078 (Istanbul)* = ج

Dated 669/1270. This manuscript seems to be closely related to أ, and is probably based on a copy of it. What lends itself to this hypothesis, apart from the many similarities between أ and ج, is that the latter's scribe, Abū Bakr Kazirūnī, tells us at the end of the manuscript that he had copied it in Tabriz, which is less than ninety-three miles north of Marāghah. One can therefore envision copies of أ, the oldest manuscript of the *Essence* that we have, being circulated outside of Marāghah and ending up in neighboring regions such as Tabriz, where further copies of it, like ج, were produced.

3. *Majlis 10190 (Tehran)* = م

Dated 1047/1637. This manuscript was copied from an older version that likely dates to 633/1235, effectively making it a copy of the second-earliest, but no longer extant, manuscript known to us. The editorial glosses and finessed readings in م might also indicate that the copyist had this older copy of the manuscript, and likely other manuscripts, at his disposal.

4. *ʿUsayrān* = ع

Alongside أ and ج, ʿUsayrān used two other late and derivative manuscripts from Berlin and Istanbul, respectively. Surprisingly, he did not know of م, and therefore did not employ it in establishing his edition. ʿUsayrān does not state his principles for establishing his text, although it seems that he relied most heavily on ج. At times, ʿUsayrān's choices are rather arbitrary or highly questionable. Incidentally, but not insignificantly for our purposes, his editorial practices have also been called into question with respect to his edition of another of ʿAyn al-Quḍāt's works.[36]

English translation

Readers of the *Essence* will surely be humbled by ʿAyn al-Quḍāt's analytical powers, erudition, and elegance, which are on full display throughout the work. At the same time, the *Essence* is a first-rate book of mysticism. Consequently, for all of the *Essence*'s logical clarity and refined philosophical analyses of some key problems in traditional Islamic metaphysics, there is an equally sublime and even poetic exposition of the limits of the human mind in grasping the true nature of reality on both sides of death. And this is to say nothing of the text's incredibly concise style.

These facts pose serious problems to any translator, for they demand an ability to strike a balance between two ways of thinking, writing, and even feeling—the philosophical and hence abstract and impersonal, and the mystical and hence concrete and personal. In other words, the use of a philosophical and detached register to translate the *Essence* will fail to convey the concreteness that is at the heart of ʿAyn al-Quḍāt's prose and worldview. If, however, the translation veers too far in the direction of the concrete and the personal, then the watertight form and internal coherence of ʿAyn al-Quḍāt's arguments can appear to have fissures and incoherence where they do not.[37]

Given the Library of Arabic Literature's focus on making texts from the Arabic literary heritage (1) accessible and (2) as idiomatic and unencumbered by awkward English as possible, some of these difficulties were rather easy to assuage. With respect to (1), I have resorted to adding titles to each of the book's chapter headings. In addressing (2), I have taken the abstract route in translation when the terminology in the *Essence* was so technical as to preclude any other choice of words in English that were not as reified. A good example involves the Arabic logical terms *jins* and *nawʿ*, which can only meaningfully be translated into English as "genus" and "species," respectively. But for the most part, I have tended in the direction of employing more concrete language in my translation, even for some words that might have specific, technical meanings in works of philosophy or philosophical theology per se. Thus, one of ʿAyn al-Quḍāt's favorite words, *azal*, I translate as "beginningless" as opposed to the more usual "sempiternal";

huwiyyah as "identity" instead of "ipseity"; *ījād* as "effectuating existence" and not "existentiation"; and the one nontechnical instance of *māhiyyah* as "what it is" rather than "quiddity."

Throughout the *Essence*, ʿAyn al-Quḍāt speaks of the *ʿulamāʾ*. This can be a blanket reference to "scholars," and in some instances by *ʿulamāʾ* he means the philosophers on the one hand, and the rationalist theologians on the other (for the latter, it is more common for him to use expressions such as *al-ʿulamāʾ al-nāẓirūn*, by which he also sometimes means "rationalists" in general). I have therefore let the context determine my translation of this term, as I have with the adjective *ʿaqlī*, which can mean "intellectual" or "rational." The same principle applies, for example, to the verbal noun *idrāk*. In technical cases, it conveys the notion of "perception," but in more generic instances that of "grasping." One translation choice that may surprise some specialists of Sufi texts is my rendering of *maʿrifah* not as "gnosis" but as "recognition," and by extension *ʿārif* as "recognizer" and not "gnostic."[38]

I have been careful to remain consistent in my choice of translations for technical and nontechnical expressions, phrases, and verbs, only making exceptions when adherence to this principle would obscure the point at hand. In preparing my translation, I greatly profited from consulting Omar Jah's English rendering of the *Essence*,[39] as well as Salimeh Maghsoudlou's unpublished French translation.[40] Needless to say, my translation differs substantially from both of them.

Furthermore, standard pious and reverential expressions such as *raḍiya Allāhu ʿanhu* ("God be pleased with him") have not been translated, and when the pleonasm *fa-ʿlam* ("Know that . . ." or "You should know that . . .") begins a paragraph, it too has not been translated. In all but a few instances, translations of Qurʾanic verses are taken, often with substantial modifications, from Nasr et al. (eds.), *The Study Quran: A New Translation and Commentary*.

Notes to the Introduction

1 For a detailed account of ʿAyn al-Quḍāt's life and times, see the introduction in Rustom, *Inrushes of the Heart: The Sufi Philosophy of ʿAyn al-Quḍāt.*

2 For this work, see the introduction in Rustom, *Inrushes of the Heart.*

3 ʿAyn al-Quḍāt, *Nāmah-hā*, 2:459.

4 For the image of Shaykh Barakah in ʿAyn al-Quḍāt's writings, see Pourjavady, *ʿAyn al-Quḍāt wa-ustādān-i ū*, 95–133.

5 A fine presentation of his life and thought can be found in Lumbard, *Aḥmad al-Ghazālī, Remembrance, and the Metaphysics of Love.*

6 ʿAyn al-Quḍāt, *Nāmah-hā*, 3:407.

7 For a discussion of this text, see the introduction in Rustom, *Inrushes of the Heart.*

8 See the introduction in Rustom, *Inrushes of the Heart*, and Safi, "The Sufi Path of Love in Iran and India," 252–56.

9 Their correspondences can be found in Aḥmad al-Ghazālī, *Mukātabāt-i Khwājah Aḥmad Ghazālī bā ʿAyn al-Quḍāt Hamadānī.*

10 For their form, content, and relationship to *Paving the Path*, see the introduction in Rustom, *Inrushes of the Heart.*

11 A study of this important dimension of ʿAyn al-Quḍāt's thought, which is intimately related to his theodicy and understanding of cosmic complementarity, can be found in Rustom, "Devil's Advocate: ʿAyn al-Quḍāt's Defence of Iblis in Context." See also Rustom, *Inrushes of the Heart*, chapter 9.

12 See the findings presented in Rustom, "ʿAyn al-Quḍāt between Divine Jealousy and Political Intrigue," and Safi, *The Politics of Knowledge in Premodern Islam: Negotiating Ideology and Religious Inquiry*, 182–200. Cf. Griffel, *The Formation of Post-Classical Philosophy in Islam*, 131–38 and 157–58.

13 I say "for the most part" because there were other factors, both overt and subtle, which ʿAyn al-Quḍāt himself identified as additional causes that led to his execution. For these other causes, see Rustom, "ʿAyn al-Quḍāt between Divine Jealousy and Political Intrigue," 67–72.

14 See the texts presented in Rustom, *Inrushes of the Heart*, chapter 2.

15 Safi, *Politics of Knowledge in Premodern Islam*, 194.

16 For the broader question of ʿAyn al-Quḍāt's engagement with Ismailism, see Landolt, "Early Evidence for Nāṣir-i Khusraw's Poetry in Sufism: ʿAyn al-Quḍāt's Letter on the Taʿlīmīs" and Safi, *Politics of Knowledge in Premodern Islam*, 176–78.

17 See the excellent English translation: ʿAyn al-Quḍāt, *A Sufi Martyr.*

18 Images of these can be found in Rustom, *Inrushes of the Heart.*

19 See Pourjavady, "Introduction."

20 Shushtarī, *Majālis al-mu'minīn*, 4:515.

21 See Arif, "Defending Sufi Metaphysics in British India: Faḍl-i Ḥaqq Khayrābādī's (d. 1277/1861) Treatise on *waḥdat al-wujūd.*"

22 Aladdin, "Aspects of Mystical Hermeneutics and the Theory of the Oneness of Being (*waḥdat al-wujūd*) in the Work of ʿAbd al-Ghanī al-Nābulusī (d. 1143/1731)," 405.

23 For a translation of this work, see al-Ghazālī, *The Niche of Lights.*

24 Maghsoudlou, "La pensée de ʿAyn al-Quḍāt al-Hamadānī (m. 525/1131), entre avicennisme et héritage ġazālien." See also Maghsoudlou, "Étude des doctrines du nom dans *al-Maqṣad al-asnā* d'al-Ghazālī et de leur origine théologique et grammaticale."

25 For which, see Ormsby, "The Taste of Truth: The Structure of Experience in al-Ghazālī's *al-Munqidh min al-ḍalāl.*"

26 For a discussion of how tasting features in ʿAyn al-Quḍāt's worldview, see Rustom, *Inrushes of the Heart*, chapter 1. A fine survey of tasting in Sufi literature can be found in Hirtenstein, "*Dhawq.*"

27 For a survey of this doctrine, which is known as *waḥdat al-wujūd* ("oneness of existence") in later Islamic thought, see Chittick, *In Search of the Lost Heart: Explorations in Islamic Thought*, chapter 8. A discussion of ʿAyn al-Quḍāt's understanding of the oneness of existence can be found in Rustom, *Inrushes of the Heart*, chapter 3.

28 See Rustom, "Ibn ʿArabī's Letter to Fakhr al-Dīn al-Rāzī: A Study and Translation."

29 For a standard, jargon-free explanation, see Hawking, *A Brief History of Time*, chapter 4.

30 For the divine attributes in Avicenna as being relations (*nisab*) and/or negations (*salbī*), and thus not ontological entities, see Adamson, "From the Necessary Existent to God."

31 For Ibn al-ʿArabī and his followers, the relationality of the divine names and attributes was a cornerstone of their highly influential Sufi metaphysical doctrine; see Ali, *The Horizons of Being: The Metaphysics of Ibn al-ʿArabī in the Muqaddimat al-Qayṣarī*, 67–91.

32 Al-Ghazālī, *al-Munqidh min al-ḍalāl*, 111, and *Niche of Lights*, 36.

33 ʿAyn al-Quḍāt, *Essence of Reality*, §176.

34 Pourjavady, ed., *Majmūʿah-yi falsafī-yi Marāghah.*

35 ʿUsayrān, "Muqaddimah-yi muṣaḥḥiḥ," 7.

36 See the substantive inquiry in Pūrnāmdāryān and Ḥafīẓī, "Nigāhī ba-taṣḥīḥ-i *Tamhīdāt* pas az nīm qarn."

37 The subtle tensions between abstraction and concretization in the art of translating Islamic philosophical and mystical texts have been deftly highlighted by William Chittick in another context. See Chittick, "The Translator's Dilemmas."

38 In doing so I follow the line of reasoning in Chittick, *Divine Love: Islamic Literature and the Path to God*, 231–32.

39 Jah, trans., *The Zubdat al-Ḥaqā'iq of 'Ayn al-Quḍāh al-Hamadānī.*

40 Maghsoudlou, trans., "La quintessence des vérités."

زبدة الحقائق

The Essence of Reality

بِسْمِ اللَّهِ الرَّحْمَٰنِ الرَّحِيمِ

رَبِّ يَسِّرْ وَتَمِّمْ بِفَضْلِكَ

ديباجة

١ أحمد الله على نعم متواصلة أرعى أطراف النهار رياضها ومنح مترادفة أرِد آناء الليل حياضها وأصلّي على سيّد ولد آدم وخير من زيّن بجماله العالم محمّد صاحب شريعة الإسلام وداعي الثقلين إلى دار السلام وعلى آله المهتدين بأنواره وأصحابه المقتدين بآثاره.

٢ وبعد فهذه اللمعة موسومة بزبدة الحقائق ومشتملة على كشف الغطاء عن الأصول الثلاثة التي تعبّد باعتقادها كافّة الخلائق وقد أودعتها مائة فصل ووشّحتها بنكت دقيقة من كلّ أصل وهي عدّة كاملة للطالبين وغنية وافية بمقاصد السالكين إلى علم اليقين.[١] وقد ذكرت في الرسالة العلائيّة التي عملتها في مذهب السلف الصالحين رضي الله عنهم وعن من سلك طريقهم ما لا يستغني عن اعتقاده العوامّ في تلك الأصول وأمّا الذي يشفي غليل الخواصّ فقد أعربت عن بيانه في هذه الفصول وقد استخرت الله عزّ وجلّ في إملائها فسلّط عليّ خواطر لم أجد بدّاً من إمضائها ولولا أنّ الخيرة كانت في ذلك لما انتهج القدر بي هذه المسالك فما استخار عبد في أمر من أمور الدين والدنيا إلّا يُسّرت له فيه أسباب الوصول إلى درجة العَلياء.[٢]

٣ ولقد كان إخواني يتوقّعون ذلك منّي إذ كنت مشتغلاً بتحصيل العلم واستفادته وقد أكببت طول الليل والنهار على استزادته ثمّ انقطع طمعهم عن ذلك بعدما أضربت عن

١ ع، م: من علم اليقين إلى عين اليقين؛ ج: من علم اليقين. ٢ ج، ع، م: درجته العُلياء.

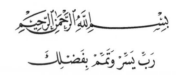

In the Name of God, the All-Merciful, the Ever-Merciful.

My Lord! Make this task easy for me and bring it to completion, by Your bounty.

Preamble

1 I praise God for His unceasing blessings, like lush gardens I tend during the day, and for His successive favors, like ponds I frequent into the night. And I invoke blessings upon the leader of humankind,[1] the best of those who have embellished the world with their beauty—Muḥammad, who came with the religion of Islam and called both humans and the jinn to the Abode of Peace;[2] and upon his family, who were guided by his light, and his Companions, who followed his footsteps.

2 This book is entitled *The Essence of Reality* and is concerned with unveiling the three principles of religion[3] in which all people, by virtue of believing in it, worship God. I have laid it out in one hundred chapters, and have adorned it with subtle points when treating each principle. It is a complete provision for seekers and an ample means for the aims of those traveling to the knowledge of certainty.[4] In the *Treatise Dedicated to ʿAlāʾ al-Dawla*,[5] which I composed according to the position of the righteous predecessors,[6] I discussed what, with respect to belief in these principles of religion, ordinary believers cannot do without. In these chapters, I have sought to clearly state what will quench the thirst of advanced seekers. In writing them, I prayed to God to bring about what is good,[7] and He thus imposed thoughts upon me, which I could not but transcribe. Destiny would not have led me down these pathways if there was no good in that. Indeed, none prays for the good to be brought about in any matter pertaining to religion or this worldly life but that the means for attaining its highest degree will assuredly be made easy for him.

3 Given the fact that I had been busy acquiring knowledge and benefiting from it—having dedicated myself night and day to augmenting it—my brethren

طلب العلم صفحاً وطويت دون الإقبال عليه كشحاً فصارت نفرة القلب عنه إلى حدّ كنت أستبعد معه من نفسي أن أتفرّغ يوماً لتمهيد تأليف أو أشتغل بتأسيس تصنيف وكان القلب في لجّ بحر لا ساحل له وقد غرق فيه الأوّلون والآخرون وليس لهم معتصم معوّل عليه ولا متمسّك يُلتجأ إليه ثمّ إنّي رأيت بعض المخلصين[1] من أعواني[2] تشوّق نفسه إلى الإحاطة بمنتهى نظر العلماء في أصول الدين وموقف أقدام السالك في طرق البراهين فلمّا رأيته محتاجاً في طريقه الذي هو بصدده إليه وقفت بضع أيّام من العمر عليه وقد تشوّشت عليّ أحوال القلب بسببه ولكن وطّن نفسي على احتمال ذلك صدق طلبه على أنّي لمّا استخرت الله عزّ وجلّ قطع الخواطر الدافعة عنّي بتقديره وسخّرني بهذا الأمر فلم أجد مدفعاً لتسخيره ثمّ كان القلب يطمئنّ إلى قوله صلّى الله عليه وسلّم ما خاب من استخار الله.[3]

فابتدأت بإملاء هذه الفصول وقد قدّمت عليها مقدّمة تتضمّن بيان الباعث ٤
الأصليّ على إملائها وأختمها بخاتمة تشتمل على ذكر الوظائف التي لا بدّ للناظر في هذا
الكتاب من أن تكون موجودة فيه حتّى تعظم فائدته من مطالعته والله عزّ وجلّ ينفع به
كلّ من ينظر فيه ويؤيّد باطنه بصفاء يستوعب به معناه ويستوفيه فهو المُستمسَك
بعروة إنعامه والمستعان في كلّ أمر على كماله وإتمامه وهو حسبي ﴿وَنِعْمَ ٱلْوَكِيلُ﴾.

---

[1] ج: المصلّين. [2] ج، ع، م: إخواني. [3] م: ما خاب من استخار ولا ندم من استشار.

had been expecting this book from me. This ambition was cut short after I renounced the pursuit of knowledge and broke free from it, effectively avoiding it altogether. My heart's aversion reached a point where I thought it highly unlikely that I would ever one day devote myself to the trouble of laying the foundations for such a work, much less preparing to compose one. My heart was at sea with no shore in sight, an ocean where early and more recent generations drowned with no one to protect them or to rely upon, and no one to cling to as their refuge. Then I saw one of my devoted supporters whose soul was filled with longing to scale the heights of theoretical reflection on the principles of religion, and to occupy the position the seeker attains on his exploration of demonstration. When I saw him thus in need upon the journey he had undertaken, I set aside a few days of my life. This caused the state of my heart to confound me, but the sincerity of my friend's request gave me the resolve to endure. Actually, when I prayed to God to bring about the good, His decree curtailed the thoughts that had been repelling me, and He enjoined this affair upon me: I could find no way to repel His injunction. Moreover, my heart sought solace in the Prophet's statement: "Whoever prays to God to bring about the good will never be at a loss."[8]

I began to dictate these chapters and included an introduction, which con- 4
tains an explanation of the initial reasons for their composition. I also provided a conclusion, which contains a discussion of certain duties incumbent upon the reader of this book—namely, that these duties be found in him—so that he may profit greatly from studying it. May God benefit all those who read this book, strengthening their inner selves with a clarity through which they can grasp and exhaust its meanings. For God's blessings are like a firm handle onto which we can cling, and His perfection and completeness allow us to beseech His aid in every matter. He alone suffices me, «and an excellent Guardian is He!»[9]

مقدّمة في بيان الباعث الأصليّ على إملاء هذه اللمعة

٥ اعلم أنّ الذي دعاني إلى ذلك غرضان مهمّان.

٦ فالغرض الأوّل أنّ جماعة من إخواني وفّقني الله للقيام بحقوق صحبتهم وصداقتهم ونهض بي لأداء ما يحبّ[1] عليّ في رفاقتهم كانوا يقترحون أن أملي فصولاً أذكر فيها ما ينتهي إليه نظر العقول في العلم بذات الله عزّ وجلّ وصفاته والإيمان بحقيقة النبوّة وباليوم الآخر وأن أنظم هذه المعاني في سلك ألفاظ يروق الفصيح إيجازُها ويروع الناظر المستقلّ بالنظر إعجازُها وكانت عوائق الزمان وصروف الحدثان تشغلني عن القيام بما حامت رغباتهم عليه وتوجّهت هممهم إليه ثمّ لمّا رأيتهم يحتاجون غاية الاحتياج إلى ذلك وخصوصاً في الإيمان بحقيقة النبوّة وحقيقة الصفات الموصوف بها فاطر السماوات والأرض رأيت صرف العناية إلى بيان ذلك من أهمّ الأمور.

٧ ولقد ذكرت في النبوّة وما يتعلّق بها من المقدّمات العلميّة في رسالتي الموسومة بغاية البحث عن معنى البعث ما يشفي غليل الطالب المستفيد ويكفي الناظر المستبدّ بنظره السديد ولكن كان الإيمان بحقيقة النبوّة إذ ذاك مستنداً إلى علم اليقين ومتلقّى من طرق البراهين وحاصل ما يدركه العقل من حقيقة النبوّة يرجع إلى إثبات وجود شيء للنبيّ عليه السلام بطريق جمليّ من غير إدراك شيء من حقيقة ذلك الشيء وماهيّته وهذا الإيمان بعيد جدّاً من الإيمان الذي يحصل لصاحب الذوق بحقيقة النبوّة ويكاد يكون التصديق المستفاد من العلم بحقيقة النبوّة شبيهاً بتصديق يحصل لمن لا ذوق له في الشعر بوجود شيء مجمل فإنّ من لم يُرزق ذوق الشعر قد يتمكّن أيضاً من تحصيل اعتقاد ما بوجود شيء لصاحب الذوق ولكن يكون ذلك الاعتقاد بعيداً عن حقيقة الخاصّيّة التي يختصّ[2] بها صاحب الذوق.

---

١ ج،ع: يجب. ٢ ج،ع: يخصّ.

Introduction: The Reason for Writing This Book

There were two important motives in this regard. 5

The first motive: A group of my brothers—God grant me success in fulfilling 6
the rights of their companionship and friendship, and impel me to carry out what He loves for me by way of camaraderie with them—suggested that I write some chapters in which I discuss where theoretical reflection ends with respect to the essence of God and His attributes, as well as faith in the reality of prophecy and the Last Day. They also suggested that I arrange these supra-sensory realities on a necklace of expressions whose terseness would please the eloquent, and whose wonder would amaze the reader reliant upon his own theoretical powers. However, time threw obstacles in my way and adversity kept me from addressing their concerns and the goal of their aspirations. But then I resolved to turn my attention to explaining these most important of matters when I saw how desperately they needed this, especially with regard to faith in the reality of prophecy and the reality of the attributes by which the Originator of the heavens and the earth is described.

I discussed prophecy and the rational premises pertaining to it in my trea- 7
tise entitled *The Investigation's End: On the Meaning of the Prophetic Mission*.[10] My discussion will quench the seeker's thirst and suffice the reader reliant upon his own sound theoretical powers. However, faith in the reality of prophecy is, at the same time, based on the knowledge of certainty[11] and is obtained through demonstrative methods. The gist of what the intellect perceives vis-à-vis the reality of prophecy goes back to an affirmation, in a very general way, of the existence of a certain something in the Prophet without at all perceiving the reality and essence of that thing. This abstract kind of faith is very far from that faith in the reality of prophecy that is obtained by the one who tastes this faith. Assent derived from knowledge of the reality of prophecy almost resembles a person's assent to the existence of something very general in a poem, though he himself has no taste for poetry. Indeed, a person who is not blessed with a taste for poetry may nevertheless have the ability to obtain some kind of belief in the existence of something unique to that person who does have a taste for poetry. However, such belief would be far from that specific reality by virtue of which the person who does have a taste for poetry stands out.

٨ وكنت إذ أمليت تلك الرسالة ابن إحدى وعشرين سنة وأنا الآن ابن أربع وعشرين سنة ولقد أفاضت عليّ الرحمة الأزليّة في هذه السنين الثلاث من أنواع المعارف الغيبيّة ونفائس الأحوال الكشفيّة ما يتعذّر عليّ شرحه ووصفه وأكثر ممّا يستحيل عنه التعبير في عالم المتناطقين بالحروف والأصوات وأنا أجتهد غاية الاجتهاد أن أذكر منه طرفاً في هذه الفصول بأحسن إشارة وأرشق عبارة.

٩ والحقّ الصريح أنّ أكثر الكلمات المذكورة في هذا الكتاب متشابهة غاية التشابه فمهما رأيتَ فيها لفظاً لم يؤدّ حقّ المعنى المسبوك في قالبه فلا تبسطنّ إليه لسان الاعتراض فلي في ذلك عذران واضحان أحدهما أنّي كنت عن ذكر المعاني في شغل شاغل عن تنقيح الألفاظ فلم أوردها على أحسن وجوه الإيراد مع أنّ ذكر تلك المعاني بعبارات تطابقها من غير تشابه فيها يكاد يكون محالاً لا بل هو كذلك قطعاً ويقيناً. والثاني أنّي أمليت هذه الفصول لقوم لا يشغلهم تشابه الألفاظ عن درك حقائق المعاني فمن كثرة ممارساتهم للحقائق العقليّة صاروا بحيث لا يقطع عليهم طريق الأنس بالملكوت الفهمُ مع عالم الملك.

١٠ الغرض الثاني أنّ الطريق إلى الله عزّ وجلّ وسلوكه صعب وفيه ما لا يحصى من البحار المغرقة والنيران المحرقة والجبال الشواهق والفلوات المملوءة بالصواعق والعقبات التي تستعصي على الأعين ويمتنع وصفُها على الألسن وكلّ واحد من السالكين يظنّ بنفسه أنّه من الواصلين وقد عمّ الضلال جميع الخلق إلّا من عصمه الله عزّ وجلّ بفضله وكرمه حتّى أُهتدي إلى الصراط المستقيم والنهج القويم والله عزّ وجلّ يعيذنا من الاغترار بلامع السراب في المشارب[1] ويعصمنا في الطريق عن القواطع المضلّة حتّى يرد بنا أعذب المشارب ﴿إِنَّهُ عَلَىٰ كُلِّ شَيْءٍ قَدِيرٌ﴾.

١١ أجل وممّا ضلّ فيه فحول العلماء الحذّاق من أهل النظر حكمهم بأنّ حصول العلم بذات الله عزّ وجلّ وصفاته من طريق التعلّم هو غاية السعادة ومنتهى الدرجات وهذا جهل عظيم قد استولى على الأكثرين من المتبحّرين في العلم والواصلين فضلاً عمّن هو بَعْدُ في

---

١ ج: بلامع السراب؛ ع: بلامع السراب في المسارب؛ م: بلامع السراب في المشارع.

I was twenty-one years old when I wrote *The Investigation's End*. Now I am twenty-four. In the intervening years, God's beginningless mercy has poured down on me such kinds of unseen knowledge and precious states of unveiling as I am unable to explain and describe. For it is impossible to express most of this in a world where people articulate themselves through words and sounds. But I will strive to the utmost of my ability to mention some of it in these chapters, through the most beautiful allusions and most elegant expressions. 8

The simple fact is that most of the terms discussed in this book are extremely ambiguous. So, whenever you encounter an expression that does not communicate the true meaning of its usual acceptation, do not be too hasty to object; for I have two clear excuses here. The first is that I was primarily concerned with discussing supra-sensory realities at the expense of refining my words. Thus, other than conveying what was intended, I did not craft these words in the most beautiful way—though to discuss these supra-sensory realities by way of fitting expressions, while not rendering them unclear, is almost impossible—rather, it is certainly the case! The second is that I wrote these chapters for people who are not diverted by the ambiguity of words from perceiving the reality of their meanings: as a result of their abundant experience with intellectual matters, they have come to a point where understanding the material realm does not bar them from the path of intimacy with the spiritual realm.[12] 9

The second motive: The path to God is difficult, containing as it does innumerable treacherous oceans, blazing fires, lofty mountains, thunder-filled deserts, and dangerous routes that confuse the eye and baffle the tongue. Every traveler thinks he is one of those who have arrived.[13] Everyone is misguided, except those whom God protects through His bounty and generosity so that they are guided along the straight path[14] and the true road. May God protect us from being deluded by a shimmering mirage, keeping us upon the path and away from misleading attacks until He brings us to that sweetest of drinking places: «Truly He is powerful over all things».[15] 10

Indeed, one area where the stalwart rationalist theologians have strayed, for all their cleverness, is their judgment to the effect that the highest felicity and the ultimate destination is to obtain knowledge of God's essence and attributes through study. This is a great misjudgment, which has overcome both the majority of people who dive deeply into rational theology, and those who have mastered it, to say nothing of those distant from traveling the spiritual path. To think 11

السلوك ومن ظنّ أنّ العلم بذات المعشوق وصفاته عين الوصول إليه فقد سحب الضلال ذيله عليه ومن صار إلى أنّ الوقوع في مخلب السبع الضاري وأنّ العلم بالوقوع واحد فهو في مهواة بعيدة من الجهل وهذا مثل هؤلاء القوم في اغترارهم بظنونهم الفاسدة وآرائهم المتناقضة على أنّ الوصول إلى ما يدّعونه من العلم المشار إليه عزيز جدّاً إذ لا يتّفق ذلك إلّا على الندور لبعض الأشخاص في آحاد العصور.

١٢ فلمّا رأيت الأمر على ذلك ورأيت نفسي مليّة بالقيام على حلّ هذا المشكل وكشف القناع عن وجه الحقّ فيه صمّمتُ عزمتي على إملاء هذه الفصول ليتّخذها الطالب ذخراً في طريق العلم ومسالكه حتّى يتيسّر له النجاة عن مهالكه فمن زاحم العلماء بركبتيه لطلب العلم ولم يعتقد أنّ وراء مقصده مقاصد كثيرة زلّ قدمه وكثر ندمه وعظم زَلَلُهُ وظهر حيث لا ينفعه خطَؤُه وهذا لأنّ الغالب على من اعتقد ذلك أنّه إذا وصل إلى مقصده وأحرز في العلم قصب السبق وقف به الطلب ولم يكن في نفسه تشوّف[١] إلى ما وراء ذلك وهذا الظنّ من السموم المهلكة لمن يسلك طريق العلم ومن لم يجرّب ذلك حقّ التجربة فلا يتصوّر أن يعرف ما أقوله.

١٣ ولقد سلكت هذا الطريق ونظرت في غثّ العلم وسمينه وطالعت منه كلّ ضارّ ونافع حتّى حصّلت ما كان يهمّني فيما كنت بصدده وأمّا ما كان قليل الغناء فما التفتّ إليه ولا عرّجت في الطريق عليه علماً بأنّ العلم كثير والعمر قصير فتضييعه في تحصيل ما لا تعظم فائدته حماقة وكان عذري إذ خضتُ كلّ مخاض في العلم واضحاً فالغريق يتمسّك بكلّ شيء رجاء الخلاص فقد كنت ﴿عَلَىٰ شَفَا حُفْرَةٍ مِّنَ ٱلنَّارِ﴾ لولا أنّ الله تعالى ينقذني بفضله وكرمه وكان السبب في ذلك أنّي كنت أُطالع كتب الكلام طلباً للارتقاع عن حضيض التقليد إلى ذروة البصيرة فلم أظفر منها بمقصودي وتشوّشت عليّ قواعدُ المذاهب حتّى تردّيت في ورطات لا يمكن حكايتها في هذه اللمعة ولا فائدة في سماعها أيضاً للأكثرين فإنّه يولّد ضرراً عظيماً للأفهام القاصرة والقلوب الضعيفة.

---

١ ج، ع: تشوّق.

that knowledge of the essence of the Beloved and His attributes is actually to reach Him is simply to be mired in misguidance. And whoever thinks that falling into the claws of a vicious predator and knowledge of falling into the claws of a vicious predator are one and the same has sunk deep into the abyss of ignorance! This is similar to remaining in a state of delusion by virtue of false opinions and contradictory views! Nevertheless, it is very difficult to reach what the rationalist theologians claim—that is, the aforementioned knowledge of God—for it is but rarely given, and at unique moments.

When I saw how things were, and found myself filled with the desire to remove this difficulty and unmask the truth, I resolved to write these chapters so that the seeker may take them as provisions for the path of knowledge and its byways until he is delivered from its perils. For those who vie with scholars in the pursuit of knowledge but do not believe that there are many goals beyond this goal will slip and experience great regret. Their errors will be severe and their mistakes will be on full display and work against them. This is because, for the most part, when those who believe this reach their goal and excel in their studies, they stop in their pursuit of knowledge and have no desire for anything further. This opinion spells fatal poison for those who walk the path of knowledge. But whoever has not actually experienced this cannot possibly recognize what I am saying! 12

As I traveled this path, I investigated all forms of knowledge, both heavy and light, and studied that which was harmful and that which was useful, until I obtained what was important for my purposes. I did not turn to what was of little profit, knowing full well that there is much to know but little time, and that it is plain old stupidity to waste this time in obtaining anything that is of little benefit. My excuse for diving into every aspect of knowledge is clear: the drowning man clutches at straws, hoping for salvation. Had God in His bounty and generosity not delivered me from it, I would have been «on the brink of a pit of fire».[16] This is because I would study the books of rational theology, seeking to raise myself from the depths of blind imitation to the summit of insight. But I did not get what I sought from these books. In fact, the foundations of the schools of rational theology so confounded me that I encountered all sorts of predicaments that cannot be recounted in this book, nor is there any benefit in hearing about them for most people—it will seriously harm puny minds and weak hearts. 13

١٤ فتحيّرت في أمري تحيّرًا تنغّص معه العيش حتّى دلّني دليل المتحيّرين على الطريق وأمدّني كرمه بالمعونة والتوفيق وعلى الجملة فما نعشني من سقطتي بعد فضل الله تعالى إلّا مطالعة كتب الشيخ الإمام حجّة الإسلام أبي حامد محمّد الغزاليّ رضي الله عنه وأرضاه فكنت أتصفّحها قريباً من أربع سنين ورأيت في هذه المدّة من الاشتغال بالعلم عجائب كثيرة ممّا استقبلني في الطريق من الكفر والضلالة والحيرة والعماية وشرح ذلك لا يفي به بيان فإنّه خارج عن حدّ الحصر والإحصاء ولا مطمع فيه لطلب الاستقصاء ثمّ لمّا حصّلت مقصودي من العلم فظننت أنّي وصلت جعلت أنشد لنفسي قول الشاعر [كامل]

انْزِلْ بِمَنْزِلِ زَيْنَبٍ وَرَبَابِ وَٱرْتَعْ فَهٰذَا مَرْبَعُ ٱلْأَحْبَابِ

١٥ فبينا أحطّ رحالي في الثرى وأنيخ المطايا لتترفّه عن السير والسُّرى إذ أخذت عين البصيرة في الانفتاح ولست أعني بصيرة العقل حتّى لا تغترّ بخاطرك فكانت عين البصيرة تنفتح قليلاً قليلاً وكنت أقف في أثناء ذلك على القواطع التي كادت تقطع عليّ طريق الطلب لما وراء العلوم وبقيت في ذلك قريباً من سنة وأنا بعد لم أقف على حقيقة الواقعة التي وقعت لي في تلك السنة حتّى أنّ سيّدي ومولاي الشيخ الإمام سلطان الطريقة وترجمان الحقيقة أبا الفتوح أحمد بن محمّد الغزاليّ متّع الله ببقائه أهل الإسلام وجزاه عنّي خير جزاية ساقه التقدير إلى همدان وهي مسقط رأسي فانكشف لي في خدمته قناع الحيرة عن وجه تلك الواقعة في أقلّ من عشرين يوماً فشاهدت جليّة الحال في ذلك ثمّ طولعت بشيء لم يُبق منّي ومن طلبي لغيره إلّا ما شاء الله وأنا الآن منذ سنين ليس لي شغل إلّا طلب الغنا في ذلك الشيء والله المستعان على إتمام ما ولّيت وجهي شطره ولو عمّرت عمر نوح وأفنيته في هذا الطلب لكان له بعد قليلاً.

١٦ ورحم الله أبا فراس حيث يقول [طويل]

تَهُونُ عَلَيْنَا فِي ٱلْمَعَالِي نُفُوسُنَا وَمَنْ خَطَبَ ٱلْحَسْنَاءَ لَمْ يُغْلِهَا ٱلْمَهْرُ

I was totally bewildered about my situation. On top of that, it ruined my life—until the "Guide of the bewildered"[17] gave me guidance and extended His generosity toward me, bestowing aid and success. In short, after God's bounty, nothing other than a study of the books of the Proof of Islam Abū Ḥāmid Muḥammad al-Ghazālī revived me from my wretched state. For almost four years, I studied his books. During this period when I was occupied with true knowledge, I beheld many wonders, which steered me away from bewilderment, blindness, error, and unbelief. Explaining this will not do it justice, for it is beyond the confines of analysis and calculation, nor is there any hope in even trying to come to terms with it. When I obtained my goal of true knowledge and was certain I had reached it, I began to recite these verses to myself: 14

> Alight at the dwellings of Zaynab and Rabāb
> and graze, for these are the pastures of lovers![18]

While I was thus encamped and my camels recovered from the voyage by day and night, suddenly, the eye of my insight began to open. Do not be deluded in your thinking: I do not mean the insight of the intellect. The eye of insight opened, little by little. I stood there, marveling at the obstacles that nearly barred me from the path of pursuing what lies beyond rational theology. I remained like this for almost a year without fathoming the reality of the situation I was in during that year, until destiny brought my master Shaykh Abū l-Futūḥ Aḥmad al-Ghazālī, that most illustrious leader, the sultan of the path and the interpreter of reality, to Hamadān, my birthplace. In his service, the veil of bewilderment was removed from my situation in under twenty days, and in that period I bore witness to an unmistakable spiritual state. For the past few years, and even now, my sole task has been to seek sufficiency in that "thing."[19] I seek God's aid to help me realize that thing in whose direction I have turned.[20] Time would still be too short were I to live as long as Noah[21] and devote all my life to this pursuit! 15

God bless Abū Firās, who says: 16

> We care not for our souls in the pursuit of glory—
> no dowry can be too high for the suitor of a beautiful maid.[22]

وكان ذلك الشيء قد طبّق الخافقين فلا يقع بصري على شيء إلّا يراه فيه [مديد] ١٧

وَجْهُـهُ فِي كُلِّ نَاحِيَـةٍ   حَيْثُ مَا قَابَلْتُهُ قَمَرُ

وكلّ نفَس لا يزيدني استغراقاً في مشاهدته فلا بورك لي فيه ولله درّ أبي الطيّب ١٨
وهذا الشعر لفاظه فيه [طويل]

تَـرَكْنَا لِأَطْرَافِ ٱلْقَنَا كُلَّ لَذَّةٍ   فَلَيْسَ لَنَـا إِلَّا بِهِنَّ لِعَـابُ
فَغَـيْرُ فُؤَادِي لِلْغَوَانِي رَمِيَّـةٌ   وَغَـيْرُ بَنَـانِي لِلزُّجَاجِ رِكَابُ

والمغبون من لم يجعل أنفاسه أثمان المعالي ولم يجتهد في طلب العزّ طول الأيّام ١٩
والليالي ولقد أجاد الموسويّ حيث يقول [طويل]

إِذَا أَنَا لَمْ أَرْكَبْ إِلَيْهَا مُخَاطِرًا   وَأُعْظِمُ قَـتْلًا دُونَهَا وَقِتَـالَا
فَهٰـذَا حُسَامِي لَمْ أُرِقْ ذُبَابَهُ   مَضَاءً وَهٰذَا ذَابِلِي لِمْ طَـالَا

وأنا أسأل الله تعالى أن يجعل لي من التوفيق ساعداً ومن القضاء الأزليّ مساعداً ٢٠
حتّى أملك ناصية سؤلي وأبلغ قاصية مأمولي [كامل]

وَلَرُبَّمَا ٱسْتَيْأَسْتُ[١] ثُمَّ أَقُولُ لَا[٢]   إِنَّ ٱلَّذِي ضَمِنَ ٱلنَّجَاحَ كَرِيـمُ

وسأزجي[٣] قلاصي حتّى يتعيّن من أسر الزمان والمكان خلاصي فأنيخ المطايا في أعزّ ٢١
مناخ وأسمو بنفسي إلى مؤاخاة من هو أجلّ مؤاخ [طويل]

مُنًى إِنْ تَكُنْ حَقًّا تَكُنْ أَحْسَنَ ٱلْمُنَى   وَإِلَّا فَقَدْ عِشْـنَا بِهَا زَمَـنًا رَغْـدَا

١ (ٱسْتَيْأَسْتُ) في ج، ع، م؛ أ: ٱسْتَشْتُّ. ٢ (لا) في ج، ع، م، ساقطة من أ. ٣ (سأزجي) في ج، ع، م: أ: سأجري.

That thing consumes me entirely, for wherever my vision alights it sees God there: 17

His face is in every direction:
wherever I turn, I see the moon.[23]

May every breath that fails to increase my immersion in witnessing Him bring me no blessing! By God! How finely Abū Ṭayyib expresses it in this poem! 18

We have abandoned every pleasure
for the spearheads—now we only dally with them.
Other hearts are prey for beautiful women,
other fingers grasp the goblet.[24]

The person who does not regard his every breath as invaluable and does not strive for greatness by day and night is truly duped. Al-Mūsawī puts it well when he says: 19

If I don't ride into danger for her,
despising death, much less battle,
why did I sharpen my sword,
and why is my spear so long?[25]

I ask God to grant me success and felicity from His beginningless decree so I can take control of my quest and fulfill my aspirations: 20

Often have I despaired, only to say,
"Despair not! The one who ensures success is generous."[26]

I will urge on my camel until I am free from the bonds of space and time, and will make it kneel in the most exalted abode. Then I will ascend to fraternity[27] with him who is the most precious of brothers: 21

Should our wishes come true—a fate most beautiful.
But if not, then at least we enjoyed their comfort.[28]

٢٢ فالهمم العليّة لا تقف بالنفوس الزكيّة دون الوصول إلى الحضرة المحمّديّة صلّى الله عليه وسلّم تسليماً كثيراً طيّباً مباركاً فيه [كامل]

فَإِذَا ٱلْمَطِيُّ بِنَا بَلَغْنَ مُحَمَّدًا فَظُهُورُهُنَّ عَلَى ٱلرِّجَالِ حَرَامُ
قَرَّبْنَنَا مِنْ خَيْرِ مَنْ وَطِئَ ٱلْحَصَا فَلَهَا عَلَيْنَا حُرْمَةٌ وَذِمَامُ

والكلام في أمثال ذلك يطول.

٢٣ وأنا أخوض في بيان الفصول وأقول أهمّ ما ينبغي أن نبدأ بذكره في هذه الفصول بعد حمد الله الذي يُفتتح كلّ كتاب بحمده والصلاة على محمّد رسوله وعبده تعريفك أنّ أكثر الخلق لا ينتفعون بمطالعة هذا الكتاب حقّ الانتفاع فإنّ بيان ذلك مهمّ في نفسه وسأنهج لك في خاتمة هذه الفصول طريقاً إذا سلكته صرت وافر الحظّ من الكتاب.

فصل ١

٢٤ اعلم أنّ المصدّقين بالسعادة الأخرويّة والطالبين لها أربعة أقسام.

٢٥ القسم الأوّل: فريق صدّقوا بما جاءت بها الرسل فآمنوا بالله وملائكته وكتبه ورسله واليوم الآخر ولم يحتاجوا في هذا الإيمان إلى بحث نظريّ كما جرت به عادة العلماء النظّار وهؤلاء لا يصلح لهم النظر في هذا الكتاب أصلاً إذ ليس واحد منهم يحتاج إلى شيء ممّا ذكر فيه نعم يجوز أن ينتفع به إذا نظر فيه للاستفادة ولكنّ النظر فيه ليس بمهمّ لأمثاله.

٢٦ القسم الثاني: فريق من علماء الظواهر سلكوا مسلكاً من البحث غير مرضيّ عند المحقّقين فقلّدوا جماعة من أرباب المذاهب في مذاهبهم وفي دلائلها جميعاً وهؤلاء

Lofty aspirations do not prevent pure souls from reaching the presence of Muḥammad: 22

> Our camels brought us to Muḥammad;
> now it's forbidden for others to ride them,
> Taking us to the best of those who graced the earth—
> now they are ours to protect and hold sacred.[29]

These kinds of discussions are extensive.

Now, I will clarify something about the following chapters. After praising God (the one with whose praise every work commences) and invoking blessings upon Muḥammad, His servant and Messenger, the most important thing, which we must first discuss in this book, is the fact that most people will not properly benefit from it. An explanation of this point is in itself vitally important. At the end of the book, I will lay out a path that will allow you to most properly profit from this work—that is, if you travel that path. 23

Chapter 1: Who Will Benefit from This Book?

Those who believe in felicity[30] in the afterlife and who seek it are in four categories: 24

Category 1: This is a group that believes in what the Prophets have brought, and thus believes in God, His angels, His Books, His Messengers, and the Last Day. They do not have a need for theoretical investigation in order to bolster their faith, as is the custom of the rationalist theologians. For this group, reading this book will basically be of no use, since not a single member of the group needs what is discussed in it. It is indeed possible for them to profit from it if they peruse it. But reading it is not important for such people. 25

Category 2: This is a group of scholars who travel a path of intellectual investigation, though that path is not the preferred way of those who have verified the truth.[31] Thus, in terms of their intellectual positions and in their proofs for these positions, they blindly imitate a number of leaders of the intellectual schools. 26

أحسن حالاً من القسم الأوّل وليس لهم حاجة إلى النظر في هذا الكتاب وربّما لا ينتفعون به إن نظروا فيه أيضاً.

٢٧ القسم الثالث: فريق من العلماء النظّار الذين يزعمون أنّهم لا يقلّدون في عقائدهم أحداً من الخلق[١] وإنّما يسلكون فيها طريق البحث العقليّ والنظر البرهانيّ وطريقة هؤلاء في طلب العلم أحمد الطرائق إلّا أنّهم إذا قطعوا منازل العلم ظنّوا أنّهم وصلوا إلى الكمال الكلّيّ في ما هم بصدده وغرور هؤلاء بما حصّلوه من العلوم النظريّة عظيم فإنّهم يظنّون أنّ تحصيل العلم بالله مثلاً وصول إليه وهو عين السعادة المطلوبة فترى الواحد منهم يكبّ طول الليل والنهار على طلب الدنيا وشهواتها ويزعم أنّ ذلك لا يضرّ أمثاله وأنّه سعي منه في طلب علف البعير وامتثال لأمر الله عزّ وجلّ حيث يقول ﴿وَلَا تَنسَ نَصِيبَكَ مِنَ ٱلدُّنْيَا﴾. وهذه حماقة عظيمة يبعد الخلاص عنها إلّا لمن يُأخذ بطبعه[٢] عناية أزليّة وهؤلاء أيضاً لا ينتفعون بمطالعة هذا الكتاب فتراهم إذا نظروا فيه يتحذلقون ويقولون نحن إذا لم نقلّد الأنبياء من غير برهان يقوم على صدق ما يقولونه فما بالنا نقلّد غيرهم وأيّ فرق بيننا وبين سائر العوامّ إذا قلّدنا واحداً من غير بصيرة سواءً كان نبيّاً أو غيره وهذه مهلكة عظيمة هلك فيها النظّار إلّا من عصمه الله بفضله ﴿وَقَلِيلٌ مَّا هُمْ﴾ ونعم الطريق طريق النظر لو لم يكن فيه أمثال هذه المهالك ومن زعم أنّه يسلك ذلك الطريق ولا تضرّه تلك المهالك فهو جاهل وسيعلم حقيقة ما ذكرتُه في سلوكه ولا ينفعه العلم.

٢٨ القسم الرابع: شرذمة قليلة يسلكون طريق العلم النظريّ فإذا فرغوا من قطع عقباته ومنازله لم يشف ذلك غليل طلبهم شفاءً كلّيّاً ومن حصل له علم يقينيّ وضروريّ بوجود الباري تعالى وتقدّس وبوجود صفاته فسكنت بذلك فورة طلبه فليس هو من القوم المشار إليهم أصلاً فهؤلاء لا يزيدهم التبحّر في العلم إلّا جدّاً في الطلب

---

١ (في عقائدهم أحداً من الخلق) في ج، ع؛ أ: لأحد من الخلق في عقائدهم؛ م: في عقائدهم حقيقة أحداً من الخلق. ٢ ج، ع: بضبعه؛ م: بصنعه.

This second group is better off than the first group, but they too have no need to read this book. If they were to read it, it is likely that they too would not profit from it.

Category 3: This is a group of rationalist theologians who claim that in their beliefs they do not blindly imitate a single person; for in their beliefs, they travel the path of intellectual investigation and demonstrative reflection. In terms of the pursuit of knowledge, this group's method is the most praiseworthy of methods, except that when they have traversed the waystations of knowledge, they think they have reached total perfection in their pursuits. The delusions this group have been led to by the theoretical knowledge they have obtained is astounding! They think, for example, that obtaining knowledge of God is tantamount to reaching Him—that very felicity which is the purpose of the pursuit of knowledge. So you will see members of this group pursue the world and its desires night and day, all the while surmising that these pursuits will not harm people like them. And they will try to equate the task of feeding their camels with obeying the command of God, since God says, «And forget not your portion in this world».[32] Only those who take the beginningless solicitude for their provision can be free from such monumental stupidity. This third group will, likewise, derive no profit from reading this book. In fact, if they were to read it, you would see them cleverly saying, "Since we do not blindly imitate even the Prophets in the absence of demonstrative proof to establish the veracity of their statements, why would we blindly imitate someone else? For what difference would there be between us and all of the simple believers if we were to blindly imitate anyone—be it a Prophet or someone else—without insight?" This is a grave danger wherein the rationalists perish, except for those God has protected out of His bounty. «And how few they are!»[33] The best of methods is the method of theoretical reflection, so long as it does not present dangers like these. To think that you can travel this path and not be harmed by these dangers is sheer ignorance. Those who do think this will on their journey come to know the reality of what I have said, and their pursuit of knowledge will be of no benefit. 27

Category 4: This is a small group that travels the path of rational theology, but whose thirst is not completely quenched once they have traversed the path's steep ascents and waystations. Those whose passions subside when they have obtained certain and necessary knowledge of the Maker and the existence of His attributes basically do not belong to this group, for the group's bewilderment in knowledge of God only increases their resolve to pursue this knowledge, their 28

وتشوّقاً إلى مزيد الاستبصار وتطلّعاً إلى ما وراء العلم والعقل من كشف ذوقيّ يختصّ به خواصّ الحقّ وهم الذين ينتفعون بهذا الكتاب ومطالعته حقّ الانتفاع ولم تصدق رغبتي في إملاء هذه الفصول إلّا لأجلهم مخافةَ أن أكون عرضة لقول الشاعر [طويل]

فَمَا خَيْرُ مَنْ لَا يَنْفَعُ ٱلْأَهْلَ عَيْشُهُ وَإِنْ مَاتَ لَمْ تَجْزَعْ عَلَيْهِ أَقَارِبُهُ

والله تعالى ينفعهم بمطالعته كما يحبّ ولا يجعله وبالاً عليّ وعليهم بفضله وجوده.

فصل ٢

٢٩ اعلم أنّ ما اتّضح فيه كلام النظّار من المسائل المطلوبة واستوفي عليه البرهان في كتبهم فإنّي لا أطوّل بذكره هذا الكتاب بل أقتصر على ذكر ما أهملوه ولم يتّضح كلامهم فيه غاية الاتّضاح كعلم الله بالجزئيّات وحقيقة النبوّة وبيان أنّها عالم من عوالم لا يُتصوّر للعقل الوصول إليها وغير ذلك من المسائل التي تاهت فيها عقول النظّار كما[١] تجد في الكتاب تفصيله فأمّا المسائل التي حقّقوا القول فيها غاية التحقيق فلا أتعرّض لها إلّا أن يجيء ذلك عرضاً في أثناء الكلام غير مقصود كما هو حكم المسألة التي أذكرها في هذا الفصل في إثبات الموجود القديم وإنّما أوردت ذلك لغرض مهمّ وهو أن يُقابل ما أذكره فيها بجميع ما ذُكر في الكتب ويُنصف أنّه هل يُتصوّر أن يكون قول أوجز وأقرب إلى التحقيق منه أم لا.

٣٠ فإنّ أهل النظر حقّقوا القول في تلك المسألة من وجوه كثيرة وأكثرهم ضلّوا فيه عن سواء السبيل كمن استدلّ على وجوده أعني على وجود القديم من طريق النظر في الحركة

١ (كما) في ع؛ أ، ج: كفا ما؛ م: كثا ما.

longing to augment their insight, and their quest for what lies beyond knowledge and the intellect. I am referring to unveiling through tasting, by which the Real's elect are singled out. It is this group that will properly benefit from studying this book. My desire in writing these chapters was for their sake alone, fearing that the words of the poet would apply to me:

> What good is there in a man whose life does not benefit his people,
> And whose kinfolk do not even mourn his death?[34]

May God benefit this group in studying this work, as He loves. And may He, by His bounty and generosity, make it a tribulation neither for me nor for them.

Chapter 2: A Proof of the Eternal

I do not mean to make my book overlong by discussing the rationalists' exposition of the topics under investigation, nor the extensive demonstrative proofs they have employed. Rather, I will restrict myself to discussing what they have disregarded and matters they are not entirely clear on, such as God's knowledge of particulars,[35] the reality of prophecy, and the fact that it is a world inconceivable for the intellect to reach, and other issues that have stymied their intellects, and that are explained in detail throughout this work. I will not broach those issues in which their statements have been entirely correct, except as may happen to arise in context. Such is the case with the issue I am going to discuss in this chapter concerning the proof of the Eternal existent.[36] I only go into this for an important reason—namely, to compare my discussion of the issue with all the discussions in their books, thus addressing, in all fairness, whether or not my statements are to be considered more succinct and closer to the truth than these statements. 29

The rationalists have spoken correctly on this issue in many cases, but most of them have strayed from the right way,[37] just as those who have tried to prove its existence—I mean, the existence of the Eternal—by means of speculating about motion. For, even if this is a clear approach and adequate to the purpose, 30

فإنّ ذلك وإن كان طريقاً واضحاً وبالمقصود وافياً فسلوكه يطول ويحتاج فيه إلى إتقان مقدّمات يستغني عنها من يسلك الطريق المستقيم. نعم لست أنكر أنّ النظر في الحركة فيه فوائد كثيرة ولكنّي أقول إنّه مستغنى عنه في تلك المسألة من حيث ذاتها وقد ذكر الإمام حجّة الإسلام الغزاليّ رضي الله عنه في كتابه الموسوم بالاقتصاد في الاعتقاد قريباً من عشر أوراق في إثبات القديم ولعمري إنّه كان معذوراً في ذلك فإنّ كتابه هذا على منهاج كتب الكلام وإن كان أكثر كلامه فيه مترقّياً عمّا يشتمل عليه كتب المتكلّمين وكثير ممّن سواه سوّدوا أوراقاً في تلك المسألة كما هو مشهور عند العلماء وذلك فضول مستغنى عنه.

٣١ والحقّ اليقين في إثبات القديم أن يُستدلّ عليه بالوجود الذي هو أعمّ الأشياء إذ لو لم يكن في الوجود قديم لما كان في الوجود موجود أصلاً والبتّة وذلك لأنّ الموجود ينقسم قسمة حاصرة إلى الحادث والقديم أعني إلى ما لوجوده بداية وإلى ما ليس لوجوده بداية فلو لم يكن في الوجود قديم لم يكن أصلاً حادث إذ ليس في طبيعة الحادث أن يوجد بذاته فإنّ الموجود بذاته يكون واجب الوجود والواجب بذاته لا يُتصوّر له بداية وينتج من هذه الكلمات قياس برهانيّ يلقّبه أهل النظر بالشرطيّ المتّصل ليكون إدراكه أسهل على المبتدي الذي لم يقوَ بعد على إدراك الحقائق المعقولة فيقال لو كان في الوجود موجود لزم بالضرورة أن يكون في الوجود قديم فهذا أصل يقينيّ لا يُتصوّر أن يشكّ فيه أحد من الخلائق. ثمّ يقال والوجود معلوم قطعاً وهذا أصل ثان وهو كالأوّل يقينيّ وبعد ذلك ينتج من الأصلين الثابتين وجود موجود قديم بالضرورة وهذا هو الاستدلال على القديم من طريق الوجود ولا يُتصوّر أن يكون وراء هذا البيان بيان لا في الإيجاز ولا في التحقيق.

٣٢ وبعد ذلك فلابدّ لك من البحث عن صفات هذا القديم الذي ثبت وجوده بطريق البرهان الضروريّ وأنّه كيف ينبغي أن يكون هذا القديم وذلك مشهور والكتب به مشحونة وليس هذا الكتاب ممّا يحتمل بيان جميع ذلك فلكلّ مقام مقال مخصوص والغرض

traveling this path will nevertheless be drawn out and require the establishment of premises with which those who travel along the straight path[38] can dispense. To be sure, I do not deny that there are merits to speculating upon motion, but I maintain that it can be dispensed with on the very issue of proving the existence of the Eternal. Indeed, in his book *Moderation in Belief*, Imam al-Ghazālī has devoted roughly ten pages to proving the Eternal.[39] By my life! He can be excused, for this book was written using the methodology of rational theology, even though most of what he says in the book far surpasses what the scholars of rational theology include in their books. Scholars are well aware that many people besides al-Ghazālī have wasted ink over this issue. But such excesses can be dispensed with.

Certain truth[40] in proving the Eternal lies in demonstrating it by way of that 31
existence which is the most general of things, for if there were not an Eternal in existence, there would, fundamentally, not be an existent in existence whatsoever. This is because existence is divided into that which encompasses the originated and the Eternal—that is, into that whose existence has a beginning and that whose existence does not have a beginning. If there were no Eternal in existence, there would, fundamentally, not be that which is originated, since it is not in the nature of that which is originated for it to exist by virtue of itself. Indeed, that which is existent by virtue of itself is the Necessary Existent.[41] And that which is necessary in itself cannot be conceived as having a beginning. From these points a demonstrative proof—referred to by logicians as a "conditional"[42]—emerges to make the point easier to comprehend for the beginner who is unable to apprehend intelligible realities. Thus, it can be said: (1) "if there were an existent in existence, it would necessarily entail that there be an Eternal in existence." This is a certain premise: it is inconceivable for anyone to doubt it. Then it can be said: (2) "existence is clearly known." This is the second premise, which, like the first, is certain. Thereafter, (3) the existence of an eternal existent necessarily follows from these two firm premises.[43] Such is the demonstrative proof of the Eternal by way of existence. Be it succinct or extended, further exposition is inconceivable.

Next, you must investigate the attributes of the Eternal—whose existence has 32
been affirmed by way of necessary demonstrative proofs—and how the Eternal must be. This type of investigation is well known, and books are replete with it. But my book does not permit an explanation of all this. For to every context there corresponds a specific mode of discourse, and the motive of my book is to

من هذا الكتاب بيان أمرهو أشرف من العلوم العقليّة فلا نطوّل بذكرها فاعلم الآن وتيقّن أنّ ما انتهى نظر النظّار فيه إلى هذا الحدّ من الوضوح فالغالب عليّ أن لا أتعرّض لذكره في هذه الفصول إلّا اذا احتجت إلى ذلك في شيء ممّا وراءه.

فصل ٣

٣٣ لا شكّ عند ذوي البصائر النافذة في حجب الغيب وسرادقات الملكوت في وجود معنى صدر عنه الوجود على أتمّ الوجوه وهو الذي عُبّر عنه خارج الحجب في لسان العرب بقولهم الله تعالى وأعني بذوي البصائر من يدرك وجود ذلك المعنى من غير مقدّمة علميّة كما هو حال أهل النظر وذلك المعنى يتعالى ويتقدّس عن أن يطمح نحو حقيقته نظر ناظر سواه وسبحانه عن أن يطمع طامع في جوازة ذلك فهو المتعزّز بذاته لا عن ذاته.

٣٤ فذاته ونفسه هي التي اقتضت هذا التعزّز على الغير كما أنّ الشمس بذاتها تقتضي في كمال سلطنة[١] إشراقها أن تكون متعزّزة عن أن تمتدّ إليها أبصار الخفافيش ﴿وَلِلَّهِ ٱلْمَثَلُ ٱلْأَعْلَىٰ﴾ . ومن آياته الشمس ولولا إذنه وكرمه الفائض المقتضي للإذن لما اجترأ أحد من البشر على ضرب مثل له وكيف لا ويستحيل ضرب المثل في حقّه إذ ﴿لَيْسَ كَمِثْلِهِ شَيْءٌ﴾ . فالشمس في المثال الذي ضربناه ليست تفي بكمال المقصود فإنّها لا تقتضي بذاتها لا تعزّزًا ولا غيره لأنّ وجودها مستفاد من الغير مع جميع صفاتها وليس في الوجود موجود له ذات يحقّ لها حقيقة الوجود سوى الواحد القهّار الذي هو متنزّه عن كلّ كمال يدركه الأنبياء والمقرّبون فضلًا عن نقصان يتخيّله فيه

---

١ (سلطنة) في ج، م؛ أ: سلطانها؛ ع: سلطان.

explain a matter nobler than the intellectual sciences themselves. So we will not prolong the book by discussing these things. You should keep in mind that in these chapters I only draw on supremely clear theoretical reflection when I need to cite it in order to launch into something beyond it.

Chapter 3: God's Transcendence

For those who have insight that penetrates the veils of the unseen and the canopies of the spiritual realm, there is no doubt that there exists a supra-sensory reality from which "existence" emerges in the most perfect of ways. Outside of these veils, this supra-sensory reality is what is called "Allāh" in Arabic. By "those who have insight" I mean people who perceive the existence of this supra-sensory reality without rational premises, unlike the rationalists. This supra-sensory reality is too exalted and holy for the gaze of anyone other than it to turn toward its reality.[44] Glory be to Him that anyone should even desire permission for this! For He is totally unapproachable by others in His essence, but not by Himself. 33

His essence and self are what demand this unapproachability of others, just as the sun in its essence demands, by virtue of its sheer splendor, that it be unapproachable by the sight of bats: «And to God belongs the loftiest similitude»;[45] and among His signs is the sun.[46] But for His permission and the abundant generosity demanded by it, not a single person would have the audacity to liken Him to something. How could it be otherwise, since likening Him to things is impossible in any case? «There is nothing like Him».[47] The sun to which we likened God does not adequately address our aim, for, in its essence, the sun demands neither unapproachability by others nor anything else. This is because the sun's existence—along with all of its attributes—is derived from something other than the sun. Indeed, in existence there is no existent with an essence that necessitates the reality of existence other than the One, the Paramount, who is far above every perfection attained by the Prophets and the angels in His proximity, let alone the deficiencies imagined by those with weak insight—those to 34

ضعفاء البصائر الذين يكنّي عنهم القديم ويقولون ويظنّون ﴿ بِٱللَّهِ ظَنَّ ٱلسَّوْءِ عَلَيْهِمْ دَآئِرَةُ ٱلسَّوْءِ ﴾ .

٣٥ فلعزّة ذاته على عموم الخلق قال في كتابه الكريم ﴿ سُبْحَٰنَ رَبِّكَ رَبِّ ٱلْعِزَّةِ عَمَّا يَصِفُونَ ﴾ . ولكمال كرمه ونهاية عنايته بعباده نزّه نفسه عن النقصان تلطّفاً بهم وتعطّفاً عليهم فقال جلّ من قائل ﴿ لَمْ يَلِدْ وَلَمْ يُولَدْ ﴾ ولم يتّخذ ﴿ صَٰحِبَةً وَلَا وَلَدًا ﴾ . وهو منزّه في بصائر العارفين عن الكمال الذي يمكن إدراكه للخلق حسب تنزّهه عند الجاهلين عن كلّ نقصان.

فصل ٤

٣٦ فالله عزّ وجلّ هو مصدر الوجود على اختلاف أجناسه وأنواعه والوجود ينقسم إلى أقسام عامّة يندرج تحتها جميع الموجودات كانقسامه إلى القديم والحادث والكامل والناقص والكثير والواحد[١] ومن أقسامه العامّة انقسامه إلى ما له من ذاته خبر وهو كلّ ما له حياة وإلى ما ليس له من ذاته خبر وهو كلّ ما ليس له حياة وكلّ واحد من هذين القسمين يمكن تقسيمه إلى أقسام مختلفة باعتبارات متعدّدة فينقسم القسم الأوّل وهو الذي له من ذاته خبر في إدراكه إلى ما لا يدرك إلّا الموافق لطبعه وإلى ما يدرك المنافي لطبعه مع الموافق له وأمّا القسم الذي لا خبر له من ذاته فينقسم عند اعتبار لونه مثلاً إلى الأبيض والأسود وغيرهما وينقسم انقسامات أُخر عند اعتبارات سواه وشرح ذلك يطول وليس الغرض متعلّقاً به فنضرب[٢] عنه صفحاً إلى ما هو الغرض المقصود.

٣٧ ونقول بعض الموجودات إذا اعتُبر نسبتها إلى القسم الذي يدرك الموافق لطبعه مع المنافي ينقسم باعتبار تلك النسبة فقط إلى الخير والشرّ والموافق للقوّة المدركة خير

١ م: القليل. ٢ م: فيضرب.

whom the Eternal has alluded as uttering and thinking «ugly thoughts about God; upon them is an ugly turn!»[48]

35 On the subject of the general inaccessibility of God's essence, He says in His book, «Glory be to your Lord, the Lord of might, above what they ascribe».[49] On the subject of the perfection of God's generosity and the height of His solicitude for His servants, He shows them great affection and tenderness and declares Himself far beyond any deficiencies. He says, «He begets not; nor was He begotten»,[50] and He takes «neither consort nor child».[51] In the eyes of the recognizers, He is far above even the perfection that people can perceive, much in the same way as, according to the ignorant, He is far above all imperfection.

Chapter 4: Categories of Existence

36 It is God who is the source of existence in all the diversity of its genera and species. Existence divides into general categories, which take in all existents, such as its division into the eternal and the temporally originated, the perfect and the deficient, and the one and the many. And among existence's general categories is its division into existents that are self-aware (namely, that which is alive) and into existents that are not self-aware (namely, that which is not alive). Each of these two categories of existents can be divided into diverse categories from numerous standpoints. The first category of existents—namely, those that are self-aware in their perception—divides into things that only perceive what conforms to their natures, and things that perceive both what precludes and what conforms to their natures. The category of existents that divides into things that are not self-aware divides, for example, with respect to color: white, black, and so on. It also divides into other categories with respect to other things. An explanation would be extensive and a distraction. So let us leave it and turn to our intended goal.

37 When the relation of some existents to the category of existents that perceive both what conforms to and what precludes their natures is considered, they divide into good and bad with respect to that relation only. That which conforms

بالنسبة إليها ما دام يوافقها إدراكه فإذا تغيّرت بينهما هذه النسبة فلم يوافقها إدراكه بل أضرّ بها كان شرًّا بالنسبة إليها ولذلك يجوز أن يكون الشيء الواحد في حالة واحدة خيرًا وشرًّا بالنسبة إلى مدركين وما أصدق القائل إذًا [طويل]

مَصَائِبُ قَوْمٍ عِنْدَ قَوْمٍ فَوَائِدُ

فصل ٥

اعلم أنّ الله الذي هو مصدر الموجودات على اختلاف أقسامها له أسامٍ كثيرة بالنسبة إلى تلك الأقسام وتكاد تلك الأسامي تخرج عن الحصر لو أراد مريد أن يستوفي جميعها فله باعتبار النسبة إلى كلّ موجود حصل منه اسم وأمّا ما سمّى به نفسه في كتابه الكريم وعلى ألسنة أنبيائه عليهم السلام وسُمّي به عند الخلق فهو محصور وهذه الكلمات ربّما تحتاج عند الضعفاء إلى زيادة شرح وإيضاح وأنا أكسّر سورة الإنكار في ذلك. ٣٨

وأقول إذا اعتُبر ذات الله عزّ وجلّ من حيث هي مصدر القسم الذي يدرك الموافق والمنافي واعتُبر مع هذا نسبة ذلك القسم إلى الشيء الذي يوافقه وينافيه من حيث يوافقه وينافيه ظهر له اسمان وهما الضارّ والنافع فإنّ الجماد لا يضرّه شيء ولا ينفعه من حيث الإدراك وإن كان يجوز أن تنعدم صورته بشيء فذلك الشيء هو الذي ضرّ صورته ولكن الاصطلاح الأصليّ الحقيقيّ في الضرّ والنفع أنهما لا يطلقان إلّا على ما له إدراك وأمّا إطلاقهما في مقتضى اللسان على غيره فهو بطريق النقل والألفاظ المنقولة كثيرة وهي أشهر من أن يُحتاج إلى بيان ولا عبرة بالألفاظ بعد ظهور المعاني. ٣٩

to the faculty of perception is good in relation to that faculty as long as its perception conforms to that faculty. But when the relationship between the two changes, its perception will no longer conform to that faculty; rather, its perception will be a detriment to that faculty and will be bad in relation to it. This is why, in relation to two perceivers, it is possible for one thing to be good and bad at the same time. How true then are the words of the one who said:

> One man's tribulation is another man's treasure.[52]

Chapter 5: Divine Names

God, who is the source of existents in all their diverse categories, has many names in relation to these categories. And these names would be virtually countless were an aspirant to try to enumerate them all. God has a "name" from the standpoint of His relation to each existent that comes about from Him. The names He gave Himself in His noble Book and which were expressed by His Prophets, and those by which He has come to be named by people, are restricted. These words might need more explanation and clarification for the weak-minded, so I will now bring down the walls of obscurity. 38

When God's essence is considered insofar as it is the source of the category of existents that perceive both what conforms to and what precludes their natures, and, alongside this, when we consider the relation of this category of existents to something that both conforms to and precludes their own natures (insofar as it does conform to and preclude them), we have two names for the source—namely, Harmer and Benefiter.[53] In terms of perception, a thing can neither harm nor benefit an inanimate object. But if its form can be nullified by a thing, then that thing is what "harms" its form. At any rate, in their original and common usage, "harm" and "benefit" only apply to that which has perception. Their application in everyday speech to other things occurs through transmission in language. And words transmitted in language are numerous and far too well known to need any explanation; for consideration need not be given to words when their meanings are evident. 39

فصل ٦

٤٠ لعلّك تقول الضارّ والنافع صفتان فكيف قلنا إنّهما اسمان وهل يجوز أن يقال صفات الله تعالى أسماؤه أم بينهما فرق فاعلم أنّا إذا نظرنا من حيث الحقيقة فالفرق ظهر بين الاسم والصفة فإنّهما متغيّران في المعنى فالاسم هو اللفظ الذي وضعه أهل الاصطلاح للدلالة على مسمّاه من غير أن يعتبر فيه صفة على حدتها وأمّا الصفة فهي بالعكس من ذلك وهذا كما أنّ اسم الحجر يدلّ على مسمّاه من غير أن يعتبر منه الصلابة أو اللين والصلب واللين صفتان لا يُطلقان إلّا عند اعتبار شيئين مخصوصين في الحجر وغيره وهذا هو الحقّ الصريح مهما نظرنا من حيث العقل.

٤١ فأمّا إذا نظرنا من حيث الشرع فقد قال الله تعالى ﴿وَلِلَّهِ ٱلْأَسْمَآءُ ٱلْحُسْنَىٰ فَٱدْعُوهُ بِهَا﴾ . وعلى هذا يندرج اللطيف الخبير[1] والرحمٰن الرحيم[2] تحت تلك الأسماء ويُشبه أن لا يكون له اسم يدلّ على حقيقة مسمّاه من غير اعتبار بعض صفاته إلّا الله فإنّ هذا الاسم له بمنزلة أسماء الأعلام[3] للغير.

فصل ٧

٤٢ إذا نظرت نظرًا شافيًا علمت أنّ كلّ ما وصف الله تعالى به نفسه أو وصفه به غيره فهو باعتبار نسبته إلى بعض الموجودات أو إلى جميعها وسيأتي لذلك مزيد إيضاح فيما بعد وأمّا الاسم الذي هو علميّ له فيشبه غاية الاشتباه أن يكون موضوعًا للدلالة على الموجود الذي انتهى إليه نظر السالك كالذي يسافر من طريق الوجود

---

١ ج،ع،م: اللطيف والحكيم. ٢ ج،ع،م: والخبير والرحيم. ٣ (الأعلام) في ع؛ أ، ج،م: الإعلام.

Chapter 6: Divine Attributes

40 You might say, Harmer and Benefiter denote two attributes, so how can we say that they are both names? And can it be said that God's attributes are His names, or is there a difference between them? When we look at it from the perspective of the intellect,[54] the difference between a name and an attribute is apparent, for they both differ in their meanings. "Name" is a term linguists use to denote a referent irrespective of the attributes it has. "Attribute" is the opposite. It is like when the name "stone" denotes its referent irrespective of its being hard or soft. For "hard" and "soft" are attributes that are only ascribed to two specific qualities found in stones and similar objects. This is the plain truth when we look at things from the perspective of the intellect.

41 But when we look at it from the perspective of revelation, we find that God says, «To God belong the most beautiful names; so call upon Him by them».[55] As such, "the Gentle, the Aware," and "the All-Merciful, the Ever-Merciful" are included among these names. Apart from the name "God," it appears that God does not have a name that can denote the reality of its referent irrespective of some of His attributes. Thus, for Him the name "God" functions as proper names do for others.

Chapter 7: The Divine Names Are Relations

42 If you think clearly about it, you will come to know that all the attributes God gives Himself or that are given to Him by others are from the standpoint of His relation to some or all existents. Further light will be shed on this later. It very much appears to be that the word "God" as a proper name is used so as to denote that Existent Being who is the ultimate end of the traveler's gaze. It is like traveling along the path of sensory existence to intellectual existence, with the traveling coming to an end when the doors of the spiritual realm[56] are opened up.

الحسّيّ إلى الوجود العقليّ ثمّ انتهى به السلوك إلى أن فُتحت له أبواب الملكوت فلمّا انتهى تغلغله في بحار الملكوت ظفر بدرّة التوحيد ووضع الاسم العلميّ للدلالة على تلك الدرّة لا باعتبار نسبتها إلى موجود صدر عنها بل باعتبار ذاتها فقط من حيث رآها موجودة.

٤٣ وأمّا الذي سمّى تلك الدرّة قديمة فإنّما سمّاها بذلك من حيث رأى مغايرتها لسائر الذوات في الحاجة إلى علّة موجدة لها وكذلك إذا نظرت إلى اسم الحيّ والحقّ علمت أنّ واضعهما نظر عند الوضع إلى موت الغير وبطلانه وأمّا الاسم الذي هو كالعَلَم له فلا تجد فيه شيئاً من ذلك وربّما يُتكلّف في ذلك أيضاً ويُتصرّف فيه بأنواع من التصرّفات الباردة التي ذكرها أهل النحو والتصريف في كتبهم واشتغالي بشرح وجوه الخلل في تلك التصرّفات لا يحتمله الوقت فإنّه أنفس من أن يُضيّع بأمثال ذلك ولا هذه اللمعة تحتمله أيضاً فإنّها تنبو مع اختصارها عن بيان ما يضاهي ذلك.

فصل ٨

٤٤ كلّ ممكن فيجب وجوده بالقديم هكذا جرت سنّة الله تعالى في الملك والملكوت ﴿وَلَن تَجِدَ لِسُنَّةِ ٱللهِ تَبۡدِيلاً﴾. وكلّ ما لم يُوجد فهو يُعدّ محالاً لوجود أعني بغيره لا بذاته والمحال لا يكون مقدوراً وما لم يصر الشيء مقدوراً فالقدرة الأزليّة لا توجده وبيان ذلك أنّ السبب في وجود الموجودات هو الله تعالى وهو موجود ولا مانع من وجود المسبّب مع وجود السبب إلّا فَقْد شرط لأنّ وجود المشروط مع عدم الشرط محال ومهما وُجدت شروط الممكن أوجبت القدرة الأزليّة وجوده بالضرورة ومادام يعوزه شرط فهو بعد ليس بممكن الوجود فإذا تحقّق ذلك فاعلم أنّ كلّ موجود

When immersion in the oceans of the spiritual realm is over, the traveler seizes the pearl of divine unity and then coins an intelligible proper name in order to denote the pearl—not from the standpoint of its relation to an existent that emerges from it, but from the standpoint only of its essence, insofar as he sees it as an existent.

The name "Eternal" is given to this pearl only with respect to its difference 43
from other essences, which need a cause to bring about their existence. Likewise, if you look at the names "the Living" and "the Real," you will come to realize that they are used with an eye on the death and unreality of something else.[57] When it comes to the name that functions like a proper name for Him,[58] you will find no aspect of this therein. A forced explanation of this name may be offered, involving all sorts of silly derivations discussed by the grammarians and scholars of morphology in their books. I have no time to be distracted with commenting upon these flawed derivations. Indeed, time is too precious to be wasted on this kind of thing. This book would also not allow it, as this would conflict with its concise treatment of such topics.

Chapter 8: Necessity, Contingency, Impossibility

The existence of every contingent is necessitated by the Eternal. It is in this way 44
that God's custom proceeds in the material realm and in the spiritual realm: «and you will find no alteration in God's custom».[59] Whatever is not yet brought into existence can be considered "impossible in existence"—that is, impossible through another, but not impossible in itself: the impossible is not yet destined to exist. And, as long as something is not yet destined to exist, the beginningless power will not bring it into existence. Here is an explanation of this point: the cause of the existence of existents is God, who is the Existent. And there is nothing to prevent the existence of the causer vis-à-vis the cause except for the absence of a certain condition: for the existence of the conditioned with the non-existence of the condition is impossible. But whenever the conditions for contingents are to be found, the beginningless power will necessarily bring about their

فهو واجب الوجود إمّا بذاته وإمّا بغيره وكلّ معدوم فهو محال الوجود إمّا بذاته وإمّا بغيره.[1]

٤٥ فقد اتّصلت إذاً حدود الواجب والمحال ولا حائل يحول بينهما وإنّما الإمكان حدّ فاصل بينهما ولا حقيقة له أصلاً كالنقطة الوهميّة التي تُفرض على خطّ مستقيم وكالحدّ الحاجز بين الماضي والمستقبل من الزمان فكان آخر حدود الماضي متّصلاً بأوّل حدود المستقبل وأمّا الحدّ الذي يتّصل بهما[2] فلا حقيقة له إلّا في الوهم فإنّك إذا فرضت نقطة وهميّة على خطّ الزمان المستقيم[3] إلى الماضي والمستقبل لم تجد شيئاً فاصلاً عن الماضي والمستقبل بقي عن خطّ الزمان حتّى يكون هو حقيقة الحدّ الفاصل وهو النقطة المفروضة في الوهم.

فصل ٩

٤٦ إن خطر ببالك أنّ الله تعالى لِمَ يوجد ألغرضٍ يرجع إليه وهو محال أم لغير غرض وهو أيضاً محال إلّا من طريق الطبع المحض ولا يوصف الله تعالى بذلك. فاعلم أنّ هذا سؤال تحيّر فيه أكثر العلماء وهو الخاطر الذي خطر لداود النبيّ عليه السلام حيث قال أي ربِّ لِمَ خلقتَ الخلق فقال له كنت كنزاً مخفيّاً فأحببتُ أن أُعرف وكان المعنى الذي يقتضي صدور الوجود عنه هو الذي كنّى عنه بقوله فأحببت أن أُعرف ولا يُتصوّر إدراك ذلك المعنى إلّا للعارفين.

٤٧ وإنّما نصيب العقل أن يُستدلّ على وجوده من وجود الموجودات وذلك بعدما تحقّق عنده أنّ الله تعالى عالم بالجزئيّات بحيث لا يتشكّك فيه فإنّ العقل إذا تحقّق استناد

١ (وكلّ معدوم . . . بغيره) ساقطة من ع. ٢ ج، ع: يفصل بينهما. ٣ ع: المنقسم.

existence. So long as the impossible lacks a certain condition, it will not become a contingent existent.[60] Once this is realized, you should then know that every existent is a necessary existent, either in itself or through another. And every nonexistent is impossible in existence, either in itself or through another.

Therefore, the opposing ends of "the necessary" and "the impossible" conjoin, with nothing to separate them. However, contingency is a barrier that separates them, although it fundamentally has no reality, like an imaginary point positioned on a straight line. Or, contingency is like a barrier of time between past and future, where the furthest end of the past conjoins with the nearest end of the future. The point at which they conjoin has no reality except in our imagination. Thus, if you position an imaginary point on a linear stretch of time going from past to future, you will find that nothing to separate the past from the future remains on the time line, serving as the real barrier that separates the past and the future—namely, the point in your imagination that you positioned on the line. 45

Chapter 9: Why Did God Effectuate Existence?

The thought may occur to you, "Why did God effectuate existence? Is it because of a motive on His part?"—which is impossible!—or, "Did He effectuate existence for a different motive"?—which is also impossible, except by way of pure nature, though God cannot be described in that way.[61] This question has perplexed many scholars, and is the very thought that occurred to the Prophet David, since he said, "O my Lord! Why did you create the universe?" God replied, "I was a Hidden Treasure and I loved to be recognized."[62] That to which God alluded in saying "I loved to be recognized" is what demands the effusion of existence from Him. However, only the recognizers can conceivably comprehend this meaning. 46

The role of the intellect is simply to demonstrate God's existence by way of the existence of existents, and then to realize beyond doubt that God knows particulars. For when the intellect realizes the dependence of all existents upon 47

الموجودات إليه وتحقّق بعد ذلك علمه بالجزئيّات ظهر له لا محالة بأنّ إيجاد الواجب مع علمه بالإيجاد صفة ضروريّة الوجود لتلك الذات كما أنّ القِدَم مثلاً صفة ضروريّة لها فكما لا يجوز للواجب أن لا يكون قديماً فلا يجوز له أن لا يكون مصدراً للخلق وكان قول القائل لِمَ كان مصدراً للوجود كقوله لِمَ كان قديماً والجواب أنّه لو لم يكن قديماً لم يكن واجباً ولو لم يكن مصدراً للوجود أيضاً لم يكن واجباً فمن تحقّق استناد الوجود إليه فلا بدّ أن يقول إنّ الإيجاد صفة له. فنقول[1] هذه الصفة إن كانت ضروريّة الوجود له فالسؤال بِلِمَ عن كونه موصوفاً بها[2] هوس فهو كالسؤال بِلِمَ عن كونه قديماً وإن كانت غير ضروريّة الوجود له فهي صفة عارضة خارجة عن ذاته والعوارض تحتاج إلى العلل والواجب يأبى بذاته أن يحتاج في شيء إلى شيء وإلّا لم يكن واجباً.

فصل ١٠

٤٨ كلّ موجود حادثٍ وُجد فهو مقدور إذ لو لم يكن مقدوراً لما وُجد فمصدر الوجود إذاً قادر وكلّ موجود مقدور فهو مراد إذ لو لم يكن مراد الوجود لما وُجد فمصدر الوجود إذاً مريد وكلّ موجود[3] فله إلى الواجب نسبة ما وله أعني للواجب إلى كلّ موجود وجه وكلّ موجود فهو حاضر للواجب والواجب معاين لكلّ موجود وما ليس بحاضر للواجب فهو معدوم إذ ليس له إليه وجه ولولا وجه القيّوم لم يكن للموجودات أصلاً وجود كما يقال في النظر العاميّ لولا وجه الشمس المقوّم لوجود الشعاعات المنبسطة على الأرض لم يكن للشعاعات أصلاً وجود واذا كان للواجب إلى كلّ شيء وجه كان بالضرورة

---

١ ع: يقول. ٢ (بها) في ج، ع، م؛ أ: فإنّها. ٣ زائدة في: مراد.

Him, and subsequently realizes His knowledge of particulars, it will become clear beyond doubt that the effectuating existence of the Necessary, given His knowledge of this, is a necessary attribute of His essence, just as eternity, for example, is a necessary attribute of His essence. And just as it is impermissible for the Necessary to not be eternal, so too is it impermissible for Him to not be the origin of the universe. Thus, to ask "Why is He the source of existence?" is like asking "Why is He eternal?" Were the Necessary not eternal, He would not be necessary. Likewise, were He not the source of existence, He would not be necessary. He who realizes the dependence of existence upon Him will inevitably say that God's effectuating existence is one of His attributes. We can thus say that if this attribute necessarily exists for God, then the question "Why is this attribute attributed to God?" is folly. For this would be like asking why God is eternal. If the attribute of effectuating existence does not necessarily exist for Him, it would be an accidental attribute, external to His essence. And accidents are contingent upon causes, while the Necessary, by virtue of His essence, cannot be contingent upon things. If it were otherwise, He would not be the Necessary.

Chapter 10: The Face of God and Existents

Each originated existent that there is is effectuated by divine power—if it were 48
not, it would not exist. The source of existence is powerful, so each existent is effectuated by divine power, which means it is desired into existence—if it were not, it would not exist. Thus, the source of existence desires. Each existent has some kind of relation to the Necessary. And it has—I mean the Necessary—its face turned to each existent. Each existent is thus present with the Necessary, for the Necessary looks at each existent, face-to-face. Whatever is not present with the Necessary is nonexistent, because the Necessary does not turn its face to it. Were it not for the face of the Self-Abiding, no existent would have existed at all. This is like the general observation, "Were it not for the face of the sun, which sustains the existence of its rays spread over the world, none of the rays would have existed at all." Since the Necessary has its face turned to each existent,

عالمًا بكلّ ذرّة من ذرّات الوجود فهذه غاية العقل في عروجه فإنّه نسبة[١] في الواجب لكلّ[٢] ما يراه ضروريًا له من طريق الاستدلال عليه بالموجودات وصفاتها كما تراه من استدلاله بالموجودات وحدوثها على قِدَمه وقدرته وإرادته وعلمه وأمّا ما وراء ذلك فليس إدراكه من شأن العقل.

فصل ١١

كلّ ما في الوجود فنسبته من سعة العلم الأزليّ كنسبة لا شيء إلى شيء[٣] لا يتناهى ٤٩
وهذا الكلام يدركه العارفون ببصائرهم تحقيقًا بحيث لا يمكنهم أن يتشكّكوا فيه كما أنّ العقلاء يدركون أنّ الكلّ أعظم من الجزء وأنّ وجود المفرد مقدَّم على وجود المركّب وهذا الإدراك يقينيّ عند العقلاء لا تشوبه شبهة أصلاً والبهائم حُرمت إدراك ذلك مع وضوحه عند العقلاء إذ عدمت حاسّة هذا الإدراك فكذلك العقلاء المعتكفون في طور العقل الذين لا يمكنهم مجاوزته يحُرمون إدراك قولنا نسبة كلّ الموجودات إلى علم الله تعالى كنسبة لا شيء إلى شيء لا يتناهى فيتحيّرون ويتيهون في كيفيّة علم الله تعالى بالجزئيّات ويظنّون أنّ تغيّر علمه لازم من تغيّر هذه الجزئيّات.

---

١ ج، ع، م: يثبت. ٢ ج، ع، م: كلّ. ٣ (كنسبة لا شيء إلى شيء) في ع؛ أ، م: نسبة لا شيء من شيء؛ ج: نسبة لا شيء إلى شيء.

it necessarily follows that He knows each and every tiny speck in existence. This is the intellect's limit in its upward ascent, for it has a relation to the Necessary only with respect to each thing that it sees as necessary for the Necessary, as a result of seeking to prove it through existents and their attributes. It is the same when you see the intellect seeking to prove, through existents and their contingency, God's eternity, power, desire, and knowledge. The intellect is unable to perceive what is beyond this.

Chapter 11: God's Infinite Knowledge

The relationship between each thing in existence and the expanse of God's beginningless knowledge is like the relationship between nothing and the infinite. Through their insight, the recognizers perceive this statement as verified truth. Thus, it is impossible for them to doubt it, much as rational people naturally perceive that the whole is greater than the part, and that the existence of something simple is logically prior to something composite. For them, such perception is certain and entirely uncontaminated by doubt. Even though this is so clear to rational people, animals cannot perceive it because they do not have the senses appropriate to this kind of perception. Likewise, rational people devoted to the scope of the intellect—which they are unable to transcend—cannot perceive the meaning of our statement to the effect that the relationship between each existent and God's knowledge is like the relationship between nothing and the infinite. Thus, they are perplexed and at a loss in understanding how God's knowledge of particulars works, conjecturing that a change in His knowledge is a concomitant of change in any of these particulars.[63] 49

فصل ١٢

٥٠ ومن عجائب آيات القرآن قوله تعالى ﴿فَلَنَقُصَّنَّ عَلَيْهِم بِعِلْمٍ وَمَا كُنَّا غَآئِبِينَ﴾ فهو مشعر بأنّ كلّ شيء حاضر له وأنّه حاضر مع كلّ شيء فلذلك لا يعزب عن علمه شيء وأمّا قوله عزّ وجلّ ﴿وَسِعَ كُلَّ شَىْءٍ عِلْمًا﴾ فإنّ استعمال السعة فيه مع ذكر العلم أعجب من كلّ عجب وبيانه أنّ الموجودات مستفادة من علمه وعلمه محيط بكلّ شيء كما قال عزّ وجلّ ﴿أَحَاطَ بِكُلِّ شَىْءٍ عِلْمًا﴾ . والحقّ أنّ الله هو الكثير والكلّ وأنّ كلّ ما عداه هو الواحد والجزء لا بل فكلّ ما سواه فليس بجزء ولا واحد أيضاً إلّا من الوجه الذي تلي كليّته وكثرته وخذ لهذا الكلام الغامض في نفسه مثالاً على قدر عماك واعلم أنّ الشمس وإن كانت واحدة فالشعاعات الفائضة منها كثيرة فالحقّ أن يقال الشمس هي الكثيرة والشعاعات هي الواحدة فإذا كان العلم المستفاد من وجود المعلوم سُمّي علماً وهو علم الخلق فكيف لا يُسمّى الصفة الإلٰهيّة التي هي ينبوع الموجودات كلّها علماً لا بل الحقّ أن لا يطلق اسم العلم إلّا عليها فإن أطلق على غيرها فبالمجاز المحض والتوسّع البعيد والاشتراك الصرف من حيث الحقيقة عند العارف وإن كان العلماء يحكمون بأنّ إطلاق لفظ العلم على علم الله عزّ وجلّ وعلم الخلق بطريق التشابه.

٥١ وقول من قال إنّ الله لا يعلم الجزئيّات تعالى عن قولهم علوّاً كبيراً كأنّه ذهب إليه معتقده من حيث أنّه رأى تلك الجزئيّات داخلة تحت الماضي والمستقبل فظنّ أنّ تغيّرها يوجب تغيّر العلم بها وهذا هوس عند أهل التحقيق لأنّ الزمان جزء من الموجودات لأنّه عبارة عن مقدار الحركة والحركة من صفات الأجسام الخاصّة ومعلوم أنّ الأجسام أخسّ الأقسام الموجودة من العلم الأزليّ والموجودات كلّها شريفها وخسيسها مستفادة منه وليس وجود العلم الأزليّ موقوفاً على وجود شيء بل وجود كلّ شيء متوقّف على وجوده فإذا كان الزمان جزءاً من الموجودات كما بُيّن فكيف يجوز أن يقال يلزم من

Chapter 12: Knowledge Is a Divine Attribute

One of the wonders of the Qur'an's verses is God's statement, «Then We will recount to them with knowledge, for We are never absent»,[64] which makes one aware that each thing is present to Him, and that He is with each thing. This is why nothing evades His knowledge. As for His statement, «He embraces all things in knowledge»,[65] the use of "embrace" alongside "knowledge" is simply wondrous. What it means is that existents are derived from God's knowledge, and that His knowledge encompasses each thing, as He says, «God embraces all things in knowledge».[66] The truth is that God is the many and the all, and that each thing apart from Him is one and particular. Indeed, everything other than God is only "particular" and "one" insofar as His all-ness and many-ness accompany it. Now, take for this discussion, which is obscure in itself, the following simile that accords with the extent of your blindness! Though the sun is one, the rays that emanate from it are many, but it is actually correct to say that the sun is many and its rays are one. If knowledge derived from the existence of known things can be called "knowledge" (namely, human knowledge), why can the divine attribute that is the fountain of all existents not be called knowledge? The truth is that it is the only thing to which the word "knowledge" can apply. In the view of the recognizer, when the word is used but not applied to this divine attribute, it is completely metaphorical, deployed with maximal license and in a purely homonymous manner with respect to the way things really are (even if scholars have decided to ambiguously apply the word "knowledge" to both God's knowledge and human knowledge). 50

It is as if those who say that God does not know particulars—exalted is He above what they say![67]—have arrived at this belief from the perspective that God sees particulars as subject to past and present. They think that change in particulars necessarily entails change in God's knowledge of them, which is stupidity in the eyes of those who have verified the truth. This is because time is a part of existents as it is an expression of the measurement of motion, and motion is one of the specific attributes of bodies. And it is well known that bodies belong to the lowest category that exists in God's beginningless knowledge. All existents—be they noble or lowly—are derived from this beginningless knowledge whose existence is not dependent upon the existence of anything. Rather, the existence of each 51

تغيّر بعض الموجودات تغيّر علمه وإنّما كان يصحّ ذلك لو كان علمه متوقّفاً على وجود الموجودات كما هو حكم علم الخلق فإذا لم يكن علمه كذلك فلم يلزم من تغيّر الجزئيّات[١] تغيّر العلم المحيط بها.

فصل ١٣

٥٢ من ظنّ أنّ تغيّر الشعاعات بسبب حجاب يمنع استعداد الأرض لقبولها كالسحاب مثلاً يلزم منه تغيّر الصفة التي هي ينبوع الشعاعات ﴿فَقَدْ ضَلَّ ضَلَـٰلًا بَعِيدًا﴾. ولعمري يجوز أن تتغيّر الشمس فتتغيّر الشعاعات عند تغيّرها ولكنّا فرضنا الكلام فيها إذا كان تغيّراً لشعاعات[٢] صادراً عن حجاب يمنع قبول الأرض لنور الشمس لست أقول يمنع فيضان الشمس فإنّ الشمس بصفاتها كما كانت لم يتغيّر منها شيء بسبب هذا الحجاب وإنّما الحجاب يمنع قبول الأرض لفيضان نور الشمس.

فصل ١٤

٥٣ الشمس بذاتها كاملة في سلطان إشراقها ليست تحتاج إلى اكتساب كمال شيء آخر فمن ظنّ أنّها إذا قابلت جسماً فظهر شعاعها عليه وبلغ أثرها إليه كان ذلك كمالاً في حقّها

---

١ ج،ع،م: الموجودات. ٢ ج،ع،م: تغيّر الشعاعات.

thing is dependent upon its existence! Since time is a part of existents, as has been shown, how can it be said that, from the change that takes place among some existents, there must also be change in God's knowledge? This could only be the case if His knowledge were dependent upon the existence of existents, as is the case with human knowledge. But since God's knowledge is not like that, why would change in particulars entail change in the knowledge that encompasses them?

Chapter 13: God's Knowledge Is Changeless

52 Whoever thinks that a change in the sun's rays, because of an obstacle that veils the earth's capacity to receive them (such as a cloud, for example), requires that there also be a change in the attribute which is the source of these rays, «has gone very far astray».[68] By my life! The sun can change and its rays can change because of that change. But what I have supposed above is that when there is a change in the sun's rays, it will have occurred as a result of an obstacle that veils the earth's reception of sunlight. I did not say that an obstacle will obstruct the emanation of light from the sun. Being what they are, the sun's attributes cannot change on account of an obstacle. So an obstacle can only obstruct the earth's reception of the light emanating from the sun.

Chapter 14: A Glimpse at the Stage beyond the Intellect

53 In itself, the sun is perfect by virtue of the power of its radiance: it is not dependent upon something else to achieve this perfection. The sun faces a body, its rays shine onto it, and its effect reaches it; to think this is a perfection belonging to the body is a sad mistake. This can never be the case! The perfection of each

هذا خطأ فاحش[1] إنّما كمال كلّ شيء في مقابلته للشمس حتّى يحظى من كمال إشراقها بنصيب ما فأمّا أن تكون مقابلة الشمس لشيء كمالاً لها فكلّا وحاشا.

٥٤ هذا من حيث النظر العاميّ مثال جليّ في تفهيم المقصود وهو عند أُولي الألباب لبّ اللبّ وكمال الكمال وهذه الألفاظ تبعد غاية البعد أن تجلّي حقائق معانيها لبصيرة العقل وإنّما إدراكها إلى طور وراء طور العقل ومهما كان في باطنك شيء منه فلو أُفيضت عليك المعقولات كلّها دفعة واحدة لم يشفِ ذلك غليلك أصلاً[2] وكما لا يسكن طلب الجائع بالماء ولا طلب العطشان بالخبز فكذلك طلب العارف المخصوص بالطور الذي وراء العقل لا يسكن بالمعقولات.

فصل ١٥

٥٥ نسبة الموجودات كلّها إلى الله عزّ وجلّ واحدة فالحاضر من الأزمنة والماضي منها والمستقبل متساوي النسبة إليه وللموجودات إذا نظرتَ إليها بنظر العقل ترتيب فإنّ لبعضها تقدّماً على البعض كتقدّم المفرد على المُركّب ولكنّها إذا أُضيفتْ إليه ونُسبتْ على الوجه الحقّ تساوت نسبتها إليه فهو تعالى واسع ﴿وَسِعَ كُلَّ شَيْءٍ عِلْمًا﴾. أي لولا علمه بوجوده لما وُجد فالذي وُجد والذي لم يُوجد داخلان على التساوي تحت علمه المحيط الذي يعجز أفهام الخلق دون إدراكه وتتلاشى عقولهم دون ملاحظة حقيقته وتنمحق قواهم دون الوصول إلى أثر من آثاره إذ لا يشبه علمه أصلاً علم الخلق كما لم يشبه

١ ج، ع، م: فقد أخطأ خطأً فاحشًا. ٢ (أصلاً) في ج، ع، م؛ أ: أيضًا.

illumined body lies in its facing the sun such that it obtains, in some measure, a part of the perfection of the sun's radiance. It is impossible and can never be the case for the sun to face a body in order to obtain a perfection that belongs to that body!

In terms of general observation, the foregoing example lucidly conveys an understanding of the point at hand. And for the people who have deep insight,[69] this example gets to the heart of the matter. Yet the insight of the intellect is very far from the reality contained in the meanings of these expressions. Perceiving their meanings only belongs to a stage beyond the intellect. When something of this stage is in your soul, your thirst would simply not be satisfied even if all of the intelligibles were to pour down upon you all at once. As a hungry person will not be satisfied by water and a thirsty person will not be satisfied by bread, so too will the apprehension of intelligibles not satisfy the quest of the recognizer singled out by that stage beyond the intellect. 54

Chapter 15: The Inability to Comprehend God's Knowledge

The relation of all existents to God is one: past, present, and future are all equal in relation to Him. Existents have order when you look at them rationally. Some precede others, just as the simple logically precedes the composite. However, when existents are ascribed and attributed to God, their relation to Him is equal. For «He embraces all things in knowledge».[70] That is, were it not for His knowledge of the existence of each thing, it would not exist. So that which exists and that which does not exist equally apply to His all-encompassing knowledge, which is beyond human understanding (let alone human perception): intellects are annihilated before they can behold His reality and their faculties obliterated before they can attain even a trace of it. For human knowledge is utterly dissimilar to His knowledge, just as the sun's rays are utterly dissimilar to its essence in the realm of sensory images to which the vision of ordinary people is confined.[71] How can it be otherwise, seeing that God's beginningless knowledge existed before time and before all existents, just as it exists right now? It is not for our 55

ذات الشمس شعاعاً أصلاً في المثال المحسوس الذي يقتصر نظر العوامّ عليه وكيف لا وعلمه الأزليّ كان موجوداً قبل الزمان وقبل جميع الموجودات كما هو الآن موجوداً وليس لعقولنا الضعيفة أن تدرك علمه بالجزئيّات على ما يجب ولكنّها تدرك عجزها عن إدراكه كما يدرك الوهم عجزه عن إدراك حقيقة موجود لا يكون داخل العالم ولا خارجه ولا متّصلاً به ولا منفصلاً عنه.

٥٦ ولا يمكن أن يُعبّر عن حقيقة العلم الأزليّ من طريق العلم إلّا بهذه العبارة الموضوعة لمعنى غير المعنى الذي أريد به هاهنا ولذلك تُشوّش العقول والأفهام دون إدراك ذلك فمن قصر همّته وعقله وعلمه عن إدراكه فليحل بالعجز على قوّته وقدرته وليكرّر نظره في تفهّمه فعساه ينفتح له باب منه وليستعن بالله عزّ وجلّ على التوفيق لما يطهّر القلب من الحجب المانعة له عن الإدراك الحقيقيّ ولايبادرنّ إلى التكذيب دون التوقّف فيه فهذا معتقد قوم اعتقدوا بضع سنين في العلم القديم ما يعتقده سائر الضُلّال حتّى هداهم الله تعالى بنوره فضلاً منه وكرماً لا استحقاقاً منهم واستيجاباً والله عزّ وجلّ يزيدهم معرفةً بعجز عقولهم عن إدراك الأمور الإلٰهيّة.

٥٧ فمن طمع أن يحيط علمه وعقله بحقيقة علم كان موجوداً قبل الكون وقبل القبل وهو سبب لوجود الموجودات ومحيط بالكلّ إحاطة لا يُتصوّر أن يكون وراءها إحاطة فقد طلب بيض الأنوق وطمع في تناول العيّوق وانخلع بالحقيقة عن غريزة العقل وبالحريّ أن يُعدّ أمثاله من المجانين عند أهل الفضل فعقولنا أعجز عن إدراك العلم الأزليّ من النمل لا بل من الجمادات عن إدراك علمنا بدرجات كثيرة ونسبة علمه إلى علمنا كنسبة قدرته إلى قدرتنا فكما يستحيل في قدرتنا اختراع شيء أعني إيجاده لا من شيء وليس ذلك يستحيل في قدرة الأزل لأنّه ﴿بَدِيعُ ٱلسَّمَٰوَٰتِ وَٱلْأَرْضِ﴾ أي موجدهما ومخترعهما لا من شيء فكذلك يستحيل في علمنا أن يتغيّر المعلوم ولا يوجب تغيّراً فيه في علمنا لأنّ علمنا مستفاد من المعلوم ولا يستحيل ذلك في علم الله تعالى الذي يُسند إليه وجود

weak minds to perceive God's knowledge of particulars as it should be. But they can perceive their own incapacity to perceive it,[72] just as sense-intuition can perceive its incapacity to perceive the reality of an existent that is neither internal nor external to the world, and neither conjoined to nor separated from it.

It is impossible to express the reality of God's beginningless knowledge by 56
means of a formal method of knowing except through an established expression that conveys a meaning distinct from the meaning intended in that context. This is why the human intellect and understanding are confounded by God's beginningless knowledge, much less able to perceive it. Thus, those constrained in their aspiration, intellect, and knowledge vis-à-vis perceiving God's beginningless knowledge should come to terms with their incapacity and inabilities but should repeatedly employ their rational powers in trying to comprehend it, for a door might be opened up. They should ask for God's assistance to attain what will free their hearts of the obstacles that prevent true perception. They should not be too hasty to deem this as false, let alone suspend judgment over it. This was a belief held by one group for some years about God's eternal knowledge that accorded with the belief of the rest of the misguided. But then God guided them with His light, as a blessing from Himself out of His generosity, without them deserving it or meriting it. May God continue to help them to recognize the incapacity of their intellects in perceiving divine matters!

Whoever desires that his knowledge and intellect encompass the reality of a 57
knowledge that existed before the cosmos and even before a "before," a knowledge which is the cause of the existence of existents, and which encompasses the totality of things so completely that no kind of encompassing that is beyond it can be conceived, would be asking camels to lay eggs, or trying to grab hold of the stars, and would truly have lost his mind. Such a person should be considered by the learned as mad! Our intellects are even less capable of perceiving God's beginningless knowledge than ants, or, rather, than inanimate bodies are able to perceive our knowledge—in fact, by many degrees less capable! The relationship between God's knowledge and our knowledge is like the relationship between His power and our power, since it is impossible for our power to create a thing—that is, to bring it into existence from nothing. But that is not impossible for God's beginningless power because He is «the originator of the heavens and the earth»[73]—that is, He is the one who brought them into existence and created them from nothing. In this vein, with respect to our knowledge, it is impossible for a known object to change without necessitating change in our

الموجودات كلّها نعم لمّا كان العقل يدرك في أوّل نظره تفاوتًا بين القدرتين ولم يدرك تفاوتًا بين العلمين تاه في الحكم فوقع في هذه الأغلوطة وتعقّد بهذه الأحبولة.

٥٨ والله تعالى فوق العقل ومحيط بالعقل فكيف يُتصوّر أن يحيط العقل به وبصفاته وإحاطة الجزء بالكلّ في غاية البعد والعقل ذرّة من ذرّات الوجود الحاصل منه وقد ذكرنا أنّ الموجودات كلّها لا نسبة[١] لها أصلاً من سعة العلم الأزليّ فكيف يليق بالعقل أن يطمع في إدراكه ومن قصر فهمه عن إدراك هذا العجز فهو لجهله وقلّة استعداده لإدراك عجزه وليس لقصوره مستند إلّا ضيق حوصلة عقله [بسيط]

عَلَيَّ نَحْتُ ٱلْقَوَافِي مِنْ مَعَادِنِهَا[٢]   وَمَا عَلَيَّ إِذَا لَمْ تَفْهَمِ[٣] ٱلْبَقَرُ

٥٩ فسبحان من أرسل محمّدًا صلّى الله عليه وسلّم إلى كافّة الخلق ونطق على لسانه بالحقّ فقال جلّ من قائل ﴿فَأَيْنَمَا تُوَلُّواْ فَثَمَّ وَجْهُ ٱللَّهِ إِنَّ ٱللَّهَ وَٰسِعٌ عَلِيمٌ﴾. ولو لم يكن في القرآن سوى هذه الآية لكان كافيًا في الشهادة على جهل الجاحدين المكذّبين بإحاطة العلم الأزليّ بالجزئيّات فكيف ولا حرف منه إلّا وهو شاهد على عماهم وذلك أنّه ذكر في تلك الآية صفة الواسع مع ذكر العلم وفرق ذلك بأن قال ﴿فَأَيْنَمَا تُوَلُّواْ فَثَمَّ وَجْهُ ٱللَّهِ﴾. وهذه إشارة لطيفة صريحة إلى أنّ كلّ موجود فله نسبة ما إلى وجهه فلولا تلك النسبة لما وُجد ذلك الشيء فإنّه يعاينه لأنّ وجهه إليه وهذا معنى علمه بالجزئيّات.

١ (نسبة) في ج، ع، م؛ أ: يشبه. ٢ م: مقاطعها. ٣ ج: إذ لم يفهم؛ م: بأن لا يفهم.

knowledge. This is because our knowledge is derived from what is known; but this is not impossible with respect to God's knowledge, upon which the existence of every existent depends. Indeed, when the intellect initially perceives that there is a difference between divine power and human power but does not perceive a difference between divine knowledge and human knowledge, it will get lost in its judgments, thereby falling into this captious question and getting caught up in this intellectual trap.[74]

God is above the intellect and encompasses it, so how is it conceivable that 58
the intellect should encompass Him and His attributes when the part can never encompass the whole? The intellect is one of the tiny specks of existence effectuated by God. We have already stated that each existent has absolutely no relation to the embrace of God's beginningless knowledge, so how is it fitting for the intellect to desire to perceive it? To be incapable of understanding the perception of this incapacity is due to ignorance and insufficient preparation. And this incapability goes back solely to the constrained capacity of the intellect.

> I am tasked with carving rhymes from the source—
> what do I care if animals cannot comprehend?[75]

Glory to Him who sent Muḥammad to all people and spoke the truth through 59
him! «Wherever you turn, there is the face of God. God is all-encompassing, knowing».[76] If the Qur'an contained only this verse, it would have been testament enough to the ignorance of those who oppose and deny that God's beginningless knowledge encompasses particulars. How could it be otherwise, given that every single letter serves as a testament to their blindness? Alongside the mention of knowledge, in the verse God mentions the divine attribute of "encompassing" and highlights it by saying, «Wherever you turn, there is the face of God».[77] This is a subtle but clear allusion to the effect that each existent has some kind of relation to God's face, without which relation the thing would not exist. So God is face-to-face with it in that His face is turned toward it. This is what is meant by God's knowledge of particulars.

فصل ١٦

٦٠ ما دمتَ تطمع في التصديق بحقيقة العلم الأزليّ من طريق المقدّمات فأنت بعد تضرب في حديد بارد وإنّما التصديق الحقيقيّ به موقوف على ظهور نور في الباطن ينشرح به صدرك وتتّسع له حوصلتك فتدرك بذلك النور أنّ الله لا يشبه علمه علم الخلائق وينقطع عند ذلك طمعك عن الإيمان المستفاد من طريق العلم تحقّق يقيناً أنّه ما لم يظهر ذلك النور في الباطن لا يُتصوّر لأحد أن يؤمن بصفة العلم وسائر الصفات حقّ الإيمان. وحقّ الإيمان أن تدع التصرّف رأساً في الصفات الأزليّة وتدع الطمع في التصرّف وما لم تصر كذلك فلا تطمع في حقيقة الإيمان وهذا النور المشار إليه يظهر في الباطن عند ظهور طور وراء العقل ولا تستبعدنّ وجود ذلك فوراء العقل أطوار كثيرة ويكاد أن لا يعرف عددها إلّا الله عزّ وجلّ وأقلّ ما يُدرك في هذا الطور مدركات يُحتاج في إدراكها إلى الاستدلال بالمقدّمات فالبصير لا يحتاج إلى الاستدلال في إدراك المبصرات إنّما الأكمه هو الذي لا يتمكّن من إدراكها إلّا من طريق الاستدلال عليها كما لو استدلّ باللمس على وجود المبصر وأمّا ما وراء الوجود من حقيقة اللون فليس ممكناً إدراكه لأنّ طريق الاستدلال في ذلك مسدود.

فصل ١٧

٦١ العقل إنّما خُلق في الأصل لإدراك الأوّليّات التي لا يُحتاج فيها إلى المقدّمات فأمّا إدراكه لغوامض النظريّات من طريق الاستدلال والاعتبار بالمقدّمات فكأنّه خارج عن

Chapter 16: True Faith

So long as you desire to assent to the reality of God's beginningless knowledge by means of premises, you will be hammering cold iron. True assent to it is dependent upon the appearance of a light within and through which your heart expands, thereby broadening your capacity. Then, through that light, you will come to perceive that God's knowledge is not similar to human knowledge. This will put an end to your desire for faith acquired by way of conventional knowledge. For you will realize with certainty that as long as this light does not appear within the self, it is inconceivable that anyone can believe properly in the divine attribute of knowledge and the other divine attributes. True faith means that, at the outset, you relinquish your attempt to grasp the beginningless divine attributes and that you even relinquish any desire for such an attempt. Without such a resolve, you will not desire true faith. The "light" discussed here appears within the self with the emergence of the stage beyond the intellect. Do not deem this stage to be far-fetched, for there are in fact many stages beyond the intellect—and none knows their number but God. At this stage, the merest things to be perceived are the objects of perception, which need demonstrative proof by way of premises in order for them to be perceived. For the person who can see does not need demonstrative proof in order to perceive the objects of his sight. It is only the one who is born blind who would need such a proof of their existence to perceive them, just as he would seek to prove the existence of an object of sight by touching it. It would be impossible for him to perceive the reality of color because he does not have a way to demonstratively prove it. 60

Chapter 17: The Intellect's Proper Place

The intellect has essentially been created to perceive primary concepts,[78] 61
which do not require premises. And when it grasps recondite points involving

طبعه الأصليّ وكذلك وهذا كما أنّ حاسّة اللمس خُلقت في الأصل لإدراك الملموسات من حيث أنّها ملموسات فأمّا إذا استعملها الأكمه للاستدلال على وجود ما يُدرك بالقوّة الباصرة كان ذلك خارجاً عن طبعها أعني عن طبع الحاسّة اللامسة وكذلك الكتابة من خاصيّة اليد فإذا كان الأقطع يكتب برجليه كان ذلك خارجاً عن طبعها فإنّ القدرة الأزليّة لم توجد الرجل للكتابة بل لأمور أخر واعلم من ذلك أنّ إدراك المعقولات الغامضة إلى طور وراء العقل يستغني في إدراكها عن المقدّمات فإنّ نسبته إلى الغوامض نسبة العقل إلى الأوّليّات.

فصل ١٨

لعلّك تقول هذا يعسر عليّ إدراكه فزده شرحاً فاعلم أنّ نسبة هذا الطور إلى مدركاته ٦٢
كنسبة قوّة ذوق الشعر إلى إدراك الفرق بين موزون الشعر ومزاحفه فتلك القوّة لا تحتاج في إدراك هذا الفرق إلى مقدّمة فكذلك الطور الذي وراء العقل لا يحتاج في إدراك الفرق بين الحقّ والباطل في غوامض المسائل إلى مقدّمات كما يحتاج إليها الناظر من طريق العقل لنقصانه وكما يحتاج الأعمى في إدراك وجود المبصرات إلى أن يتحرّك بقدمه إليها ثمّ يدرك وجودها بقوّة اللمس وكما يحتاج الذي لا ذوق له إلى مقدّمات العروض حتّى يدرك بواسطتها الموزون والمنزحف من الشعر.

theoretical reflection through demonstrative proof and the articulation of premises, it is as if it has had to depart from its original nature in order to do so. Likewise, since the sense of touch has essentially been created in order to perceive objects of touch insofar as they are objects of touch, were a person born blind to use it in order to demonstratively prove the existence of that which is perceived by the faculty of vision, that would be a departure from its nature (that is, from the nature of the sense of touch). Such too is the case with the act of writing, which is specific to the hand. Were an amputee who had lost a hand to write with his feet, that would be a departure from the foot's nature. For God's beginningless power did not bring feet into existence for the act of writing, but for other functions. From this you should know that the stage beyond the intellect does not require the perception of obscure intelligibles based on premises. Indeed, the relationship between it and such obscure matters is like the relationship between the intellect and primary concepts.

Chapter 18: The Stage beyond the Intellect and Premises

You might say, "This is difficult for me to grasp, so explain a little more." The relationship between the stage beyond the intellect and the objects of perception is like the relationship between the ability to taste poetry and being able to perceive the distinction between poetry with its meter correct and poetry that drags its feet. This ability does not need premises in order for such a distinction to be grasped. Likewise, the stage that is beyond the intellect does not need premises in order for the distinction between truth and falsehood in recondite matters to be perceived, unlike the rational thinker who needs intellectual methods to do so because of the intellect's deficiency. It is also unlike the blind man when it comes to perceiving the existence of the objects of sight—he needs to perceive them by going to them and touching them. And it is unlike the one who does not have a taste for the principles of prosody—he needs to perceive them through the medium of the accuracy and inaccuracy of meters and feet. 62

فصل ١٩

اعلم أنّ للعقل طريقاً إلى أن يدرك معنى القليل والكثير فإنّهما صفتان إضافيّتان ٦٣
للعدد وله طريق إلى أن يدرك أنّ القليل المطلق الذي لا أقلّ منه في الأعداد هو الاثنان وليس له طريق إلى إدراك الكثير المطلق الذي لا أكثر منه فاعلم أنّ نسبة الكثير المطلق في الإدراك إلى العلم الأزليّ كنسبة القليل المطلق فلا فرق في علم الله من إدراك الكثير المطلق والقليل المطلق ولا يمكن للعقل أن يدرك كيفيّة إحاطة العلم الأزليّ بذلك بل إدراكها موقوف على انفتاح عين في باطن الآدميّ يختصّ بها العارفون وحينئذ يتبيّن له حقيقة الطور الذي وراء العقل ونسبة العقل من هذه العين كنسبة الشعاع من الشمس وقصور العقل عن إدراك مدركات مملوكات هذه العين يضاهي قصور الوهم عن إدراك مدركات العقل فمن صادف من باطنه تصديقاً ضروريّاً لا مجال فيه للشكّ.

ولا ريب أنّ الكثير المطلق في علم الله عزّ وجلّ كالقليل المطلق من غير تفاوت فليتحقّق ٦٤
أنّ عين المعرفة قد انفتحت في باطنه وستصير ينبوعاً على القرب لأمثال هذه الحكم فإيّاه ثمّ إيّاه وأن يدع للعمى إليها طريقاً فكثيرًا ما يقع لها من الوقائع ما يعمّشها ويعديها وعلى الجملة يخرجها عن كونها مدركة لما يخصّها وليعتبر في ذلك بقوله تعالى ﴿مَثَلُهُمْ كَمَثَلِ ٱلَّذِى ٱسْتَوْقَدَ نَارًا﴾ . واعلم أنّ نسبة تلك الوقائع من عين المعرفة كنسبة الوقائع التي تقع للأرض وتبطل استعدادها قبولها لفيضان نور الشمس من الأرض.

Chapter 19: The Inner Eye

The intellect has a method by which it perceives the meaning of magnitude and paucity, which are relational attributes appropriate to numbers. The intellect has a method to perceive the fact that the absolutely smallest number (which no number can be smaller than) is two,[79] but it does not have a method to perceive the largest number possible, which no number is greater than. In terms of perception, the relationship between the largest number and God's beginningless knowledge is like the relationship between that number and the smallest possible number. For there is no distinction in God's knowledge between the greatest number and the smallest number, but the intellect cannot perceive how it is that God's beginningless knowledge encompasses them. Rather, the perception of this is dependent upon the opening of an eye inside the human self—the eye for which the recognizers have been singled out. It is then that the reality of the stage beyond the intellect will be made clear. The relationship between the intellect and this eye is like the relationship between the rays of the sun and the sun. And the intellect's deficiency in perceiving the objects of perception appropriate to this eye can be compared to the imaginal faculty's deficiency in perceiving the intellect's objects of perception—but for those in whom an assent necessarily occurs, there is no room for doubt. 63

There is no doubt that in God's knowledge the largest possible number is like the smallest possible number—there is no distinction between them. We should realize that, were the eye of recognition to open up inside of us, it would quickly become a source for this kind of wisdom. We should thus be on guard to ensure that this eye does not get blinded in the many ways that it can, by being afflicted with some kind of blight and obstruction of its vision—in a nutshell, causing it to lose its status as a special, perceptive faculty. One should take a lesson from God's words: «Their parable is that of one who kindled a fire».[80] The relationship between the eye of recognition and these things that can happen to it is like the relationship between the sun and those things that can happen to the earth, destroying its ability to receive the effusion of the sun's light. 64

فصل ٢٠

٦٥ من خواصّ الطور الذي بعد العقل أنّه إذا أدرك وجود الحقّ تعالى لزمه شوق عظيم إليه لا تُصوّر عنه العبارة وطلب تامّ والعقل أيضاً يلتذّ بإدراك وجود الحقّ ولكنّه ليس ذلك التذاذاً بإدراك كماله بل هو التذاذ به من حيث أنّه معلوم كما يلتذّ بسائر المعلومات من الحساب والطبّ وغيرهما ولعمري لا أنكر التفاوت في التذاذه بين إدراك الحقّ وبين إدراك مسألة حسابيّة ولكنّه كالتفاوت الذي يراه في سائر المعلومات من حيث شرفها وخسّتها بل من حيث أنّ بعضها فوق البعض بالطبع وكان العقل إذا التذّ بإدراك وجود الحقّ من حيث كونه معلوماً فهو شبيه بالبصر الظاهر إذا التذّ بإدراك مشموم طيّب من حيث أنّه مبصر ذو لون حسن فإنّ هذا الالتذاذ بعيد عن التذاذ حاسّة الشمّ برائحته عند إدراكها فكما أنّ إدراك البصير لوجود المسك بحاسّة البصر والتذاذه بإدراك لونه لا يظهر فيه عظيم شوق وكثير طلب للمسك كما هو في حقّ من يدرك رائحته بحاسّة الشمّ فكذلك من أدرك وجود الحقّ تعالى من طريق المقدّمات العقليّة فلا يلزم إدراكه الشوق الذي يلزم العارف وإنّما يلتذّ العقل بإدراك ذلك من حيث أنّه معلوم فقط.

فصل ٢١

٦٦ إذا انفتحت للسالك عين المعرفة فبقدر كمالها واستعدادها للإدراك تفيض عليه لطائف الأمور الإلٰهيّة وبقدر فيضان ذلك عليه يحصل له إلف مع عالم الملكوت

Chapter 20: Longing for God

65 One of the special attributes of the stage after the intellect is that when one perceives the existence of the Real there necessarily follows a tremendous longing for Him, which cannot be conceived through expressions or a thorough search. The intellect delights in perceiving the existence of the Real. However, this is not a delight in the perception of His perfection. Rather, it is delight insofar as He is an object of knowledge, as is the case with other objects of knowledge, such as mathematics, medicine, and the like. By my life! I do not deny that there is a difference between perceiving God and grasping a problem in mathematics. But this is the kind of difference that we notice in every form of knowledge, however noble or base, and insofar as some of them are naturally above others. But when the intellect delights in perceiving the existence of God insofar as He is an object of knowledge, it is similar to the delight the external eye takes in a pleasant scent insofar as it is an object of vision with a beautiful color. But such delight is far removed from the delight the sense of smell takes in the object's scent when this scent is perceived. Thus, when we perceive musk with the sense of sight and take delight in the perception of its color we will not experience a tremendous longing for the musk and will not want it as much as those who perceive its scent with the sense of smell. Likewise, the perception of the one who perceives God's existence by way of intellectual premises will not excite the same longing as that of the recognizer, for the intellect can only perceive God's existence insofar as He is an object of knowledge.

Chapter 21: Familiarity with the Spiritual World

66 When the eye of recognition is opened for the traveler, subtle and divine matters will, in accordance with its perfection and capacity for perception, pour down on him. And, in accordance with this outpouring, the traveler will obtain

وأنس بألطاف الحقّ وعشق لجمال الحضرة الأزليّة فيتناقص أنسه بهذا العالم على التدريج شيئاً فشيئاً ويتزايد بقدر ذلك أنسه بالعالم الإلهيّ وربّما تقيس الآن هذا الأنس على ما يحصل للنظّار من الأنس بالعلوم النظريّة وذلك ظنّ فاسد وخطأ شنيع[١] وخاطر فاحش وإنّما استُعير هاهنا لفظ الأنس وغيره من العشق والجمال وغيرهما ضرورةً فلا يغرّنّك تشابهها في المعاني المختلفة فتضلّ من حيث لا تدري وتقنع من مسمّيّاتها بترّهات تخيّلها عقلك الضعيف منها.

فصل ٢٢

من لم يُرزق من هذا الطور شيئاً ولم يصدّق عقله من طريق المقدّمات بوجوده ٦٧
فيكاد يستحيل له الإيمان بالنبوّة إذ النبوّة عبارة عن طور وراء هذا الطور الذي سبقت الإشارة إليه ومن لم يصدّق بذلك فهو بعيد غير مصدّق بالنبوّة أصلاً فما ظنّك بمن يكذّب بطور الوَلاية وهو الذي يظهر بعد العقل ولا يظهر طور النبوّة إلّا بعده وإن صدّق باللسان أو اعتقد بالقلب أنّه مصدّق بحقيقة النبوّة فهو مخطئ ويكون مثاله في اعتقاده هذا مثال الأكمه إذا اعتقد أنّه قد صدّق بوجود اللون وأدرك حقيقته حيث أدرك وجود المتلوّن بقوّة اللمس وهيهات فذلك بعيد عن إدراك حقيقة اللون.

١ (شنيع) في ج، ع، م؛ أ: لا يقرأ.

familiarity with the spiritual world, intimacy with God's subtle blessings, and love for the beauty of God's presence. The traveler's intimacy with the world will gradually diminish, and his intimacy with the divine world will proportionately increase. You may now want to compare this intimacy with what the rationalist theologians know "intimacy" to be through rational knowledge. But such a conjecture would be bad—a horrible mistake, a terrible thought. The word "intimacy" and other terms such as "love," "beauty," and the like are used metaphorically here, out of necessity. So do not let their ambiguous resemblance to various other meanings delude you, for you will then fall into error in ways that you do not know, contenting yourself with fanciful expressions dreamed up by your weak intellect!

Chapter 22: The Stage of Prophecy

The intellect of a person who has not been blessed with even a little experience 67
of this stage will not accept its existence as true merely by way of premises. Faith in prophecy is almost impossible for him since prophecy is an expression of a stage beyond that stage to which I have alluded. And whoever does not believe in this is far away, essentially not accepting prophecy as true. What then do you think of those who disbelieve in the stage of friendship with God,[81] which appears beyond the intellect, and beyond which the stage of prophecy appears? For even if they were to state or believe that they accept the reality of prophecy as true, they would still be wrong. Their belief would be like a blind man when he believes in the existence of color and perceives its reality insofar as he perceives something colorful, but does so with his sense of touch. That is absurd, being very far as it is from perceiving the reality of color!

فصل ٢٣

الإيمــان بالنبوّة إيمان بالغيب عند العقل فإن شبّه العقل هذا الغيب بشيء ممّا هو حاضر لإدراكه فهو بعيد جدّاً عمّا هو الحقّ فإن حصل لك مثل هذا الإيمان فاعلم أنّك تؤمن بالنبوّة وإلّا فحرام عليك أن تأكل أو تشرب أو تنام إلّا عن ضرورة حتّى تصل إلى هذا الإيمان فإن قبلت هذه النصيحة أفلحت وإن أهملتها أُهملت ﴿وَمَن جَٰهَدَ فَإِنَّمَا يُجَٰهِدُ لِنَفْسِهِۦٓ إِنَّ ٱللَّهَ لَغَنِيٌّ عَنِ ٱلْعَٰلَمِينَ﴾ . وسيتبيّن أمثالك عند ظهور صفة الموت قوله تعالى ﴿وَبَدَا لَهُم مِّنَ ٱللَّهِ مَا لَمْ يَكُونُوا۟ يَحْتَسِبُونَ﴾ . ٦٨

فصل ٢٤

تقولــــ فما السبيل الذي يجب سلوكه على العاقل حتّى يتمكّن من الإيمان بالنبوّة فأقول سبيله سبيل من لا ذوق له في الشعر في مجالسته أهل الذوق حتّى يحصل غرضه فكثير ممّن لا يكون لهم ذوق الشعر ولا يدركون فرقاً بين المنظوم والمنثور صدّقوا بوجود قوّة في غيرهم شأنها إدراك ذلك الفرق وذلك لكثرة مجالستهم لأقوام لم يُحرموا تلك القوّة فصاروا مؤمنين بالغيب إيماناً يقينيّاً. ٦٩

Chapter 23: Faith in the Unseen

For the intellect, faith in prophecy means faith in the unseen. Were it to liken the unseen to something within the purview of its perception, it would be very far from the truth. If you have faith in the unseen, then you believe in prophecy. And if you do not have faith in the unseen, then you should be forbidden to eat, drink, and sleep (except when necessary) until you arrive at this faith! Take this counsel and prosper. But if you disregard it, then you will be disregarded: «And whoever strives, strives only for himself. Truly God is beyond need of the worlds»;[82] and it will all become clear to those like you when death prevails: «And from God there will appear to them what they had not expected».[83] 68

Chapter 24: The Path to Faith in Prophecy

You might ask, "What is the path the intelligent person must follow in order to have firm faith in prophecy?" I would say that this path should be that of a person who does not have a taste for poetry but spends time with those who do, in order to achieve his goal. There are many people who do not have a taste for poetry and cannot grasp the difference between verse and prose but who believe in the existence of this ability in others. By spending enough time with those who do not lack this ability, they become believers—with faith and certainty—in something unseen. 69

فصل ٢٥

٧٠ صفات الله تعالى منقسمة إلى ما يُدرك من طريق النظر في بعض الموجودات واتّصافها بصفات مخصوصة كالحكيم والصانع والخالق وهذه الصفات يُتصوّر للعقل إدراكها فأمّا الصفات التي لا تعلّق لها بموجود أصلاً فإدراك ذلك وحقيقته موقوف على ظهور الطور الذي بعد العقل وذلك كصفة الكبرياء والعظمة والجمال والبهاء فإنّ كلّ ما يدركه العقل من معاني هذه الألفاظ بعيد عن حقائقها فإيّاك وأن تغترّ بظواهر الأمور فإنّ الطبع مجبول على التجلّي بكلّ كمال مع التعرّي عنه فلا يعترف بالعجز بل يخوض فيما يجوز له الخوض فيه وفيما لا يجوز ويزاحم فيما يمكن له إدراكه وفيما لا يمكن مزاحمة الوهم للعقل من مدركاته وحسّك شاهد على تكذيب الطبع إذا قال لك إنّ العقل يمكن له إدراك الجمال الأزليّ أن تقول له الجميل يُترك للأجمل فما بالك لا تترك له ما سوّاه مع أنّ أجمل الأشياء بالإضافة إلى جماله أقبح من كلّ قبيح وعند ذلك يفزع الطبع إلى هَذَيانات أشفق على زماني أن أضيّعه في ذكرها وفي وجه الخلل في كلّ واحد منها ومن ساعدته هذه الدولة فرُزق شيئاً من الطور المشار إليه حتّى أدرك به من الجمال الأزليّ قدراً قُدّر له إدراكه فهذا القدر يكفيه شاهداً على الغرض المطلوب.

Chapter 25: The Stage beyond the Intellect and the Divine Attributes

God's attributes can be perceived by reflecting upon certain existents and qualifying them with specific attributes, such as "wise," "artisan," and "creator." The intellect can conceivably grasp these attributes. As for those attributes that are not tied to any existent in any way, perceiving them and their reality is dependent upon the appearance of the stage beyond the intellect. These would be attributes like pride, greatness, beauty, and splendor. Indeed, all of the meanings of these terms that the intellect perceives are far removed from what they really are. So be careful not to be deluded by externalities, for people are naturally inclined toward all things that appear to be perfect, even though they may be devoid of perfection. And they never acknowledge their incapacity to know, but instead dive into things that admit of being dived into and those that do not, thus disputing over what they can perceive and what they cannot. The fact that the imaginal faculty can compete with the intellect over its objects of perception and your senses is proof of the falsity of this natural inclination. Now, if someone were to say to you, "It is indeed possible for the intellect to perceive beauty," you should respond, "If a thing of beauty is to be put aside for something more beautiful, why would you then not put aside all things for God, for the most beautiful thing in relation to His beauty is the vilest of things out there!" At that point, the questioner will naturally resort to nonsensical statements—but time is too precious for me to waste in discussing them and addressing all of their defects. Whoever is aided by that realm, and is blessed with some of the aforementioned stage so that thereby he can grasp whatever portion of God's beauty has been assigned to him, will have enough proof for the point being made. 70

فصل ٢٦

٧١ العشق من خواصّ هذا الطور فلا شكّ عند من شاهد أحوال العشق أنّ العقل معزول عن إدراك تلك الأحوال إذ لا سبيل للعاشق إلى اتّصال معنى العشق الذي هو ملابس له إلى فهم عاقل لم يلابسه ذوقاً حتّى يكون هو بمنزلة العاشق الذي ذاقه وهذا شأن العقل في جميع الأحوال من الغضب والفرح والخجل فالعقل يدرك العلوم وليس إلى إدراك الأحوال له سبيل نعم يدرك وجودها ويحكم على كلّ واحد منها بأحكام كثيرة فأمّا ماهيّة العشق وسائر الأحوال فلا يدركها العقل من طريق المقدّمات كما يدرك المدركات المعقولة إذا سمع مقدّماتها من غيره حتّى ساواه في الإدراك.

فصل ٢٧

٧٢ العشق يتبعه الطلب[١] وحقيقة الطلب أن يكون نظر الطالب بكلّيّته متوجّهاً إلى المطلوب وحينئذ يكون الطلب والوجدان توأمان واعتُبر في حقيقة الطلب بانجذاب الحديد إلى المغناطيس فإنّ الحديد إذا كان خالصاً انجذبه بكلّيّته إليه ولم يكن في طلبه تفرقة فإن اختلط بشيء من الذهب أو الفضّة أو غيرهما اقتضى ذلك نقصاناً في كمال الانجذاب ومهما لم يكن فيه شوب من غيره فالطلب الحقيقيّ وحينئذ يكون الوجدان أي الوصول إلى المغناطيس ضرورياً وهذا معنى قولنا الطلب والوجدان توأمان.

١ ع، م: الطلب للمعشوق؛ ج: الطلب.

Chapter 26: The Intellect's Relationship to Love

Love is one of the things specific to the stage beyond the intellect. For those who have witnessed the states of love, there is no doubt that the intellect is far from perceiving these states. To the understanding of the person restricted by his intellect and who has no taste of an intimate experience with love, there is no way for the lover to convey the meaning of that love with which he is so intimate. That can only happen when such a person stands in the same position as the lover who tastes love. This is what the intellect is like in every state, such as anger, joy, and shame. For the intellect perceives knowable things, but has no way to perceive such states. To be sure, it can perceive their existence and pronounce judgments about every single one of them in various ways. But the intellect cannot perceive what love and other states are about by way of premises in the way a person can perceive intelligible, perceptible objects when he hears of their premises from someone else, and then uses those premises to perceive those objects as adequately as the other person does. 71

Chapter 27: The Lover's Attraction to the Beloved

The pursuit of the beloved follows on from falling in love. This pursuit is fully actualized when the gaze of the pursuer is entirely turned toward the pursued. It is then that pursuit and ecstasy are twins. The reality of this pursuit can be expressed by the attraction of iron to a magnet: if the iron is unalloyed, the magnet will attract it, with nothing to impede the iron's attraction to the magnet. But if the iron is mixed with some gold, silver, or the like, this will compromise its attraction. Likewise, when the iron is uncontaminated, its fully actualized attraction to the magnet will ensue. It is then that ecstasy—namely, the iron reaching the magnet—will necessarily occur. This is the meaning of our statement, "pursuit and ecstasy are twins." 72

٧٣ ثمّ الحديد قد يعوقه عن الانجذاب عائق من خارج فلا يكون قادحاً في كمال الطلب إنّما القادح أن يكون في ذاته شوب أو جصّ أو غيرهما ممّا اختلط به في معدنه والعائق الخارج قد لا يكون له عظيم تأثير في قطع طريق الطلب إلى الانجذاب عليه ومهما لم يكن في ذات العاشق شوب من شيء يولّي[1] وجهه للمعشوق كان بكلّيّته ملبياً للإحرام إلى قبلته المطلوبة وهي وجه المعشوق وحينئذ يكون الطالب من أهل البداية في الطلب ويتجلّى له حقيقة قوله تعالى ﴿أَسۡلَمۡتُ وَجۡهِيَ لِلَّهِ﴾، وقوله تعالى ﴿إِنَّ ٱلدِّينَ عِندَ ٱللَّهِ ٱلۡإِسۡلَٰمُ﴾ وقوله تعالى ﴿فِطۡرَتَ ٱللَّهِ ٱلَّتِي فَطَرَ ٱلنَّاسَ عَلَيۡهَا﴾ وقوله تعالى ﴿أَلَا لِلَّهِ ٱلدِّينُ ٱلۡخَالِصُ﴾ وقوله تعالى ﴿لَآ إِكۡرَاهَ فِي ٱلدِّينِ﴾ وقوله تعالى ﴿فَلَا ٱقۡتَحَمَ ٱلۡعَقَبَةَ﴾ الآية.

٧٤ والفرق بين ما يعوق العاشق من داخل ويكون[2] منزلته منه منزلة الذهب إذا اختلط بالحديد وبين ما يعوقه من خارج ويكون منزلته منزلة يد قاصرة تمنع الحديد عن الانجذاب يكاد يعسر إدراكه إلّا على من صار له قدم راسخ في ذلك وإيّاك ثمّ إيّاك يا جامداً على علمك ومغروراً بعقلك أن تنظر إلى هذا الفصل وأمثاله بعين الاستحقار وتمنح لها سنبلتك وتظنّ أنّ ذلك من الطامّات التي سلف بها بعض الجمع من الطالبين[3] ولم يصل إلى شيء من معانيها ذوقاً فيكون ممّن يقول فيه القرآن ﴿وَإِذۡ لَمۡ يَهۡتَدُواْ بِهِۦ فَسَيَقُولُونَ هَٰذَآ إِفۡكٞ قَدِيمٞ﴾ وبقوله ﴿بَلۡ كَذَّبُواْ بِمَا لَمۡ يُحِيطُواْ بِعِلۡمِهِۦ وَلَمَّا يَأۡتِهِمۡ تَأۡوِيلُهُۥ﴾. هذا نصيبك من الواجب عليّ في نصيحتك وأمّا العارفون فسواء عليهم إيمانك وكفرك فمنزلة علمك الذي تدلّ به عندهم كمنزلة علم الخياطة والحجامة عند أهل التحقيق من العلماء وماذا على العالم المحيط علمه بحقائق المعلومات لو لم يحط بعلم الخياطة والحجامة.

١ (يوّلي) في ع، م؛ أ، ج: ليس يوّلي. ٢ (ويكون) في ج، ع، م؛ أ: وبين ما يعوقه من خارج ويكون. ٣ ج: تلقفها بعض الحمقى من الضالين؛ ع: يلفقها بعض الحمقى الضالين من الباطلين؛ م: يتلقّنها بعض الحمقى من الباطلين.

Moreover, iron may be prevented from being attracted to the magnet by an external object, but this will not cancel out its attraction to the magnet. The only thing that will do so is if, in its essence, there is a contaminant, or plaster, or some other substance mixed in with its ore. Indeed, an external impediment may not greatly affect the iron's ability to cover the path of its attraction toward the magnet. As long as the lover's essence does not contain a contaminant that will cause it to turn its face away from the Beloved, he will obey the call to consecrate himself in turning toward the object of his pursuit—namely, the face of the Beloved.[84] It is then that he will become a novice in his pursuit, and the reality of God's statements will become clear: «I submit to the Lord of the worlds»;[85] «Truly the religion in the sight of God is submission»;[86] «the primordial nature from God, upon which He originated people»;[87] «Indeed, pure religion is for God»;[88] «There is no coercion in religion»;[89] «Yet he has not assailed the steep pass».[90] 73

The difference between what impedes the lover internally (this is like gold mixed in with iron) and what impedes him externally (this is like a feeble hand that prevents the iron's attraction to the magnet) is quite difficult to perceive—but not for a person firmly rooted in this kind of an inquiry. You who are lifeless in your knowledge and deluded by your intellect, be wary of reading this and similar chapters with derision, puzzling over them and deeming them to be those ecstatic utterances[91] that have brought ruin to a certain group of seekers who did not obtain a single taste of their meanings![92] Be wary, otherwise you will be among those about whom the Qur'an says, «Since they will not be guided by it, they will say, "This is an ancient perversion"»;[93] «Nay, but they disbelieve in that whose knowledge they cannot comprehend and whose interpretation has not yet come to them».[94] This is your share of the counsel that I am obliged to offer to you. It is all the same to the recognizers whether you believe or disbelieve them. To them, the knowledge you refer to is similar to how erudite scholars view weaving and cupping. What would a scholar whose knowledge encompasses the realities of things care if he did not know weaving and cupping? 74

فصـل ٢٨

٧٥ كلّ من كان أوفر حظّاً من هذا الطور كان عقله أبصر بعجزه عن إدراك حقيقة الأوّل وإدراك حقيقة صفاته وآخر عالم من عوالم المدركات المعقولة أن يدرك العقل عجزه عن إدراك كثير من الموجودات وهذا العجز من أوائل ما يلوح في الطور الذي بعد العقل فكان آخر حدود طور العقل متّصلاً بأوّل حدود الطور الذي بعده كما أنّ آخر حدود التمييز متّصل بأوّل حدود العقل فمن خاصّيّة العالم إذا كمل في علمه أن يعلم يقيناً أنّه لا يُتصوّر له إدراك الحقيقة الإلٰهيّة وإنّما يدرك ذلك بعد إتقان مقدّمات كثيرة مشهورة عند العلماء النظّار ثمّ يكون بين إدراك العقل لعجزه بالمقدّمات وبين إدراك العارف لذلك العجز أعني لعجز العقل عن إدراك مدركات العارف بون بعيد وفرق عظيم ويكاد يكون ذلك العجز الذي يلوح للعقل بمنزلة العجز الذي يلوح للوهم عن إدراك مدركات العقل فإنّ عجز الوهم عن المعقولات الغامضة مستفاد عند الوهم من المقدّمات وأمّا العقل فإنّه يدرك عجز الوهم عن مدركاته من غير مقدّمة فغاية الوهم أن يعترف بالعجز عن إدراك العقليّات إذا قرّر العقل ذلك عنده بمقدّمات مسلّمة عند الوهم فكذلك العاقل إذا تقرّر عنده عجز العقل عن مدركات العارفين فقد بلغ آخر منازل العقل وأدرك منتهى ما يمكن إدراكه بالعقل فيستوطن حينئذ كعبة طلبه وها هنا يوافي السالك أوّل منزل من منازل طور المعرفة.

Chapter 28: The Last Stage of the Intellect

The intellect of those fortunate enough to access this stage will "see" its incapacity to perceive the reality of the First and the reality of His attributes. The last of worlds containing intellectual objects of perception is where the intellect will perceive its incapacity to perceive many existents. This incapacity is one of the first things to appear in the stage after the intellect. For the last border of the stage of the intellect is connected to the first border of the stage that comes after it, just as the last border of distinction-making is connected to the first border of the intellect. One of the special attributes of a true knower, when he perfects his knowledge, is that he comes to know with certainty that it is inconceivable for him to perceive the divine reality. According to the rationalists, he can only know this after having mastered many well-known premises. At any rate, there is a great distance and a tremendous divide between the intellect's perception of its incapacity to perceive by way of these premises and the recognizer's perception of this incapacity (which is to say that the intellect is incapable of perceiving the recognizer's objects of perception). This incapacity that appears to the intellect is almost like the incapacity that appears to the imaginal faculty when attempting to perceive the intellect's objects of perception. For the imaginal faculty's incapacity to perceive obscure intelligibles is obtained from premises. The intellect can perceive the imaginal faculty's incapacity through its own objects of perception and without any premises; therefore, the imaginal faculty's objective is for it to acknowledge its incapacity to perceive intellectual matters when the intellect affirms them by way of premises incontrovertible to the imaginal faculty. Likewise, when the intelligent person affirms the incapacity of the intellect to perceive the recognizer's objects of perception, he reaches the last station of the intellect and comes to perceive the ultimate end that is possible for him to perceive through the intellect. Permanently residing in the Kaaba of his quest, it is here that the traveler encounters the first waystation in the stage of recognition. 75

فصل ٢٩

العقل عاجز بالضرورة عن إدراك عجزه الحقيقيّ وعن إدراك مدركات العارف كما أنّ الوهم بالضرورة عاجز عن إدراك حقيقة عجزه عن إدراك المعقولات والعقل هو الذي يدرك العجز الحقيقيّ الذي يلازم الوهم عن إدراك الأمور العقليّة فإذا كان العقل عاجز عن إدراك عجزه الحقيقيّ فكيف تعجّب المتعجّبون من قولنا إنّه عاجز عن إدراك حقيقة الحقّ وحقيقة علمه الذي هو ينبوع الوجود فاذاً يرجع تفاوت العقول في هذا النظر إلى تفاوت في الاستعداد لإدراك العجز فليس العجز الذي اعترف به محمّد صلّى الله عليه وسلّم مثل العجز الذي يعترف به أبو بكر لا بل وفي الاعتراف بالعجز عن الاعتراف بالعجز أيضاً تفاوت عظيم ولعلّ النفس إذا استغرقها العجز عن إدراك كمال العجز فقد صارت مدركة للعجز من طريق المعرفة لا من طريق المقدّمات ولعلّ قول الصدّيق الأكبر العجز عن درك الإدراك إدراك كان إشارة إلى شيء يشبه ذلك ولعلّ المعرفة المذكورة في قول الصوفيّة من عرف الله كَلَّ لسانه قريبة في المعنى ممّا أشير اليه. ٧٦

فصل ٣٠

قد انتهى في الكلام إلى أن جاوزتُ حدود النظر العقليّ ويكاد ما خضتُ فيه يضرّ سماعه بأكثر الخلق فقليل منهم من يدرك ذلك ولا ينكره فالأولى بي الرجوع إلى الغرض المقصود وأقول ما أحوجك إلى استتمام سماع المعنى الذي كنّا فيه من قبل في حديث الصفات ودلالة أقسام الوجود على أقسام الصفات المتعدّدة التي هي بالحقيقة لا عين ٧٧

Chapter 29: "The Incapacity to Perceive Is Perception"

The intellect is necessarily incapable of perceiving its true incapacity and of perceiving the recognizer's objects of perception, just as the imaginal faculty is necessarily incapable of perceiving the reality of its incapacity to perceive intelligibles. It is the intellect that perceives the true incapacity that accompanies the imaginal faculty in terms of perceiving intellectual matters. Since the intellect is incapable of perceiving its true incapacity, how can anyone wonder at our statement that the intellect is incapable of perceiving the reality of God and the reality of His knowledge, the fountain of existence? Thus, the different ways intellects understand this point go back to their different capacities to perceive "incapacity." To be sure, the incapacity acknowledged by Muḥammad[95] is not like the incapacity acknowledged by Abū Bakr.[96] Indeed, the disparities in acknowledging incapacity are also great. It might be that, when the soul is engulfed by the incapacity to perceive the fullness of its incapacity, it will perceive its incapacity by way of recognition, not by way of premises. Perhaps the statement of Abū Bakr the Truthful,[97] "The incapacity to perceive is perception,"[98] is an allusion to something similar. Or perhaps the recognition mentioned in the Sufi saying, "Whoever recognizes God becomes speechless,"[99] comes close to the meaning alluded to here. 76

Chapter 30: A Transition

My discussion has now gone beyond the boundaries of intellectual reflection, and what I have delved into may just about harm many a listener. Indeed, the people who can grasp it and not reject it are few. It is thus fitting that I return to my purpose. You are in much greater need of a clear discussion about the points I was making concerning the divine attributes and about my demonstration of the divisions of existence into numerous attributes, which in reality are not the 77

الذات ولا غيرها كما قال أهل الحقّ وأجمعوا عليه من عند آخرهم فإنّ الحكم بأمثال ذلك مستنكرٌ عند العقول الضعيفة.

فصل ٣١

لعلّك تقول من المحال الظاهر في العقل الأوّليّ أن يكون الشيء لا عين شيء ولا ٧٨
غيره فهل لك أن تزيد ذلك بياناً فربّما يشفي به بعض الغليل فاعلم قول القائل أنّ هذا الشيء مثلاً لا عين ذلك الشيء ولا غيره من وجه واحد محال وليس أحد من العقلاء يصير إلى اعتقاد أمثاله ولكن إذا وُجد اعتباران لم يكن محالاً كما أن يقال مثلاً هذا الشيء ليس بمعدوم ولا موجود فإنّ ذلك محال قطعاً واستحالته للعقل في غاية الوضوح ولكنّه ظاهر الصدق إذا اعتُبر في معناه وجهان وأُطلق على مقتضى معنيين مختلفين وبيانه أنّ الشيء قد يكون موجوداً من وجه ومعدوماً من وجه وهذا حكم كلّ موجود سوى الموجود الذي وجوده قائم بذاته فإنّ كلّ ممكن إذا نُظر إلى ذاته ولم يعتبر قيّوميّة الواجب له كان معدوماً من حيث ذاته ومهما نُظر إليه من الوجه الذي يلي قيّوميّة الواجب كان موجوداً وإلى مثل ذلك يشير القرآن العظيم والكلام القديم حيث يقول ﴿كُلُّ مَنْ عَلَيْهَا فَانٍ﴾. وعلى شيء شبيه لذلك ينبّه قوله عليه السلام حيث يقول أصدق بيت قالته العرب بيت لبيد[١] [طويل]

أَلَا كُلُّ شَيْءٍ مَا خَلَا ٱللّٰهَ بَاطِلُ

١ (لبيد) في ج، ع، م؛ أ: كثير.

divine essence itself and are not other than it,[100] as the people of truth have said and agreed upon—every last one of them. But judgments like this are disdained by weak intellects!

Chapter 31: God's Essence and Attributes

You might say, "To the intellect, it is manifestly impossible for a thing to both not be that thing itself and yet not be other than it. Can you explain a little bit more so that perhaps my thirst may be partially quenched?" The statement to the effect that a thing, for example, is not that very thing itself and not other than it is impossible from one perspective. Not a single intelligent person would believe such a thing. However, this is not impossible when there are two standpoints. For example, it can be said that something is neither nonexistent nor existent. This is totally impossible, and its impossibility is extremely clear for the intellect. However, this would only be the outward aspect of such an assent if this statement, in terms of meaning, were expressed as having two senses and if it equally applied to what is demanded by these two different meanings. To explain: something might be existent in one sense and nonexistent in another. This is the situation of everything other than the One Existent whose existence abides through itself. Any contingent, seen in itself and without consideration of the self-abidingness of the Necessary with respect to it, would be nonexistent in terms of itself. But seen from the perspective of the self-abidingness of the Necessary, it is existent. The majestic Qur'an and the eternal Word allude to this when it says, «All that is on the earth passes away».[101] The Prophet's statement also called attention to something similar when he said, "The truest words uttered by the Arabs are those of Labīd: 78

> Truly, everything other than God is unreal."[102]

فصـل ٣٢

٧٩ الصفـات عين الذات إذا نُظر إليها من الوجه الذي يلي الذات[١] وهي غير الذات إذا نُظر إليها من الوجه الذي يلي انقسام[٢] إلى الأقسـام المتعدّدة وعلى هذا الوجه تكون الصفات متغايرة متعدّدة وهذا له مثال واضح ولعلّ نفسك لا تقنع إلّا بعد سماعه فهو الذي يكسر سورة استبعاده لِما نحن فيه بالكلّيّة ويقطع دابر إنكار المتحذلقين عليه.

٨٠ فاعلم أنّ العشرة لها في ذاتها معنى مفهوم وذلك المعنى واحد لا ينقسم ويدلّ عليه لفظ العشرة فأمّا إذا اعتُبر منها نسبة إلى الخمسة دُلّ عليها بلفظ الضعف وإذا اعتُبر نسبتها إلى العشرين دلّ عليها بلفظ النصف وإذا اعتُبر نسبتها إل الثلاثين دلّ عليها بلفظ الثلث وهكذا يمكن أن يدلّ عليها بألفاظ أُخر[٣] وهذه الصفات التي وصفت بها العشرة عند اختلاف تلك النسبة واحدة من وجه وكثيرة من وجه فإذا اعتُبر منها الوجه الذي يلي ذات العشرة لم يوجد فيها تعدّد وإذا اعتُبر منها الوجه الذي يلي أقسام الأعداد التي نسبت العشرة إليها تعدّدت باعتبار تلك النسب لتعدّد أعداد ونسبت إليها.

٨١ وكذلك ذات واجب الوجود الحقّ يلزمها الوحدة وكيف لا يلزمها الوحدة والأحديّة التي هي أخصّ من الوحدة لازمة لها إذ لا يمكن أن يوجد لغيرها من الذوات خاصّيّتها الموجودة لها فالوحدة لازمة للشمس إذ ليس لها ثانية في الوجود لكن الأحديّة ليست لازمة لها إذ يمكن وجود ثانية لها فاذا نظرتَ[٤] عين الذات الواجبة إلى نسبتها[٥] صادفتها متّحَدة غير متكثّرة بوجه من الوجوه وإذا نظرت قلوب السالكين بعيونها إلى تلك الذات صادفتها كذلك من غير فرق ولكن لكثرة نسب تلك الذات إلى الموجودات الأُخر التي استحقّت الوجود من تلك الذات لا من نفسها احتاج السالكون بالضرورة إلى تغيير

١ زائدة في ج،ع،م: وعلى هذه لا يكون فيها تغايرًا أصلاً والبتّة. ٢ ج،ع: هو انقسام الوجود؛ م: يلي أقسام الوجود. ٣ زائدة في ج،ع،م: عند اختلاف نسبتها إلى أعداد أُخر. ٤ زائدة في ج،ع: إلى نسبة. ٥ ج،ع،م: نفسها.

Chapter 32: The Divine Essence and Its Standpoints

When viewed from the perspective of God's essence, the divine attributes are the essence itself. But they are other than it when viewed from the perspective of existence into multiple divisions. It is from this perspective that the divine attributes are different and multiple. This point is illustrated with a clear example—perhaps you will only be satisfied after hearing it. It will raze the walls of your rejection, leaving not so much as a trace of denial among those pretending to be clever. 79

In its essence, the number ten has one obvious meaning, which cannot be divided, and which is indicated by the expression "ten." When ten is considered in relation to the number five, it is indicated by the expression "double." When considered in relation to twenty, it is indicated by the expression "half." And when considered in relation to thirty, it is indicated by the expression "one-third." In this way, ten can be indicated by other expressions. From one perspective, the attributes by which ten can be described in accordance with the diversity of their relations to it are one, and from another, many. If these attributes are considered from the perspective of the essence of ten, no multiplicity will be found in ten. But if these attributes are considered from the perspective of the divisions of numbers relative to ten, it will be multiple from this standpoint, on account of the multiplicity of numbers related to it. 80

Oneness is a concomitant of the essence of the true Necessary Existent. How can oneness not be its concomitant when uniqueness, which is more particular than oneness, is a concomitant of it, as it is impossible for any other essence with its own existent characteristic to be brought into existence for it? On the contrary, oneness is a concomitant of the sun since there is not a second sun in existence, but uniqueness is not a concomitant of the sun since it is possible for there to be a second sun. If you reflect upon the relation of the essence as such, which is Necessary in itself, you will discover that it is one, without multiplicity in any way whatsoever. When the travelers look at this essence with the eyes of their hearts, they discover it to be this way, with no distinction. However, on account of the multiplicity of the relations of this essence to the other existents that derive existence from it—not from themselves—the travelers have to depend upon the alternation of its standpoints such that the realities of these 81

العبارات عنها حتّى تتأدّى حقائق تلك النسب بواسطتها إلى أفهام الضعفاء فإذا نسبت تلك الذات إلى صدور الموجودات منها وعُلم أنّها ممكنات وأنّ الممكن لا بدّ له من واجب يوجده سُمّيت عند اعتبار هذه النسبة التي بينها وبين الموجودات قدرة وربّما سمّيت إرادة عند اعتبار نسبة أخرى فالقلوب لضعفها تظنّ مغايرة بين القادر والقدرة والإرادة والمريد فهذا منتهى نظر العقل.

فصل ٣٣

فاعلم إذاً أنّ قولنا الصفات لا عين الذات ولا غير الذات حقّ وصدق ولا يجوز ٨٢
المصير إلى خلافه لأحد من المسلمين أصلاً ومن صار إليه فقد خلع من عنقه ربقة الدين فهو مذهب السلف الصالحين والأئمّة المنقرضين ولنا فيهم أسوة حسنة وقدوة مرضيّة وقد أجمعوا على ذلك قاطبة للضرورة التي يعرفها المحقّقون من كبار العلماء دون أهل الظاهر من الرسميّين فمن صار إلى إثبات الذات ولم يثبت الصفات كان جاهلاً مبتدعاً ومن صار إلى إثبات صفات مغايرة للذات حقيقة المغايرة فهو ثنويّ كافر ومع كفره جاهل.

relations can be conveyed, by way of these standpoints, for the weak-minded to understand. Thus, since this essence is related to the effusion of the existents that emerge from it, and it is known that they are contingents and that it must be the Necessary who brings the contingent into existence, it is called "power" from the standpoint of this relation between it and the existents, and sometimes it is called "desire" from the standpoint of another relation. But the weak-minded think there is a difference between power and the Powerful, and desire and the Desiring! This is the very limit of intellectual reflection.

Chapter 33: The Way of the Righteous Predecessors

Therefore, our statement that the divine attributes are not the divine essence 82
itself nor are they other than it is true, and it is definitely impermissible for any Muslim to go against it. To do so is to stray in one's religion. This is the position of the righteous predecessors and leaders who have come before us. In them, we have a beautiful example and a most pleasing model. They were unanimous in their agreement on this thanks to its necessity as recognized by those scholars who have verified the truth (with no care for the exoterically minded among the religious formalists!). To affirm the divine essence and not affirm the divine attributes is to be guilty of ignorant innovation in religion; and to affirm the divine attributes as actually different from the divine essence is to be guilty of dualism[103] and disbelief, and ignorance to boot.

فصل ٣٤

اعلم أنّ الله تعالى وصف نفسه في كتابه الكريم غير مرّة بصفات متعدّدة كالقدرة ٨٣
والمشيئة والإعزاز والإذلال والسمع والبصر والإحياء والإماتة فقال عزّ من قائل ﴿إِنَّ ٱللَّهَ عَلَىٰ كُلِّ شَيْءٍ قَدِيرٌ﴾. وقال أيضاً ﴿وَمَا تَشَآءُونَ إِلَّآ أَن يَشَآءَ ٱللَّهُ﴾. وقال ﴿وَتُعِزُّ مَن تَشَآءُ وَتُذِلُّ مَن تَشَآءُ﴾. وقال ﴿لَيْسَ كَمِثْلِهِۦ شَيْءٌ وَهُوَ ٱلسَّمِيعُ ٱلْبَصِيرُ﴾. وقال ﴿هُوَ ٱلَّذِى يُحْىِۦ وَيُمِيتُ﴾. فانظر كيف تعدّدت هذه الصفات بتعدّد نسب الموجودات إلى ذاته التي هي مصدرها وكيف اتّحدت هي في ذواتها من الوجه الذي يلي الذات ثمّ قِس على ذلك سائر الصفات فما أراك تعجز عن إدراك شيء من النسب في كلّ صفة إن كنت من الممارسين للغوامض العقليّة واجتهد أوّلاً في فهم ما أقول لك.

فصل ٣٥

من المعلوم الظاهر الذي لا يجوز أن يتمارى فيه أنّ الحقيقة الأزليّة التي صدر عنها ٨٤
الوجود إذا نُظر إليها واعتُبر ما وُجد منها وما لم يوجد منها بعد ولكنّه يوجد في أجله المسمّى ووقته المعلوم كان لِما وُجد منها نسبة لا توجد تلك النسبة لِما لم يصدر عنها بعد فهذا هو اختلاف الموجودات والمعدومات في النسبة إليه ثمّ الموجودات تختلف في نسبتها إليه فليست نسبة الملك إلى ذاته كنسبة الإنسان ولا نسبة الإنسان كنسبة البهائم ولا نسبة البهائم كنسبة النبات ولا نسبة النبات كنسبة الأرض

Chapter 34: Scriptural Evidence

On several occasions, God describes Himself in His noble book with multiple attributes, such as power, will, exaltation, abasing, hearing, seeing, life-giving, and death-causing: «Truly God is powerful over all things»;[104] «And you do not will until God wills»;[105] "You exalt whomever You want, and abase whomever You want";[106] «There is nothing like Him, and He is the Hearing, the Seeing»;[107] «He is the one who gives life and causes death».[108] Look at how these divine attributes are multiple by virtue of the multiple relations of the existents to the divine essence (which is their source), but how they are united in their essences from the perspective of the divine essence. Make analogous judgments based on this for the remaining divine attributes, for I do not think you are incapable of perceiving some relations in each divine attribute—if you are in fact one of those who delve into recondite, intellectual matters. But first, strive to understand what I am saying! 83

Chapter 35: The Divine Attributes Are Relations

One of the things that are well known and cannot be doubted is that when the beginningless Reality from which existence emerged is looked at, taking into consideration what has come into existence from it, what has not come into existence from it, and what will come into existence from it at an appointed moment and specified time, it will be seen that whatever has come into existence from the beginningless Reality has a relation that is not there for anything that has not yet emerged from it. This explains the diversity of existents and nonexistents in relation to God. Moreover, the existents themselves are diverse in their relation to God. An angel's relationship to God's essence is not like a human's relationship to it; a human's relationship to God's essence is not like an animal's; an animal's relationship to God's essence is not like a plant's; a plant's relationship 84

والسموات ولا نسبة البياض كنسبة الحمرة ولا نسبة العزيز في الدنيا والآخرة كنسبة الذليل فيهما.

٨٥ واعلم أنّ الله عزّ وجلّ إذا نسبت إليه كلّ من عزّ بوجه من الوجوه اقتضت هذه النسبة أن يُسمّى معزًّا وإذا نسبت إليه أهل الذلّ اقتضت النسبة أن يُسمّى مذلًّا فإذا نُظر إليه من حيث هو مصوّر الحياة والموت قيل ﴿هُوَ ٱلَّذِى يُحْيِۦ وَيُمِيتُ﴾. وإذا نُظر إلى إحاطة علمه بوجودات يدركها الإنسان بحاسّتَي السمع والبصر قيل ﴿هُوَ ٱلسَّمِيعُ ٱلْبَصِيرُ﴾. وإذا نُسبت إليه جميع الموجودات ورُؤي كلّ واحد منها متعلّقا به قيل ما شاء الله كان وما لم يشأ لم يكن وإذا نُسبت إليه الموجودات الحاصلة منه والمعدومات التي لم تحصل منه بعد وجودها قيل ﴿هُوَ عَلَىٰ كُلِّ شَىْءٍ قَدِيرٌ﴾. فالقدرة متلقّاة من نسبة الموجودات والمعدومات إليه والإرادة والمشيئة من نسبة الموجودات إليه فقط وأمّا الإرادة فمتلقّاة من الموجودات المَلَكوتيّة[1] وأمّا المشيئة فمتلقّاة من الموجودات المُلْكيّة[2] والمحيي والمميت متلقّيان من نسبة كلّ حيّ وميّت إليه وقِس بهذا القدر سائر الصفات.

فصل ٣٦

٨٦ ذواتنا ناقصة وإنّما يكمّلها تمام الصفات ولذلك تحتاج قدرتنا إلى الإرادة وإرادتنا إلى العلم فالقدرة لا تكفي في حصول المقدور إلّا مع الإرادة هذا في حقّنا أمّا ذات الله تعالى فهي كاملة لا تحتاج في شيء إلى شيء وكلّ ما يحتاج إلى شيء فهو ناقص

١ (المَلَكوتيّة) في ج، ع، م؛ أ: المعلقيّة. ٢ (المُلْكيّة) في ج، ع، م؛ أ: المدركيّة.

to God's essence is not like that of the heavens and the earth; the color white's relationship to God's essence is not like that of the color red; and the relationship to God's essence of an individual exalted in this world and in the next is not like that of a person abased in both of these worlds.

The relationship of someone exalted in some way to God requires that God be called "the Exalter." And the relationship of abased people to God requires that He be called "the Abaser." When God is viewed as the source of life and death, it is said that «He is the one who gives life and causes death».[109] When people look at the manner in which His knowledge encompasses all existents and grasps it with the senses of hearing and sight, it is said that «He is the Hearing, the Seeing».[110] When all existents stand in relation to God and each of them are seen as connected to Him, it is said, "Whatever God wills is, and whatever He does not will is not."[111] When the existents that issue from Him and the nonexistents whose existence has not yet issued from Him stand in relation to God, it is said, «And He is powerful over all things».[112] Divine power comes about from the relation between God and existents and nonexistents, while the divine desire and will come about from the relation between God and existent things only. The divine desire comes about from the existents that belong to the spiritual world, while the divine will comes about from the existents that belong to the sensory world. The divine names "Life-Giver" and "Death-Giver" come about from the relation between God and things that are respectively living and dead. Now, go on and make analogous judgments based on this for the remaining divine attributes. 85

Chapter 36: Nonduality

Our essences are deficient and are only perfected by attributes that complete them. This is why our power needs desire, and our desire needs knowledge. Power alone can only acquire its object of power with desire. This is as it pertains to us. God's essence is complete and is never in need of anything at all, for that which is in need of something is deficient, and deficiency does not pertain 86

والنقصان لا يليق بالموجود الواجب فعلم الله تعالى بالشيء لا يغاير إرادته ولا إرادته تغاير قدرته فذاته كافية الكلّ في الكلّ فهي بالنسبة إلى المعلومات علم وبالنسبة إلى المقدورات قدرة وبالنسبة إلى المرادات إرادة وهي واحدة ليس فيها اثنينيّة بوجه من الوجوه.

٨٧ والاثنينيّة لا يُتصوّر وجودها في الواجب أصلاً إذ لا يجوز أن يكون شيئان وكلّ واحد منهما واجب بذاته وذلك لأنّ كلّ شيئين فلا بدّ وأن يكون بينهما مغايرة في شيء وإلّا لم يتحقّق بينهما اثنينيّة ولو كان في الوجود واجبان لا فرقًا في شيء ثمّ كان ما يفترقان فيه لا يخلو إمّا أن يكون ضروريًّا لكلّ ما هو واجب بذاته[١] أو لا يكون ضروريًّا ولو كان ضروريًّا لكان موجودًا في الواجبين على التساوي ولو لم يكن ضروريًّا لزم أن يكون وجوده مُعلّلاً بسبب وكلّ ما كان كذلك فالواجب يتنزّه عنه فإن لم يكفيك هذا القدر في هذه المسألة فعليك بطلبها من كتب استوفى أصحابها كلامَهم عليها فإنّ وقتي لا يتّسع لأكثر من ذلك وليس غرضي في هذا الكتاب تطويل ما فرغ العلماء من إقامة البرهان عليه فليُطلب من معدنه.

فصل ٣٧

٨٨ فإن قلت فما قولك في النسبة التي بين الواجب وبين السموات والأرض مثلاً هل كانت موجودة في كلّ وقت أم لا فإن كانت موجودة في كلّ وقت فهذا يفضي إلى قدم السموات والأرض وإن لم تكن موجودة فكيف وُجدت بعد العدم ألعلّة ظهرت في ذات الواجب بعدما لم تكن وذلك محال أو لأثر ظهر في معدوم كان مستمرّ العدم إلى وقت

---

١ (وذلك . . . واجب بذاته) في ج، م؛ ع: وذلك لأنّ كلّ شيئين فلا بدّ وأن يكون بينهما مغايرة في شيء وإلّا لم يتحقّق منهما اثنينيّة فلو كان في الوجود واجبان لافتقرا في شيء ثمّ كان ما يفترقان فيه لا يخلو إمّا أن يكون ضروريًّا لكلّ ما هو واجب بذاته؛ أ: واجب بذاته.

to the Necessary Existent. Thus, God's knowledge of something is not other than His desire, and His desire is not other than His power. His essence is entirely self-sufficient. It has "knowledge" in relation to things that are known, "power" in relation to objects of power, and "desire" in relation to things that are desired. God's essence is one and contains no duality in any way whatsoever.

The existence of duality is totally inconceivable with respect to the Neces- 87
sary, for there cannot exist two things, each part of which is necessary in itself. Indeed, there must be a difference between the two things in some sense. If not, there would be no duality with respect to them. And if there were two necessary beings in existence with no distinction between them in any sense, then that which they lacked would either be necessary for each thing that is necessary in itself, or it would not be necessary. If necessary, it would equally exist in the two necessary beings.[113] If not necessary, then its existence would have to be the effect of some cause.[114] But the Necessary is far removed from anything like this! If this is not enough for you on the topic, then you must seek it out in those books whose authors have fully dealt with it, for my time does not permit me to say anything more, and my intention—in this book at any rate—is to not prolong a discussion that the rational theologians have already dedicated themselves to proving through demonstrative methods—so feel free to go to those sources.[115]

Chapter 37: A Note on the Eternity of the World

You may ask, "What do you say about the relationship between the Necessary 88
and the heavens and the earth? For example, has the relationship always existed or not? If it has always existed, this would entail the pre-eternity of the heavens and the earth. But if the relationship has not always existed, then how did they come into existence after having been nonexistent? Was it due to a cause that appeared in the essence of the Necessary after not having been there? But this would be impossible. Or was it because of an effect that appeared in something nonexistent and that continued to be nonexistent until a specific time, prior to which this effect had not appeared? This would also be impossible. Or did it

مخصوص ولم يكن يظهر هذا الأثر فيه وذلك أيضاً محال أو وُجد من غير ظهور شيء حادث بعدما لم يكن وذلك أيضاً محال.

٨٩ فاعلم أنّ العلماء قد أكثروا في ذلك والحقّ الذي لا ريب فيه أصلاً عند أولي البصائر أنّ نسبة السموات والأرض إلى الله عزّ وجلّ نسبة شيء هو الآن معدوم ويحصل وجوده غداً مثلاً فليت شعري ماذا يقول القائل في معدوم ظاهر العدم إذا وُجد بعد ذلك يقول ظهر في القديم أثر أو في هذا المعدوم أثر أو وُجد المعدوم من غير ظهور أثر وكلّ ذلك محال ولا يبقى إلّا أن يقال العلّة في وجوده هو الله تعالى وهو موجود على حالة واحدة أزلاً وأبداً وإنّما لم يحصل منه وجوده قبل ذلك لفقد شرط جعل وجوده مستحقّاً للوجود ومستعدّاً لقبول نور الموجود[1] الأزليّ.

فصل ٣٨

٩٠ المعــدوم إذا أفاض عليه صورة الوجود كصورة فاكهة مثلاً كانت معدومة ثمّ صارت بعد العدم موجودة فلا بدّ وأن يكون لوجود الصورة بعد عدمها سبب والسبب في وجود كلّ موجود هو الله تعالى فإنّ كلّ موجود سواه ليس له ذات من حيث الحقيقة ولا وجود فكيف يكون سبباً. نعم يجوز أن يُسمّى سبباً في النظر العاميّ كما يُسمّى موجوداً فكما أنّ كونه موجوداً ليس له أصل إلّا من حيث يلي الذات القديمة فكذلك كونه سبباً لا يجوز أن يكون له أصل إلّا من ذلك الوجه فكما لا حقيقة لوجوده فلا حقيقة لسببيّته التي هي صفة[2] تابعة من توابع الوجود ولا يبقى هاهنا إلّا أن يقال إن كان السبب هو الله

١ ج،ع،م: الوجود. ٢ (صفة) في ج،ع،م؛ أ: منه.

come to exist without the appearance of something originated in time? Yet this, too, would be impossible."

Many scholars have addressed this matter in abundance.[116] For those who have insight, the truth beyond a shadow of a doubt is that the relation of the heavens and the earth to God is, for example, like the relation of something that is at this very moment nonexistent but that then comes into existence tomorrow. I would like to know what the poser of this question would say about a nonexistent thing that appears to be nonexistent even when it is subsequently brought into existence. He would say that an effect has appeared in the Eternal, or that an effect has appeared in this nonexistent thing, or that the nonexistent thing came to exist without the appearance of an effect. But all of that is impossible! There remains no option but to say that the cause of the existence of the nonexistent thing is God, who exists, beginninglessly and endlessly, at one and the same moment. The only reason God did not bring about the nonexistent thing's existence before is because of the absence of a condition that would cause it to warrant existence and be prepared to receive the light of the beginningless Existent. 89

Chapter 38: Divine Causation

When the form of existence flows into a nonexistent thing, like, for example, the form of a fruit that was nonexistent and then, after nonexistence, became an existent thing, that must be a cause for the form's existence after its nonexistence. The cause for the existence of every existent is God. Since every existent other than God does not have an essence insofar as its reality is concerned, and does not have existence, how can it be a cause? Indeed, in general observation it can be called a "cause," just as it can be called an existent, and just as its being an existent only has an ontological root insofar as God's eternal essence is concerned. Likewise, its being a cause only entails that it has an ontological root from that perspective. Just as there is no reality to its existence, so too is there no reality to its causality (which is an attribute that is one of the concomitants of existence). There is nothing left to say but that the cause is God. Now, why 90

فلِمَ لم يُوجد المسبَّب والسبب موجود فنقول لفقد شرط من شروطه وأنا أزيد ذلك بياناً فالحاجة داعية.

فصل ٣٩

لعلّك تقول من المعلوم الظاهر عند أهل النظر أنّ الله تعالى لا يكون سبباً إلّا لشيء واحد من الموجودات ثمّ يكون ذلك الشيء سبباً لوجود شيء آخر وهذا الشيء الثاني سبباً لشيء ثالث وهكذا يتداعى هذا الأمر إلى وجود الإنسان والواحد من كلّ وجه لا يجوز أن يصدر عنه إلّا شيء واحد فاعلم أنّ هذه مجازفة عظيمة من الكلام لا يجوز أن يطلق اللسان بأمثاله فهو كفر صريح عند ذوي البصائر فلا فرق بين من يثبت قديمين كلّ واحد منهما واجب بذاته وبين من يثبت سببين كلّ واحد منهما يصلح للإيجاد. ٩١

لا بل الحقّ الذي لا مرية فيه أنّه ليس في الوجود موجود يصلح لأن يكون سبباً لوجود شيء آخر إلّا الله عزّ وجلّ. وحقيقة السببيّة ترجع إلى إيجاد صورة الوجود في معدوم ولا ترسم في[1] وجود السبب حتّى يوجد منه المسبّب فإنّ المعدوم لا يصلح للسببيّة ولا بدّ للسبب من دوام الوجود حتّى يصلح لأن يحفظ دوام الوجود على المسبّب وليس من الموجودات الممكنة ذات بوجود حقيقيّ وإنّما الوجود الحقيقيّ والذات الواجبة لله تعالى. فما لا وجود له من حيث الحقيقة فكيف يكون سبباً لغيره وما لا وجود لنفسه كيف يوجد غيره والسبب بالحقيقة ما كان كامل الذات بذاته ثمّ فضل فيه الوجود حتّى فاض على المعدومات وخلع عليها صور الوجود وأمّا ما لا يكون كاملاً بذاته بل وجوده وصفات وجوده متعلّقة بوجود غيره وقائمة به فيكون في ذاته في غاية النقصان لا يستحقّ الإيجاد ولا الوجود.

---

١ ج، ع، م: لا بدّ من.

was the effect not brought into existence when the cause existed? Because of the absence of one of the cause's conditions. Since greater detail is needed, I will explain further.

Chapter 39: The True Nature of Causation

You might say, "It is clearly known by the rationalists that God is only a cause for one existent, and then that thing is a cause for the existence of another thing, and then that second thing is a cause for a third thing, and so on until it comes to the existence of human beings. In every respect, only one thing can emanate from the One."[117] No tongue should utter the likes of this astonishingly audacious statement, for it is outright unbelief as far as those with insight are concerned. There is no difference between affirming two eternal existents, with each being Necessary in itself, and affirming two causes, with each effectuating existence. Rather, the indubitable truth is that, apart from God, there is no existent that can be a cause for the existence of something else. The reality of causation stems from the act of imposing the form of existence onto a nonexistent. And you cannot conceive of the existence of a cause until an effect is found, since causation cannot apply to a nonexistent. There must then be a perpetual cause of existence so that it can uphold the existence of the effect perpetually. Among possible existents there is no essence that has true existence. True existence and a necessary essence belong to God alone. So how can a thing that does not have existence insofar as its reality is concerned be a cause for another thing? And how can a thing that does not have existence in itself bring another thing into existence? In reality, the Cause is that which is complete in its essence and which abounds in existence, overflowing onto the nonexistents and draping them with the form of existence. But whatever is not complete in its essence—or rather, whose existence and the attributes of whose existence are attached to the existence of some other thing, and by which it subsists—is in fact extremely deficient in its essence and is not fit to bring things into existence, let alone exist itself. 91

فصل ٤٠

هـذا له مثال في الأمثلة العامّيّة فإنّ الشمس إذا فاض عنها النور على القمر ليلاً ٩٢
وفاض نور القمر على الأرض فلا شكّ أنّ نور القمر غير مستحقّ الوجود بذاته بل من الشمس فكيف يصلح نور القمر مع هذا النقصان أن يُجعل سبباً لوجود النور الفائض على الأرض وليتأمّل الناظر في هذا تأمّلاً شافياً وليستفت في ذلك نفسَه فلا شكّ في أنّه لو نظر بعين الإنصاف رأى نور الشمس أولى بأن يجعل سبباً لنور الأرض من نور القمر فإنّ نور القمر إذا لم يكن له وجود فكيف يكون له إيجاد والإيجاد فوق الوجود بالضرورة والوجود قبل الإيجاد بالطبع ثمّ لن يُسمّي نور القمر سبباً من طريق الاصطلاح فلا مشاحّة في ذلك ولكن لا يجوز أن يغفل عن تبعيّة نور القمر لنور الشمس وأنّه لولا نور الشمس لم يكن لنور القمر أصلاً وجودٌ. فالحقّ أنّ من أثبت صلاحيّة السبب بغير الواجب الحقّ بذاته القيّوم في صفاته فقد أشرك وأثبت له نظيراً وكان كمن أثبت القمر مشاركاً للشمس في إيجاد النور ولا شكّ أنّ الواجب لو فُرض عدمه لم يبق في الوجود شيء أصلاً فإذا لا يستغني عن الواجب شيء في شيء أصلاً إذ ليس يبقى مع عدمه وجود شيء أصلاً فالعجب كلّ العجب من عاقل يفهم ذلك الفهم ثمّ يتوقّف في كونه عن أولى بالسببيّة من غيره.

Chapter 40: An Example Using Natural Phenomena

There is an everyday example of the preceding discussion. When the sun shines its light on the moon at night and the moon's light shines on the earth, there is no doubt that the moonlight does not merit existence in itself—rather, its light comes from the sun. So, given this deficiency, how can the moonlight be a cause for the existence of the light that shines upon the earth? Let the contemplative person ponder this carefully, consulting his soul for the answer. There is no doubt that if he looks at this example with a fair eye, he will see that it is more appropriate that the light of the sun and not the light of the moon be the cause of the earth's light. How can the moonlight bring something into existence if it does not have existence? For bringing something into existence is necessarily built off of existence, and existence is naturally prior to the act of bringing into existence. Moreover, the moonlight is never called a cause, technically speaking, and that is indisputable. At the same time, one should not forget the subordination of the moon's light to the light of the sun, and that, were it not for the sun's light, the light of the moon would basically not have existence. The truth is that affirming that the cause could be something other than the Necessary, who is the Real in His essence and the Self-Abiding in His attributes, is to assign an associate to Him and to affirm that He has an equal. This would be tantamount to affirming that the moon is the sun's partner in the act of bringing about light. There is no doubt that, if the Necessary were posited as nonexistent, nothing at all would remain in existence. Since nothing can in any way do without the Necessary, nothing at all would remain in existence were He to be nonexistent. How truly astonishing is the intelligent person who understands this but then hesitates to say that God is better suited to have causal efficacy than others! 92

فصل ٤١

٩٣ الحقّ أنّ قولنا الواجب أولى بالسببيّة من غيره يُشعر بنقصان عظيم في الواجب وكأنّه يشير إلى استحقاق غيره لشيء ولكنّه أولى بالاستحقاق واستحقاق غيره لشيء محال[١] إلّا من ذاته الواجبة ويبقى هاهنا من الإشكال أن يقال إن كان الواجب كاملاً في السببيّة فلِمَ تأخّر وجود المسبّب عنه وتأخّر وجود المسبّب عن السبب الموجود بكماله محال وإن كان ناقصاً في السببيّة وتمّ ببعض الشروط سببيّتُه فقد ثبت له شريك في كونه سبباً فما بالكم لا تجوّزون تسمية غيره سبباً مع اعترافكم بأنّ وجود بعض الأشياء شرط في وجود البعض.

٩٤ وهذا إشكال يسهل علينا دفعه فإنّا نقول وجود الشرط إنّما أثّر في استعداد المشروط في الوجود[٢] لا في سببيّة الذات الواجبة كما أنّ انقشاع السحاب إنّما يؤثّر في استعداد الأرض لإشراق نور الشمس وليس له تأثير أصلاً في تكميل الشمس وليس لقائل أن يقول إنّ انقشاع السحاب شرط تتمّ به سببيّة الشمس لوجود المشروط وهو إشراق الأرض[٣] وهذا غاية في البيان لا يُتصوّر وراءها غاية في التمثّل وصناعته ونور القمر إذا كان مستفاداً من نور الشمس وهو في ذاته فان وهالك ومعدوم فلا نور من حيث الحقيقة إلّا نور الشمس فكان نور القمر هو نور الشمس حتّى كأنّه هو هو فكيف يجوز مع ذلك أن يُجعل القمر شريكاً للشمس في إفاضة النور وكما لا نور إلّا نور الشمس فلا وجود إلّا وجود الحقّ فكان وجود الموجودات ليس خارجاً من وجود الحقّ كأنّه[٤] هو هو.

---

١ (بالاستحقاق واستحقاق غيره لشيء محال) في ج، ع، م: أ: بالاستحقاق غيره لشيء واستحقاق غيره محال. ٢ ج: المشروط لوجود المشروط؛ ع، م: المشروط للوجود. ٣ زائدة في: لأنّا نقول انقشاع السحاب زواله والزوال أمر عدميّ والعدميّ لا يصلح للشرطيّة في أمر وجوديّ وهو الإيجاد للشيء فكيف يصلح للسببيّة. ٤ ج، ع: بل.

Chapter 41: The Oneness of Existence and Causation

The truth is that my statement that the Necessary is "better suited to have causal efficacy than others" gives one the impression of a significant deficiency in the Necessary, for it seems to indicate that these "others" have a rightful claim to something. But God is better suited to have a rightful claim. In fact, the "rightful claim" of these others to something is only possible by virtue of God's necessary essence. At this juncture an ambiguity persists: "If the Necessary has complete causal efficacy, why then does He delay the existence of the effect, seeing that it is impossible to put off the existence of an effect from its existing cause when the cause is complete? If God is deficient in terms of causal efficacy and His causal efficacy can only be complete with the presence of certain conditions, then He has a partner in His being a cause. So why then do you maintain that something other than God cannot be called a 'cause,' despite the fact that you acknowledge that the existence of certain things is a condition for the existence of other things?" 93

It is easy for me to resolve this ambiguity. The existence of a condition only has an effect on the conditioned thing's capacity to exist, not on the causal efficacy of God's necessary essence. It is just like the disappearance of a cloud, which only has an effect on the earth's capacity to be illuminated by the light of the sun—but the disappearance of the cloud itself has absolutely no effect on bringing the light of the sun to completion. One cannot say that, through the disappearance of the cloud, the sun's causal efficacy for the existence of the conditioned thing is completed—namely, the earth's being illumined. In its design and imagery, this example represents the highest kind of explanation, beyond which nothing greater can be conceived. If the light of the moon is derived from the light of the sun, but the moon in its essence is vanishing, perishing, and nonexistent, then in reality the moon only has the light of the sun. So the light of the moon is the light of the sun—it is as if they are one and the same. Given this, how can the moon be a partner with the sun in diffusing light? Just as there is no light other than the light of the sun, so too is there no existence other than the existence of God. Thus, the existence of existents is not external to the existence of God—it is as if they are one and the same. 94

فصل ٤٢

٩٥ كلّ ما في الوجود فهو فان من حيث الحقيقة ولا بقاء إلّا لوجه[١] الحيّ القيّوم كما أنّ الصورة التي في المرآة فانية بالحقيقة ولا بقاء إلّا للصورة الخارجة هذا من حيث النظر العاميّ في القناعة بالأمثلة المحسوسة وإلّا فالصورة الخارجة مع المرآة في نظر العارف فانية أيضاً حسب فناء الصورة الداخلة في المرآة من غير تفاوت.

فصل ٤٣

٩٦ المـرآة عبرة عظيمة لأُولي الألباب ومن نظر في المرآة نظرًا شافيًا ولم ينحلّ له كثير من المشكلات فليس يستحقّ أن يُعدّ في زمرة العقلاء ولعمري لم ينظر في المرآة عاقل إلّا ويعتور عقله إشكالات عظيمة وتشكّك في جليّات الأمور ولكن تنحلّ له مع ذلك مشكلات كثيرة[٢] ولو لم يكن من منافع الحديد سوى المرآة لكان يكفي ذلك شاهداً على صدق قوله تعالى ﴿وَأَنزَلۡنَا ٱلۡحَدِيدَ فِيهِ بَأۡسٌ شَدِيدٌ وَمَنَٰفِعُ لِلنَّاسِ﴾ . وكيف وفيه من المنافع ما يستحقر معها المرآة على أنّ فيها من المنافع عجائب عظيمة كثيرة لا يمكن إحصاؤها للعقل والمرآة بالحقيقة مرآة العقلاء إذ يرون فيها صورة العقل العاجز عن إدراك حقائق كثيرة فحسبك بها شاهدة على أنّ العقل معزول عن إدراك كثير من المحسوسات الظاهرة فضلاً عن المعقولات الخفيّة فمن أراد أن يشاهد عقله على صورته التي هو عليها من العجز فليكثر النظر في المرآة فنعمت مبصرة للعقل[٣] بعجزه وكذبه في دعاويه العريضة الطويلة لنفسه من إدراك حقائق الأمور الإلٰهيّة ولست أنكر أنّ للعقل

---

١ ع: لوجود. ٢ (ولكنّ تنحلّ له مع ذلك مشكلات كثيرة) في ج، ع؛ أ: وكذلك يتخيّل له مشكلات كثيرة؛ م: ولكنّ تنحلّ له كثير من المشكلات. ٣ (للعقل) في ج، ع، م؛ أ: للعقلاء.

Chapter 42: An Example Using Mirrors

95 From the perspective of reality, everything in existence is transitory, and the only thing that remains is the face of the Living, the Self-Abiding. It is just like a transitory form in a mirror—only the form outside the mirror remains insofar as general observation is concerned, satisfied as it is with sensory imagery. In the eyes of the recognizer, the form outside the mirror is also transitory, just like the form inside the mirror, with no distinction between them.

Chapter 43: The Mirror of the Intellect

96 A mirror is a tremendous example for those who are intelligent. If you look into one properly and still do not have many of your difficulties resolved, you do not deserve to be considered intelligent. By my life! When an intelligent person looks into a mirror, he is beset by tremendous problems and comes to doubt many things he had taken for granted. Nevertheless, many difficulties will be resolved. If the forging of mirrors was the only benefit to be derived from iron, that alone would testify to the truth of God's statement, «And We sent down iron which has great might, and benefits for people».[118] How can it be otherwise, given that the benefits derived from iron include those that would make even mirrors look insignificant, despite the fact that mirrors contain many tremendous wonders, which the intellect cannot enumerate? In reality, mirrors function as "mirrors" for the intelligent, since in them they can see the form of the intellect, which is incapable of perceiving many realities. This should be sufficient testimony for you of the fact that the intellect can barely perceive many sensory objects that are in plain sight, let alone intelligibles that are hidden. Spend a great deal of time looking into a mirror if you want to witness your intellect's incapacity. How fine an aid it is for the intellect to see its own incapacity and its deceit in making long-standing claims about its ability to perceive the realities of divine matters!

خُلُق[1] لأدراك أمور عظيمة من الغوامض ولكنّه لا يُجبني إذا عدا طوره في دعواه وجاوز قدره وتخطّاه.

فصل ٤٤

٩٧ المرآة تظهر فيها صورة مطابقة للصورة خارجة عن طريق الانطباع والعقل في أوّل النظر وبادئ الرأي يفرق بين الوجود الخارج والوجود الداخل فأحدهما مستتبع والآخر تابع ولا يُتصوّر أن يشكّ أحد في ذلك وحاصل الوجود التابع يرجع إلى نسبة حاصلة على وجه مخصوص بين صورة خارجة وبين المرآة. فإذا طالع البصر تلك النسبة الحاصلة بينهما أدرك الصورة الداخلة التابعة المعدومة من حيث الحقيقة الموجودة من حيث الظاهر ولا يشكّ العقل في أنّ وجود الصورة الداخلة ليس موجوداً بذاته مستقلاً بالوجود[2] بل هو موجود بالإضافة إلى أربعة أمور وهي المرآة والصورة الخارجة والنسبة الحاصلة بمطالعة البصر[3] لذلك وإذا بطلت هذه النسبة بطل وجود تلك الصورة الداخلة وعلم العاقل أنّ تلك الصورة لم يكن لها استقلال بالوجود وإن تصوّر وجود المرآة أو الماء أو ما يضاهيهما في محاكاة الصورة[4] بحيث كان يحاكي الصور ولا يتصوّر عليه تغيّر لم يدرك أحد من الخلائق أنّ تلك الصورة الداخلة تابعة في الوجود للصورة الخارجة وأنّ هذه الخاصّيّة للمرآة والماء لا يشاركهما فيه جسم من الأجسام كالطين والجصّ وأمثالهما ولكن لمّا كانت الصورة الخارجة تتغيّر وكانت النسب الحاصلة أيضاً تتغيّر وعند ذلك تتغيّر الصورة الداخلة حسب تغيّر الصورة الخارجة على منهاج واحد

١ ج، ع، م: العقل خُلق. ٢ ج: ليس ذاتيًا أعني به أنّه ليس موجودًا بذاته مستقلاً بالوجود؛ ع، م مثل ج. ٣ ع: ومطالعة البصير؛ ج، م: ومطالعة البصر. ٤ ج، ع، م: الصور.

I do not deny that the intellect has the disposition to perceive many great, recondite matters. I am just unimpressed when it steps outside of its scope in its claims and seeks to go further than it can.

Chapter 44: The Forms in Mirrors Are Relations

In a mirror, an imprinted form appears that corresponds to the form outside 97
of it. At first glance, the intellect makes a distinction between the existence of the form outside of the mirror and the one inside it, with the first preceding the second. It is inconceivable for anyone to doubt this. The actual existence of the form inside the mirror goes back to a relation, which comes about in a specific way, between the form outside the mirror and the mirror itself. When the eye sees the relation that obtains between the two, it perceives the form inside the mirror as nonexistent in relation to the existent reality of the external image. But the intellect never doubts that the form inside the mirror is not independent and existent in its essence—it does not have an existence of its own. Rather, it is an existent in relation to four things: (1) the mirror, (2) the external form, and (3) the relation that obtains between them when (4) seen by the eye. That is, when this relation terminates, the existence of the form inside the mirror also terminates. Intelligent people know that this form does not have an existence of its own. If we conceive of the existence of the mirror, or of water, or of anything corresponding to them that produces images of forms, and conceive of them as unchanging, not a single one of us would fail to perceive that the existence of the forms inside the mirror derives from a form outside it, and this is because no other body, such as clay, plaster, and the like, shares the special attribute that belongs to mirrors and water. But when the form outside the mirror changes, the relationships between it and the mirror also change—and that is when the form inside the mirror changes in accordance with the change of the form outside it, in one and the same manner. An intelligent person would not even bother

لم يتخالج العقلاء ريب في أنّ الداخلة تابعة الوجود للخارجة وأنّ الخارجة متقدّمة الوجود[١] على الداخلة تقدّماً رتبياً لا زمانياً.

فصل ٤٥

٩٨ ليتأمّل العاقل تأمّلاً صادقاً أنه لو لم تكن المرآة موجودة وحُكي له ما يشاهده منها من انطباع الصور فيها هل كان يصدّق بوجود ذلك أو لا فما عندي أنّ واحداً من أهل الإنصاف الناظرين بالبصائر الصافية يشكّ في أنّه كان يكذّب بوجود ذلك ويقيم على استحالته برهاناً وكان يستحيل أن يظهر له وجه الخلل في برهانه ذلك. فاعتبر الآن ولا تبادر إلى التكذيب فيما لا يدركه عقلك الضعيف فإنّ العقل خُلق لإدراك بعض الموجودات كما أنّ البصر خُلق لإدراك بعض الموجودات وهو عاجز عن إدراك المشمومات والمسموعات والمذوقات وكذلك العقل يعجز عن إدراك كثير من الموجودات نعم هو مدرك لأشياء محصورة قليلة بالإضافة إلى كثرة الموجودات التي هو عاجز عن إدراكها ثمّ جميع الموجودات بالإضافة إلى العلم الأزليّ كالذرّة بالإضافة إلى العرش لا بل والذرّة بالإضافة إلى العرش شيء ما والموجودات كلّها بالنسبة إلى علم الله تعالى ليست شيئاً أصلاً وإنّما ذكرت ذلك مخافةَ أن يبادر عقلك الضعيف ويقول المعقولات لا تتناهى فكيف جعلتها محصورة متناهية فإنّ من كانت الموجودات كلّها في نظره محصورة لا بل ولا تكون شيئاً فلا يكون عنده للحكم بذلك[٢] عظم خطر إنّما امتناع الحصر في نظره يوجد في الصفات الأزليّة كالقدرة والإرادة والعلم والكرم المفيض صور الموجودات عليها وهذا الكرم لازم للذات فإنّها لمّا كانت كاملة وفوق الكمال لا جرم كان الكرم المقتضي لإفاضة خلع الوجود على المعدومات لازماً لها كما أنّ الوجوب لازم لها مثلاً.

---

١ ج، ع، م: في الوجود. ٢ ج، ع، م: بأمثال ذلك.

to doubt that the form inside the mirror comes from the existence of the form outside it, and that the existence of the latter precedes the former in terms of hierarchy, not in terms of time.

Chapter 45: A Note on the Limits of the Intellect

The intelligent person should truthfully ponder this: if the mirror were not exis- 98
tent and if someone were told about how he could see forms imprinted in it, would he believe in the existence of such a thing or not? I do not think that a single fair-minded person who looks at this clearly would doubt that he would not believe in the existence of such a thing. He might even set out to prove its impossibility by way of demonstration, and it would indeed be impossible for there to be flaws in his proof. Now, consider this, and do not be so quick to reject what your weak intellect cannot grasp: the intellect was created to perceive some existents just as the eye was created to perceive some existents; but the eye is incapable of perceiving objects of smell, hearing, and taste. Likewise, the intellect is incapable of perceiving many existents. To be sure, what it perceives are limited and restricted in relation to the many existents it cannot perceive. Moreover, in relation to God's beginningless knowledge, all existents are like specks in relation to His Throne. But these specks in relation to the Throne are things in some sense, whereas all existents in relation to God's knowledge are nothing at all! I only mention this out of fear that your weak intellect would hastily say, "The intelligibles are infinite, so how can you say they are restricted and yet infinite?" For the One in whose eyes each existent is restricted—and indeed is nothing!—such a proposition is not of great consequence. The beginningless divine attributes, such as power, desire, knowledge, and the generosity that flows onto the forms of existents, are the only things in God's eyes that are impossible to be restricted. This generosity is a concomitant of the divine essence, and since the essence is perfect and above perfection, there is no doubt that the generosity which requires that nonexistents be dressed in the robe of existence is a concomitant of the divine essence, just as, for example, necessity is a concomitant of the essence. The divine essence would be

ولو خلت الذات عن هذا الكرم كانت ناقصة وهذا كما أنّ الشمس إذا أشرقت بها الآفاق كان ذلك من كمال إشراقها ولو لم تكن هذه الصفة موجودة للشمس كانت ناقصة وكان يعوزها شيء من كمال نورانيتّها ولله ﴿ٱلْمَثَلُ ٱلْأَعْلَىٰ فِى ٱلسَّمَـٰوَٰتِ وَٱلْأَرْضِ وَهُوَ ٱلْعَزِيزُ ٱلْحَكِيمُ﴾.

فصل ٤٦

٩٩ أولو الألباب يعتبرون بالمرآة من وجوه كثيرة ويكاد حصر تلك العبر يستحيل وممّا يعتبرون به أنّهم إذا نظروا فيها شاهدوا حقيقة قوله تعالى ﴿كُلُّ شَىْءٍ هَالِكٌ إِلَّا وَجْهَهُۥ﴾ وقوله عليه السلام الناس نيام فإذا ماتوا انتبهوا. وعلموا أنّ نسبة الملك والملكوت في الوجود إلى وجه الحيّ القيّوم نسبة الصورة الداخلة في المرآة إلى الصورة الخارجة إذ ليس للملك والملكوت حقيقة الوجود وإنّما وجودهما تابع لوجود الوجه الحقّ الحقيقيّ الوجود فإنّ بعض الخلق لا بل أكثرهم يظنّون أنّ الموجودات التي يشاهدونها في الدنيا لها وجود حقيقيّ. فإذا بطلت النسبة الحاصلة بين أبصارهم وبين تلك الموجودات المحسوسة انكشف الغطاء عن أبصارهم وارتفع اللبس[١] وانتبهوا من نومهم وعلموا يقيناً أنّ ﴿كُلُّ شَىْءٍ هَالِكٌ إِلَّا وَجْهَهُۥ﴾. اللّهمّ إلّا إذا قام موجود أزلاً وأبداً بقيّوميّة وجهه الباقي فيكون القائم من موجود الأبديّة وجود القيّوم وسرمديّته جلّ الواحد القهّار. وحينئذ ينادى الخلقَ[٢] من بطنان العرش بقوله تعالى ﴿لِّمَنِ ٱلْمُلْكُ ٱلْيَوْمَ لِلَّهِ ٱلْوَٰحِدِ ٱلْقَهَّارِ﴾، ويشاهدون[٣] ذلك مشاهدة لا يبقى معها ريب ومن طالع هذه الألفاظ ولم يقف على حقائق معانيها فليتوقّف في الإنكار فوراءها من عجائب الأسرار ما لا يفي بشرحه لسان ولا يعرب عن حقيقته بيان.

---

١ ج، ع، م: التلبيس. ٢ (ينادى الخلقَ) في ج، ع، م؛ أ: ينادى الحق. ٣ (يشاهدون) في ع؛ أ، ج، م: يشاهد.

deficient were it bereft of this generosity. It is like the sun: when it illuminates the horizon, its illumination is an aspect of its perfection. The sun would be deficient if this attribute did not exist in it and something was needed in order to perfect its luminosity. But to God «belongs the loftiest description in the heavens and the earth, and He is the mighty, the wise».[119]

Chapter 46: Mirrors and the State of Dreaming

The people of intelligence take lessons from mirrors from many different perspectives, and it is nearly impossible to enumerate them. One lesson is that, when they look into mirrors, they witness the reality of God's words, «All things perish, except His face»,[120] and the Prophet's statement, "People are asleep; when they die, they awaken."[121] They know that the relationship between the existence of the earthly and spiritual realms to the face of the Living and the Self-Abiding is like the relationship between forms inside mirrors to forms outside of them. For there is no reality to the existence of the earthly and spiritual realms—their existence comes from the existence of the face of the Real, the one to whom existence truly belongs. Some, or rather most people, think that the existents they behold in this world have true existence. But when the relation between their eyes and these sensible existents is negated, the veil will be lifted from their eyes and the delusion disclosed. They will then awaken from their state of sleep and come to know with certainty that «All things perish, except His face»[122] (unless of a course there is another existent that has always abided through God's subsisting face and is thereby also endless thanks to the existence of the Self-Abiding and His everlastingness!). At that time, from the very depths of the Throne, people will be summoned with His words, «Whose is the sovereignty this day? It is God's, the One, the Paramount».[123] They will witness this in a way that leaves no room for doubt. Those who study these statements and do not understand the realities of their meanings should hesitate before rejecting them. For indeed, beyond these statements lie wondrous mysteries that speech cannot expound, nor can their reality be expressed through explanation. 99

فصــل ٤٧

رجعــنا إلى حديث السرى. لا شكّ أنّ الله عزّ وجلّ خلق في الإنسان معنى يسمّى في ١٠٠
اصطلاح الخلق قدرة والإنسان يقدر بذلك المعنى على أن يتكلّم بعد سكوته متى شاء فالسبب الظاهر من حيث نظر عوامّ الخلق لوجود الكلام بعد عدمه هو المسمّى قدرة ومعلوم أنّ القدرة تكون موجودة ولا يوجد المسبَّب وهو الكلام لا لخلل في السبب بل لفقد شرط وهو المشيئة فوجود الكلام من سببه المسمّى قدرة في الاصطلاح موقوف على وجود شرط المشيئة ومحال أن يحصل المشروط والشرط معدوم والمحال لا يكون مقدوراً إذ لا يظهر أثر القدرة إلّا في مقدور كما لا يظهر أثر البصر إلّا في مبصر ولا أثر الشمّ إلّا في مشموم وكذلك في سائر المدركات فإنّ الكواكب المحجوبة بسحاب مثلاً إذا لم تتمكّن القوّة الباصرة من إدراكها لم يكن ذلك دليلاً على خلل في الأبصار فكذلك إذا كان الشيء المعدوم محجوباً بحجاب عدم الشرط فإنّ القدرة الأزليّة لا توجده ما لم ينقشع حجاب عدم الشرط لا لخلل في القدرة بل لأنّ المعدوم بعد محال الوجود فإذا انقشع عنه الحجاب صار ممكناً ويصير من القدرة الأزليّة واجباً كما لو انقشع حجاب السحاب فصارت الأرض مستعدّة لقبول نور الشمس عند الانقشاع.

Chapter 47: Divine Power and Human Power

Let us return to our earlier discussion. There is no doubt that God created a supra-sensory reality in people, which in conventional terms is called "power." After having been silent, they can decide to speak whenever they want by virtue of this supra-sensory reality. In the eyes of the majority of people, the apparent cause for the existence of speech after its nonexistence is what is called "power." It is known that this power can exist without its effect—speech—being brought into existence. And that would not be on account of any defect in the cause, but because of the absence of a certain condition—namely, volition. The coming into existence of speech from its cause, called "power" in conventional terms, depends on the existence of the condition of volition. But it is impossible for that which is conditioned to come about when the condition is itself nonexistent! Yet something impossible cannot be an object of power since the effect of power can only appear in an object of power, just as the effect of sight can only appear in an object of sight and the effect of smell in an object of smell. This applies to all sensible objects. For example, when planets are veiled by clouds and the faculty of vision does not have the ability to perceive them, this is not proof of an ocular defect. In the same vein, if a nonexistent is veiled by the nonexistence of a condition, then God's beginningless power will not bring it into existence as long as the veil of the nonexistence of the condition is present. This is not due to a defect in God's beginningless power. Rather, it is because it is as yet impossible for the nonexistent to exist. But when the veil is removed, it will become a contingent thing, necessarily existent through God's beginningless power.[124] This is just like when a veil of clouds disappears, and the earth is then prepared to receive the light of the sun. 100

فصل ٤٨

نسبة المحال إلى القدرة الأزليّة كنسبة المشموم مثلاً إلى العين المبصرة فلا يصير المشموم أبدًا مبصرًا لا لخلل في قوّة الأبصار بل لأنّه ليس بمبصر والمحال لا يفيض عليه الوجود من القدرة الأزليّة لا لخلل في القدرة بل لأنّ المحال غير مقدور ونسبة المعدوم الممكن بذاته إلى القدرة الأزليّة كنسبة المبصر المحجوب بحجاب إلى قوّة البصر. فإنّه إذا ارتفع الحجاب أدركته القوّة المبصرة فكذلك المعدوم الممكن بذاته إذا وُجد شروطه أوجدته القدرة الأزليّة وما دام يعوزه شرط فهو بعد محال الوجود لغيره لا لذاته والممكن بذاته ما يجب وجود شروطه والمحال بذاته ما يستحيل وجود شروطه وتأمّل في ذلك تأمّلاً شافيًا ولا تعترض عليه بتحذلقك فتزلّ قدمك وأنت لا تدري. ١٠١

فصل ٤٩

قد يقول أهل النظر إنّ الإمكان للمكن من ذاته والاستحالة للمستحيل بذاته ومن ذاته فيتخيّل الضعيف من هذه الألفاظ معانٍ فاسدة ويخطئ فيها بأنواع فاحشة من الخطأ وكيف يكون الممكن من ذاته[١] وذاته ليست من ذاته بل من غيره. فإذا كانت ذاته من غيره كان الإمكان الذي هو صفة من صفاته أولى أن يكون من غيره فإنّ استناد ١٠٢

١ ج،ع،م: الإمكان للممكن من ذاته.

Chapter 48: The Possible and the Impossible

101 The relationship between the impossible and God's beginningless power is like the relationship between an object of smell and an eye that is able to see. An object of smell will never become an object of vision, not because of some defect in the faculty of vision but because it simply cannot be seen. Existence cannot flow from God's beginningless power to something impossible, not because of a defect in God's power, but because the impossible is simply not an object of power. And the relationship between the nonexistent that is contingent in its essence and God's beginningless power is like the relationship between a veiled object of vision and the power of vision. If the veil were removed, the faculty of vision would perceive the veiled object. Likewise, when the conditions are there for the nonexistent that is contingent in its essence, God's beginningless power will bring it into existence. However, for as long as it is in need of a condition, it will be impossible for it to exist through another (let alone through itself).[125] The contingent in itself is that whose conditions for its existence are necessary, whereas the impossible in itself is that whose conditions for its existence are impossible. So reflect upon this properly and do not object to it with your pretend cleverness—otherwise your foot will slip, and you will not even know.

Chapter 49: Possibility Means Contingency

102 A person given to rational consideration might say, "A contingent thing's contingency is from itself, whereas an impossible thing's impossibility is in itself and from itself." A dimwit might concoct some corrupt notions from these words, erring in several dreadful ways. How can the contingent be from itself when its essence is not from itself but is from another? If its essence is from another, then it is even more fitting that contingency, one of the attributes of the contingent, is from another. For the dependence of essences that are qualified by what brings

الذوات الموصوفة إلى موجدها بدرجة واستناد الصفات التابعة إليه بدرجتين. هذا حكم الممكنات في إمكانها إذا وُجدت وأمّا الممكن الذي لم يوجد فليس له بعد ذات ولا صفات فكيف يُطلب له ولصفاته سبب والمعدوم لا يُطلب له سبب وإنّما يُطلب السبب لموجود بعد العدم وإنّما ذكرت ذلك لأنّ قولهم الإمكان للممكن من ذاته له معنى صحيح وكثيرًا ما تغلط الأوهام فيه فليُستعن بما ذكرته في الاحتراز من تغليط الوهم وهذا بعينه هو الجواب عن قولهم الاستحالة للمستحيل من ذاته فالمستحيل إذا لم يكن له ذات فكيف يُطلب لاستحالته التي هي صفة تابعة سبب وإذا قيل العدم للعدم[1] من ذاته كان له معنى صحيح عند الراسخين في العلم ولا يجوز أن يُتوهّم للمعدوم ذات ثمّ يُتوهّم العدم شيئًا موجودًا لتلك الذات فإنّ العدم معناه صفة والصفة لا توجد إلّا بعد وجود الموصوف فكيف يوجد العدم والمعدوم الذي هو موصوفه معدوم فأوهام الضعفاء تغلط كثيرًا في أمثال ذلك والمحقّقون يتيسّر[2] عليهم الاحتراز ممّا يضاهي هذه الأغاليط.

فصل ٥٠

والسموات والأرضون وُجدت حين وجدت من القدرة الأزليّة ولم يكن قبل وجودها قبل ولا بعد حتّى يقال لِما لم يوجد قبل ذلك فإنّ القبل والبعد عارضان من عوارض الزمان[3] لا يوجد إلّا بعد وجود الأجسام فكما لا يجوز أن يكون قبل وجود الأجسام فوق ولا تحت لأنّهما عارضان من عوارض المكان فكذلك لا يجوز أن يكون قبل وجود ١٠٣

---

١ ج، ع، م: للمعدوم. ٢ (يتيسّر) في ج، ع، م؛ أ: يتعسّر. ٣ ج، ع، م: الزمان، والزمان.

them into existence is on one level, but the dependence of attributes that come from these essences is on a level twice removed. This pertains to contingents in their contingency, when they are brought into existence. The contingent that is not yet brought into existence has neither essence nor attributes. So how can a cause be sought for it and its attributes when a cause cannot be sought for a nonexistent? A cause can only be sought for an existent after its having been nonexistent. I mention this because the statement, "A contingent thing's contingency is from itself," has a true meaning, but most minds fall into error about it. So one should seek help from my words, being wary of falling into errors of the mind. The same remarks apply in answering the statement, "An impossible thing's impossibility is from itself." Since that which is impossible does not have an essence, how can one seek its impossibility, which itself is an attribute that would follow from a cause? The statement that a nonexistent's nonexistence is from itself does have a true meaning for those who are firmly rooted in knowledge. But one cannot imagine an essence for a nonexistent, let alone imagine nonexistence to be an existent for that essence. Indeed, "nonexistence" indicates an attribute, but an attribute can only come into existence after the existence of that which is qualified. So how can nonexistence be brought into existence when a nonexistent, which is what qualifies nonexistence, is itself nonexistent? Weak minds have erred many times in matters like this, but it is rather easy for those who have verified the truth to avoid these kinds of errors.

Chapter 50: The Creation of the World and Time

The heavens and the earth came to exist when they were brought into existence 103
by God's beginningless power. Before their existence there was no "before" or "after." There is thus no point in asking why God did not bring them into existence "before" that point. Indeed, before and after are accidents of time, which itself only comes to exist after the existence of bodies. So, just as there cannot have been an "above" and a "below" before the existence of bodies—since they are both accidents of space—so too, before the existence of bodies, could there

الأجسام قبل ولا بعد لأنّ ذلك موقوف الوجود على وجود الزمان والزمان موقوف الوجود على وجود الحركة والحركة موقوفة الوجود على وجود الأجسام وكان الزمان ظرف الحركة كما أنّ المكان ظرف الجسم.

فصل ٥١

قولــــه القائل العالم قديم بالزمان هوس محض لا طائل تحته إذ يقال له ما الذي تعني ١٠٤
بالعالم فإمّا أن يقول أعني به الأجسام كلّها كالسموات والأمّهات وإمّا أن يقول أعني به كلّ موجود سوى الله تعالى وعلى هذا تكون النفوس والعقول والأجسام كلّها داخلة تحت لفظ العالم فإن قال أعني بالعالم كلّ موجود ممكن من الأجسام وغيرها فعلى هذا يكون أكثر الموجودات المندرجة تحت لفظ العالم غير متوقّف الوجود على وجود الزمان بل يكون بالضرورة سابق الوجود عليه فكيف يقال العالم قديم بالزمان وأكثر موجودات العالم سابق الوجود على الزمان، وإن قال أعني بالعالم الأجسام كلّها فلا يجوز على هذا الوجه أيضاً أن يقال الأجسام قديمة بالزمان فإنّ معنى ذلك أنّ الأجسام موجودة مذ كان الزمان موجوداً فيكون مشعراً بأنّ الزمان سابق على الأجسام في الوجود وليس كذلك فإنّ الأجسام سابقة الوجود على الزمان والزمان متأخّر الوجود عنها وإن كان كذلك بالرتبة والذات. فإن قال قائل ليس المراد بقولنا العالم قديم بالزمان ما ذكرتموه فنحن لا نفهم من قوله إلّا ذلك وقد تكلّمنا على ما فهمنا وأمّا ما لم نفهمه من مقاصده فالكلام عليه من شأن العميان فعليه أن يبيّن معناه على ما فهمه فإن كان صدقاً وحقّاً وافقناه في ذلك وإلّا تكلّمنا عليه حسب الوسع والطاقة.

not have been a "before" and an "after." This is undoubtedly because their existence is dependent upon the existence of time, and the existence of time is dependent upon the existence of motion, and the existence of motion is dependent upon the existence of bodies. Indeed, time is a locus for motion, just as space is a locus for bodies.

Chapter 51: Clarifications on the Term "World"

A person's statement to the effect that the world is eternal in time is pure and outright foolishness. For, if asked, "What do you mean by 'world'?," he will say, "By 'world' I mean all bodies, such as the heavens and the elements."[126] Or he will say, "By 'world' I mean every existent other than God"—the word "world" in this sense would thus comprise all souls, intellects, and bodies. If he says, "By 'world' I mean every existent that is contingent, such as bodies and the like," the existence of most existents subsumed under the word "world" would not be dependent upon the existence of time, for they would necessarily precede its existence. How then can it be said that the world is eternal in time when most of the existents in the world precede the existence of time? If the person says, "By 'world' I mean all bodies," this idea would also not be tenable, for it would amount to saying, "Bodies are eternal in time." That would mean that bodies were existent from when time was existent, which would indicate that time preceded bodies in existence; but such is not the case since bodies precede time in existence, and the existence of time comes after them (even if it is only with respect to logical hierarchy and essence). If this person were to say, "In proposing that the world is eternal in time, I did not have in mind the things you mentioned," well, I would be unable to understand his proposition in any other way. Our discussion is based on what we have understood this person's proposition to be. As for what he does mean but which we cannot understand, that would be like groping for something in the dark. The onus is on him to explain what he means, as he understands it. If his point is correct, I will accept it. But if not, then I will have already done my best to address his proposition. 104

فصل ٥٢

١٠٥ الحقّ ـــ في ذلك أن يقال كان الزمان موجوداً مذ كانت الحركة موجودة وليس يجوز أن يقال كانت الحركة موجودة مذ كان الزمان موجوداً فإنّ ذلك وإن كان له وجه ما فهو فاسد النظر[١] جدّاً فإذا لم يجز ذلك فكيف يجوز أن يقال كانت الأجسام موجودة مذ كان الزمان موجوداً ولو لم تُوجد الأجسام[٢] إلى الآن لعدم شرط ثمّ إن وُجدت الآن لوجود ذلك الشرط كان ذلك جائزاً ولم يكن قبل وجودها قبل ولا بعد ولا حين وُجدت فإنّما وُجدت كذلك من غير فرق فإن زعمت أنّ الأجسام كانت موجودة مذ كان الحقّ موجوداً فهو خطأ عظيم وهو اعتقاد أكثر العلماء الذين يزعمون أنّهم أربوا في صدق النظر على الأوّلين والآخرين وممّا لابدّ لك في هذا المقام من الإحاطة به أن تعلم أنّ الأجسام لا تُوجد أصلاً حيث يوجد الحقّ لا الآن ولا قبله ولا بعده ومن صار إلى أنّ العالم موجود الآن مع وجود الحقّ فهو مخطئ خطأ عظيماً حيث الحقّ فلا زمان ولا مكان وهو محيط بالزمان والمكان وسائر الموجودات فإن سبق وجوده على كلّ شيء مساو فإنّه سابق الوجود على وجود العالم كما إنّه سابق الوجود على وجود صورة هذه الكلمات المسطورة في هذا الكتاب مثلاً من غير فرق أصلاً ومن فرّق بينهما فهو بعد في مضيق النسبة[٣] ولم يتنزّه عنده الحقّ عن الزمان كما لم يتنزّه عن المكان عند العوامّ الذين يزعمون أنّه جسم كسائر المحسوسات ومثل هذا الإيمان بالله بعيد عن الإيمان الحقيقيّ الحاصل للعارف في أوّل سلوكه ونظره.

١٠٦ والله عزّ وجلّ سابق على الزمان المستقبل حسب سبقه على الزمان الماضي من غير فرق وهذا يقينيّ عند العارف والعلماء عاجزون عن إدراكه بالضرورة ولو لم يعجزوا عن إدراكه لما قالوا إنّ العقل الأوّل مساوق الوجود لوجود الحقّ الأوّل كما لم يقولوا إنّ صورة هذه الحروف المنقوشة بهذا القرطاس مثلاً مساوقة في الوجود لله الحقّ المنزّه عن أمثال

---

١ ج،ع،م: النظم. ٢ ج،ع: الأجسام مثلاً. ٣ ج،ع،م: التشبيه.

Chapter 52: The Eternity of the World in the Eyes of the Recognizer

The truth of the matter is to say that time was existent from when motion was existent, but one cannot say that motion was existent from when time was existent. Even though there is a way to consider this, it would be an extremely corrupt view. If this cannot be, then how can one say that bodies were existent when time was existent? For if bodies were not brought into existence up until now because of the nonexistence of a condition, and then were brought into existence at this very moment because of the existence of that condition, that could be the case. Yet neither before the existence nor at the moment of the existence of these bodies was there a before or an after. Bodies came into existence without any distinction between before and after. Now, it would be a tremendous error to claim that bodies are existent with God's existence; such is the view of most philosophers, who claim that, in reflecting correctly, they have gone beyond all those who went before and those who are to come after them. At this point, one of the things you must comprehend is that bodies do not exist in any way whatsoever insofar as God exists—be it in the past, the present, or the future. To maintain that the world exists right now insofar as God exists is to be guilty of a great error. With respect to God, there is neither time nor space, as He encompasses time, space, and every existent. Indeed, the precedence of God's existence to every thing is one and the same. God is precedent in existence over the existence of the world just as, for example, He is precedent in existence over the existence of the form of the words inscribed in this book, without any difference at all in His precedence over both things. To differentiate between them is to be far from the mark, for it delimits the true nature of God's relationship to them. According to this view, God does not transcend time, just as He does not transcend space in the opinion of ordinary people who claim that God is a body like other sensible objects. This kind of belief is far removed from the true faith obtained by the recognizer at the outset of his journey and at the beginning of his spiritual vision. 105

God precedes the future just as He precedes the past, without any difference between them. This is certain knowledge for the recognizer, but the philosophers are perforce incapable of perceiving this. If they were not incapable of perceiving this, they would not have said that the First Intellect is coextensive in 106

هذه الظنون وعن ظنون الأنبياء والمقرّبين وانظر في ذلك نظرًا شافيًا فلا بدّ أن يحظى عقلك القاصر من معناه بنصيب ما وإن كان فهم المراد الحقيقيّ منه موقوفًا على انفتاح عين المعرفة التي منزلتها من بصيرة العقل منزلة الجنين من الرحم لا بل منزلة العقل من العين التي تراها موجودة لابن المهد وسأزيد لذلك شرحًا في موضوع آخر أليق به لعلّ القاصرين[١] يشمّون من روائحه شيئًا.

فصل ٥٣

الحقّ أنّ الله تعالى كان موجودًا ولم يكن معه شيء وهو الآن موجود وليس معه شيء ١٠٧
ويكون موجودًا ولا يكون معه شيء فأزليّته حاضرة مع أبديّته من غير فرق[٢] وحيث سلطنة كمال إشراق الشمس فلا يُتصوّر للخفافيش وجودها أصلاً فخذ إليك هذا المثال العاميّ على قدر ضعف عقلك القاصر وعلمك المزخرف واجتهد لعلّ فهمك الضعيف ينتفع بشيء من هذا المثال واحذر من التشبيه.

١٠٨ وليس وجود الواحد الحقّ زمانيًا حتّى يحسن مثلاً أن يقال كان الله ولم يكن معه شيء ولا يحسن أن يقال يكون ولا يكون معه شيء وإيّاك ثمّ إيّاك ألف مرّة أن تطمع في الإحاطة بهذا الذي تسمعه بعقلك الذي نسبته من إدراكه نسبة الخفافيش من إدراك نور الشمس فإمّا أن لا تلتفت إلى ما في هذا الفصل وأمثاله أصلاً ولا تتلقّاها بردّ ولا قبول وإمّا أن تحفظ هذه الكلمات وسل الله عزّ وجلّ أن يخصّك بعين عند تدرّك أمثال ذلك لا من اللفظ فإنّ ذلك محال بل من وجه آخر[٣] فإن أدركته[٤]

١ زائدة في أ: الإقبال. ٢ ج، ع، م: فرق وحيث سلطانه فلا موجود غيره ولا أيضًا يُتصوّر وجود ذلك. ٣ زائدة في أ: فإنّ إدراكه من وجه آخر. ٤ (فإن أدركته من هذا الوجه) في ج، ع، م؛ أ: فإنّ إدراكه.

existence with God's existence,[127] nor could they say, for example, that the form of these letters imprinted on this page is coextensive with God's existence (who is exalted far beyond the likes of their opinions, and even those of the Prophets and the proximate angels!). Look at this carefully, and your puny intellect will inevitably grasp some of its meaning to some degree—even if understanding what is truly intended depends on opening the eye of recognition, which, in relation to the vision of the intellect, is like a womb is to a fetus, or like the intellect is to a baby's eye. I will explain this further in a more suitable context so that hopefully the puny-minded will catch a whiff of its fragrance.

Chapter 53: Do "Was" and "Is" Apply to God?

The truth is that God was existent and there was nothing with Him. And right now He is existent and there is nothing with Him.[128] And He will be existent, and nothing will be with Him. His beginninglessness is present with His endlessness, with no distinction between them. But bats cannot conceive of the power of the sun's radiance at all. So take from this general example whatever the weakness of your puny intellect and your vain learning can bear, and strive hard so that maybe your weak understanding will still derive some benefit from it. But be wary of declaring God to be similar to anything. 107

The existence of the Real One is not temporal such that it can be said that "God 'was,' and nothing was with Him." Nor can it be said that "He 'is,' and nothing is with Him." You should take a thousand precautions not to desire to comprehend what you have heard with your intellect, which in relation to perceiving God is like the relation of bats to perceiving the light of the sun. So you should either completely turn away from the contents of this and similar chapters, neither rejecting them nor accepting them; or you should remember these words and ask God to single you out with an eye that can perceive what this is like, not by means of words (for that would be impossible), but from another standpoint. If you perceive it from that standpoint, then you will undoubtedly know that no expression concerning existence can convey the truth of what you have 108

من هذا الوجه فحينئذ تعلم قطعاً أن لا عبارة في الوجود تؤدّي حقّ ما أدركته أحسن من هذا الذي ذكرته وتعلم قطعاً أنّ من أودع أمثال تلك المعاني في الألفاظ المذكورة فهو ظالم غاية الظلم.

١٠٩ واعلم أنّا إذا قلنا لها كان الله ولم يكن معه شيء موجود فهو متشابه فإنّ لفظ كان يدلّ على وجود موجود في زمان ماض فإذا قلنا ولم يكن معه موجود فكيف يكون الزمان معه موجوداً ومهما كان كذلك فلا فرق بين قولنا كان ولم يكن معه موجود وبين قولنا يكون وليس معه موجود فهذا غاية ما يمكن ذكره في مضيق الألفاظ والعبارات.

فصل ٥٤

١١٠ إذا انفتحت من باطنك روزنة إلى عالم الملكوت فكلّ ما اتّفق طيرانك إليه شاهدت جليّة الحال في ذلك كلّه فاستغنيت عن سماع حكاياته ولعلّك الآن تشتهي أن تعرف معنى الأزليّة وكيفيّة الطيران إلى الملكوت فإنّ ظاهر ذلك كالمحال فاعلم أنّ من ظنّ أنّ الأزليّة شيء ماض فقد أخطأ خطأً فاحشاً وهذا وهم غالب على الغالبة فحيث الأزليّة فلا ماض ولا مستقبل وهي محيطة بالزمان المستقبل كإحاطتها بالزمان الماضي من غير فرق ومن اختلج في ضميره فرق بينهما فعقله بعد أسير في يد وهمه فليس زمن آدم أقرب إلى الأزليّة من زماننا هذا بل نسبة الأزمنة كلّها إلى الأزليّة واحدة ولعلّ نسبة الأزليّة إلى الأزمنة كنسبة العلوم مثلاً إلى الأمكنة إذ لا تُوصف العلوم بكونها قريبة من مكان أو بعيدة من مكان بل نسبتها واحدة إلى كلّ مكان فهي مع كلّ مكان ومع ذلك فقد خلا عنها كلّ مكان وهذا يسهل إدراكه على ما نظر في

perceived better than my discussion. And you will also undoubtedly know that it is extremely unjust to try to put the likes of these supra-sensory realities into words.

It is ambiguous to say that God "was" and that there was no existent with Him 109
because the word "was" points to the existence of an existent at a time in the past. And when we say that no existent "was" with God, how can time be an existent thing with God? Since this is the case, there is no difference between our saying that God "was" and that there was no existent with Him, and our saying that He "is" and that there is no existent with Him. This is the extent of what can be discussed within the limitations of words and expressions.

Chapter 54: God's Beginninglessness and Time

When a window inside of you opens up onto the spiritual realm, you will come 110
to see all that will happen during your flight in their true state of affairs, thus freeing you from having to listen to representations of it. Maybe even now you have the desire to recognize the meaning of God's beginninglessness and how to fly to the spiritual realm, although these seem to be impossible to get at. It is an egregious error to think that God's beginninglessness extends to the past. This is an illusion that most people labor under. In terms of God's beginninglessness, there is neither past nor future, for it encompasses the future in the same way that it encompasses the past, without any distinction between them. If your mind busies itself with any distinction between them, then your intellect is still a captive to your illusion! Adam's era is not closer in time to God's beginninglessness than our era because the relation of all eras to it is one and the same. Perhaps the relationship between God's beginninglessness and time is like the relationship, for example, between forms of knowledge and location. For forms of knowledge are not described in terms of proximity to or distance from a given location, because their relationship to every location is one and the same since they are "with" every location; but, by the same logic, every location is devoid of them. This is easy to perceive for anyone who has studied the rational sciences

العلوم العقليّة قليلاً وإنّما يعسر على من بعد[١] به القصور في عالم الملك ولم يفتح بعد عينه الجوّالة في الملكوت.

١١١ وكذلك ينبغي أن تُعتقد نسبته إلى كلّ زمان فإنّها مع كلّ زمان وفي كلّ زمن ومع ذلك فإنّها محيطة بكلّ زمن وسابقة الوجود على كلّ زمان ولا يسعها زمن كما لا يسع العلم مكان فإذا فهمت هذه المعاني فاعلم أنّه لا مغايرة بين الأزليّة والأبديّة في المعنى أصلاً بل إذا اعتبروا وجود ذلك المعنى مع نسبته إلى الماضي من الأزمنة استُعير له لفظة الأزليّة وإن اعتُبر وجوده مع نسبته إلى المستقبل من الأزمنة استعير له لفظة الأبديّة ولا بدّ من لفظتين مختلفتين لاختلاف النسبتين وإلّا ضلّ الخلق في إدراكه عن سواء السبيل. واعلم الآن أنّا إذا قلنا أراد الحقّ تعالى ويريد وعلم ويعلم وقدر ويقدر فهو لمثل هذه الضرورة وإلّا فإذا لم يكن له ماض ومستقبل فلا معنى للاختلاف في فعله أن يتعلق في الماضي أو المستقبل نعم إذا نُسبت الإرادة إلى زمن ماض قيل أراد وإذا نُسبت إلى مستقبل قيل يريد وهذا مفتاح أسرار كثيرة ومشكلات عظيمة وإذا كان كذلك فمن المحال الظاهر أن يصل السالك إلى الأزليّة من طريق العلم. نعم، يجوز أن يدرك معناها بالعلم ولكنّ إدراك معنى الشيء غير والوصول إليه غير وإنّما قلنا يستحيل الوصول إليها من طريق العلم لأنّ المتفرّغ للطلب العلميّ في أسر الزمان بعد ولا وصول إلى الأزليّة إلّا بعد حلّ ذلك الأسر.

١ ج،ع،م: قعد.

even a little; it is only hard for those whose shortcomings hold them back in the material realm, and whose roaming eyes have not yet been opened up to the spiritual realm.

You should therefore believe in the relationship between God's beginning- 111
lessness and every temporal referent in this manner. For it is with every time, is in every time, and encompasses every time; in existence it precedes every time (but time cannot embrace it, just as location cannot embrace knowledge). When you have understood these points, you should know that, in their supra-sensory reality, there is absolutely no difference between God's beginninglessness and His endlessness. Indeed, if the existence of this supra-sensory reality is communicated in relation to the past, the term "beginninglessness" is used as a metaphor for it. And if its existence is communicated in relation to the future, the term "endlessness" is used as its metaphor. The two terms must differ because of the different relations involved. If it were not for these terms, people would stray far from the right way. Now, when we say that God desired and desires, knew and knows, and determined and determines, the same obtains necessarily. Otherwise, it would be meaningless to apply differentiation to His actions, be they in the past or the present, since He does not have a past or a present. Indeed, when God's desire is related to the past one says, "He desired," and when it is related to the future one says, "He desires." This is a key to unlocking many mysteries and great difficulties. Since this is the case, it is evidently impossible for the traveler to arrive at the meaning of God's beginninglessness by way of formal knowledge. True, he can perceive its meaning through this kind of knowledge; however, perceiving the meaning of a thing is one thing, and attaining it is quite something else. I only say that it is impossible to arrive at God's beginninglessness by way of formal knowledge because the person who is exclusively devoted to the pursuit of formal knowledge remains a prisoner of time. And he can only arrive at God's beginninglessness after breaking free from this prison.

فصل ٥٥

١١٢ واعلم أنّ إشراق الأرض بنور الشمس يستدعي نسبة مخصوصة بين الأرض والشمس لو بطلت تلك النسبة بطل استعدادها لقبول نور الشمس ولو دامت هذه النسبة بينهما دام القبول وبقدر دوامها يدوم القبول فأيّ نَفَس وجدت هذه النسبة وجد القبول وأيّ نفس بطلت هذه النسبة بطل القبول ثمّ إن دامت هذه النسبة في أنفاس متعدّدة دام القبول في تلك الأنفاس على منهاج واحد فيظنّ القاصرون أنّ الشعاع الموجود في كلّ نفس مثلاً عين الشعاع الموجود في النفس الذي قبله أو بعده وهو خطأ عند أهل المعرفة الناظرين بنور الله عزّ وجلّ بل الشعاع الموجود في كلّ نَفَس مقتضى النسبة الموجودة في ذلك النفس والنسبة الموجودة في تلك الأنفاس متغايرة بالضرورة ولذلك يجوز أن يحكم على نسبة واحدة من جملتها بأحكام لا يجوز الحكم في تلك الأحكام على نسبة أخرى كما يقال مثلاً إنّ النسبة الفلانيّة كانت مساوقة الوجود للحركة الفلانيّة وإنّ النسبة التي بعدها لم تكن مساوقة الوجود لتلك الحركة وبهذا تحقّق المغايرة بين النسبتين قطعاً .

١١٣ فإذا كانت تلك النسب متغايرة كان القبول في كلّ نَفَس مقتضى نسبة أخرى على حدتها واستقلالها فاعلم أنّ الشعاع الذي يكون موجوداً في نفس مخصوص غير الشعاع الذي يكون موجوداً قبله أو بعده ولو بنفس واحد نعم لمّا كانت هذه النسب المتغايرة واحدة في كونها مقتضية للقبول على وتيرة واحدة ظنّ بعض الضعفاء أنّ هذا الشعاع الموجود في هذا النفس عين الشعاع الموجود في النفس الذي يُرى قبله وبعده كمن يرى زيداً وعَمْراً أو خالداً وبكراً واحداً في معنى الإنسانيّة فيظنّ أنّ كلّ واحد منهم عين صاحبه وليتحقّق هذا فإنّه محتاج إليه من طريق ضرب المثال العاميّ في الفصل الذي يلي هذا الفصل وهو يُبنى عليه أصل عظيم .

Chapter 55: A Hint at Perpetual Renewal

112 The illumination of the earth by the light of the sun calls for a specific relationship between the earth and the sun. If that relationship is nullified, the earth's capacity to receive the light of the sun will also be nullified. But were this relationship between them to persist, the earth's reception of the sun's light would persist in keeping with the persistence of this relationship. So every moment that this relationship exists, the earth's reception of the sun's light will exist, and every moment that this relationship is nullified, the earth's reception of the sun's light will also be nullified. Moreover, were this relationship to persist over the course of a number of moments, the earth's reception of the sun's light would be unchanged over the course of these moments. But the puny-minded think, for example, that the sun's rays that exist at every moment are the selfsame rays that exist in preceding and successive moments, which is an error in the eyes of the recognizers who see with the light of God. Rather, in every moment, the rays that exist are demanded by the relationship that exists at that given moment, for the relationship that exists in each moment necessarily changes. This is why one can make a pronouncement about one such relationship in a way that cannot apply to other relationships, as, for example, when it is said that a given relationship is coextensive in existence with a given motion, but that any subsequent relationship is not coextensive in existence with this motion. In this way can you assuredly verify the difference between these two relationships.

113 Since these relationships are different, the earth's reception of the sun's light at every moment is demanded by another relationship, independent and unique. The rays that exist in a specific moment are different from the rays that exist before and after it, even if it is in one moment.[129] Indeed, since these changing relationships are one in demanding the earth's reception of the sun's light in exactly the same way, some weak-minded people think the rays that exist in this given moment are the selfsame rays that are seen in preceding and successive moments. This is like viewing Zayd, ʿAmr, Khālid, and Bakr as "one" in the sense of being human, and then thinking that each is identical to the other! This should be verified, for it will form the basis of a general example in the next chapter, and a tremendous foundational principle will be built upon it.

فصل ٥٦

لا شكّ أنّ إشراق المعدوم بنور الوجود يستدعي نسبة مخصوصة بينه وبين ١١٤
القدرة الأزليّة ولو دامت هذه النسبة دام قبول المعدوم لإشراق نور القدرة ولو بطلت النسبة بطل القبول وبقدر دوام النسبة يدوم القبول والقبول في كلّ نَفَس مقتضى النسبة الموجودة في ذلك النفس والنسب تتغاير فإذا القبول الذي في هذا النفس مثلاً غير القبول الذي في ذلك النفس وإن تشابهت أنفاس متعدّدة في القبول فذلك لتشابه النسب المتغايرة فاتّحادها في معنى الاقتضاء للقبول فإذا رأيت الشيء مثلاً موجوداً سنين كثيرة على منهاج واحد فذلك لدوام النسب المقتضية للوجود في تلك السنين نفساً بعد نفس فاعلم يقيناً أنّ الوجود في كلّ نفس مقتضى النسبة الموجودة في ذلك النفس فالوجود الذي تراه في هذا النفس للسماء والأرض وسائر الموجودات غير الوجود الذي تراه فيما بعد ورأيته فيما قبل. نعم لمّا كانت النسب المتغايرة المقتضية لوجود تلك الموجودات واحدة في كون كلّ نسبة منها مقتضية للوجود وقع الوهم للأوّلين من عند آخرهم في هذا الغلط ﴿إِلَّا مَن شَآءَ ٱللَّهُ﴾ ﴿وَقَلِيلٌ مَّا هُمْ﴾.

وهذا الفصل غامض شديد الغموض صعب المتناول عسير المدرك ممتنع على الأفهام ١١٥
وزلل الأقدام في أمثاله تكثّر والعقل لا يُتصوّر له إدراك ذلك إلّا بتأمّل عظيم ونظر شاف وبحث واف وذكاء عظيم وجدّ بليغ نعم يدركه العارفون بعين المعرفة في أوّل نظرة من غير احتياج إلى تكلّف ومن استعان من العقلاء في فهم هذا الفصل بنور السراج الذي تجدّد له في كلّ نفَس وجود آخر سهل عليه إدراكه فإنّ الصبيان يظنّون أنّ نور السراج الذي يرونه مشتعلاً على منهاج واحد وهو شيء واحد والعلماء يعلمون قطعاً

Chapter 56: Perpetual Renewal

There is no doubt that the illumination of a nonexistent by the light of existence calls for a specific relationship between it and God's beginningless power. If this relationship were to persist, the reception by the nonexistent of illumination from the light of God's power would persist. If this relationship were to be nullified, the reception by the nonexistent of this illumination would also be nullified. So it persists in accordance with the persistence of this relationship and, at every moment, the reception by the nonexistent of this illumination is determined by a relationship that exists at that moment—and these relationships vary. So if, for example, the reception of this illumination by the nonexistent at moment *x* is different from its reception of this illumination at moment *y*, even though the numerous moments resemble one another as far as the reception of this illumination is concerned, because the different moments themselves resemble one another, then it is the conjunction of these moments that demands the reception of this illumination by the nonexistent.[130] So if, for example, over the course of many years you see something as existent in one and the same manner, that would be on account of the persistence of the relationships that demand existence during these years, moment by moment. You should know with certainty that, at every moment, it is existence which is demanded by an existing relationship. Thus, the existence that you see at this very moment in the heavens, the earth, and in other existents is different from the existence that you saw previously and will see afterward. Indeed, since the different relationships that demand the existence of these existents are one and the same in respect of every such relationship that demands existence, most people fall into the illusion of this mistake, «except those whom God wills»,[131] «And how few they are!»[132] 114

This chapter is very obscure, hard to grasp, difficult to perceive, and forbidding to the human mind—indeed, many have slipped over the likes of this. The only way the intellect can perceive these points is through deep reflection, careful study, extensive investigation, mental acuity, and serious application. To be sure, with the eye of recognition the recognizers perceive this without any difficulty at the start of their spiritual quest. The points in this chapter will be easy to grasp by those intellectuals who seek aid in understanding it with the light of the lamp whose existence is renewed at every moment. For children think that 115

أنه في كلّ نفَس تجدّد له صورة أخرى وهذا مقتضى نظر العارف في كلّ موجود سوى الله عزّ وجلّ فلعلّ عقلك يحيط بشيء من ذلك إن أدمت النظر إليه ووقفت فهمك عليه والغالب أنّ هذا الباب لا ينفتح للعقل.

فصل ٥٧

١١٦ اعلم أنّ الله عزّ وجلّ كان موجودًا ولم يكن معه شيء ولا أيضاً يُتصوّر أبدًا أن يكون معه شيء إذ ليس لشيء مع وجوده رتبة المعيّة فالله عزّ وجلّ ليس معه شيء ولكنّه مع كلّ شيء ولولا معيّته مع كلّ شيء لما بقي في الوجود موجود والموجودات في حصولها منه لها ترتيب فبعضها متقدّم كالمفرد وبعضها متأخّر كالمركّب هذا إذا نظرنا بنظر العقل الصحيح فإن نظرنا بنظر المعرفة فهو خطأ والعقل لا يدرك حقيقة ذلك أصلاً فيراه إذا سمع ذلك يفور فائرة ويثور ثائرة ويقول الشيء الواحد كيف يكون صحيحًا وخطأ وعليك أن تُسكّن فورته بهذا المثال العاميّ إن سكنت به وإلّا فدونك والتكذيب به والإنكار عليه ما دمت أسيرًا في عالم العقل محبوساً في مضيقه.[1]

١١٧ وهذا المثال العاميّ هو أنّ الصبيّ إذا حكم على شخصين مثلاً بأنّ أحدهما أقرب إليه من الآخر فقال له بعض البالغين من أهل التحقيق حكمك هذا صادق إذ نظرت بنظر الحسّ وأمّا إذا نظرت بنظر العقل علمت أنّ حكمك خطأ فإنّ الأقرب بنظر الحسّ هو الأبعد

---

١ (مضيقه) في ج، ع، م؛ أ: لا يقرأ.

the light of the lamp that they see is lit in one and the same manner and is one thing. But those who understand know with certainty that, at every moment, the light is renewed in another form. This is what is required by the vision of the recognizers with respect to every existent other than God. Perhaps your intellect will encompass some of this if you persistently reflect on this point, applying all of your understanding to it. But in most cases, this door will remain closed to the intellect.

Chapter 57: Divine Withness

God is existent, and there is nothing with Him, nor can it ever be conceived that something will be with Him. For nothing shares the rank of withness[133] with His existence. Thus, nothing is with God, but He is with each thing. Were it not for His withness with each thing, no existent would remain in existence.[134] In acquiring their existence from Him, existents are hierarchically ordered with some preceding, such as the simple, and others following, such as the composite. This is how it is when we look at it with the eye of a sound intellect. But if we look at it with the eye of recognition, it is incorrect. Yet the intellect cannot perceive the reality of this vision at all. When presented to an intellectual, he will be up in arms, inveighing against this vision: "How can one thing be both correct and incorrect?" If possible, you should try to assuage his perturbation with the following everyday example, saying to him, "If you are assuaged thereby, well and good. But if not, be careful not to disbelieve in and reject it as long as you remain a captive to the realm of the intellect, imprisoned within its confines." 116

Here is the everyday example. A child makes a judgment, for example, between two people, saying that one of them is physically closer to him than the other. But then he is told by an adult, who happens to be an exacting scholar, "Your judgment is correct, if you view the two people with the sensory eye. But if you look with the eye of your intellect, you will come to know that your judgment is wrong. For that which is closer for the sensory eye is more distant for 117

في نظر العقل فإنّ قول العاقل[١] صحيح ونظر الصبيّ صحيح عند العاقل وتكذيبه للعاقل في دعواه خطأ وهذا التكذيب له ضروريّ لا يتمكّن من اعتقاد غيره وطريق تفهيمه مسدود على العاقل.

١١٨ فإذًا لا بدّ من بيان صدور الموجودات من القدرة الأزليّة بطريق يمكن للعقل إدراكه وإن كان ذلك خطأ في نظر العارف وقد أكثر في بيانه النظّار وحاصلهم فيه يرجع إلى ظنون يرجمونها والحقّ في ذلك على ما يلوح لعقولنا أن يقال إنّ الله تعالى فاض منه الوجود أوّلاً على الموجود الأوّل وهو أقرب الملائكة إليه وأقرب الموجودات كلّها في نظر العقل وشبيه أن يكون الروح المذكور في قوله تعالى ﴿يَوْمَ يَقُومُ ٱلرُّوحُ وَٱلْمَلَٰٓئِكَةُ صَفًّا﴾، عبارة عنه.

١١٩ وكان وجود هذه الروح شرطاً تمّ به استعداد شيء آخر لقبول نور القدرة الأزليّة فكان استعداد هذا الشيء الثاني بشرط وجود الروح كاستعداد الروح من غير شرط ثمّ كان وجود هذا الثاني شرطاً في وجود شيء ثالث ويجوز أن يكون شرطاً في وجود شيئين ثالث ورابع وليس للعقول الضعيفة أن تدرك حقيقة هذا الأمر على ما يجب إلّا أنّ لها أن تدرك جواز الوجهين المشار إليهما وهو أنّ وجود الثاني يجوز أن يكون شرطاً في وجود شيئين ويجوز أن يكون شرطاً في وجود شيء واحد وهو أن يكون باعتبار ذاته على حدتها شرطاً لشيء ويكون باعتبار ذاته مع اعتبار الروح شرطاً لشيء آخر. وكلا الوجهين معقول وهذا القدر يكفيك في كيفيّة صدور الموجودات الكثيرة من الواحد الحقّ فإنّه إذا جاز أن يكون الثاني شرطاً لشيئين جاز أن يكون كلّ واحد من الشيئين[٢] شرطاً لوجود ثالث ورابع من الموجودات.

---

١ ج، ع: قائل. ٢ (الشيئين) في ج، ع، م؛ أ: الشرطين.

the eye of the intellect."[135] Now, this statement is correct, as is the child's statement (as far as the scholar is concerned). But the child would be wrong were he to disbelieve in the scholar's claim. Yet the child will necessarily disbelieve him because he cannot believe otherwise, as the scholar has no way to make him understand.

Therefore, the effusion of existents from God's beginningless power must be 118
clarified in a way that the intellect can perceive, even if it is incorrect in the eyes of the recognizer. The philosophers have explained this process often, but their conclusions about it are based on their own conjectures. The truth is what is clear to our intellects, which is to say that existence first emanated from God upon the first existent—namely, the angel most proximate to Him,[136] the closest of all existents to God in the eyes of the intellect. It is probable that this is the spirit referred to in God's statement «That day the spirit and the angels will stand in rows».[137]

The existence of this spirit is a condition through which the capacity of some- 119
thing else to receive the light of God's beginningless power becomes complete. The capacity of this second thing with the condition of the existence of the spirit is like the capacity of the unconditioned spirit. The existence of this second thing is a condition for the existence of a third thing, and can be a condition for the existence of two things—namely, a third and a fourth thing. It is not for weak intellects to perceive the reality of this point as it must be understood. Rather, they can only perceive the possibility of these two aforementioned things—namely, that the existence of the second thing can be a condition for the existence of two things and that the second thing can also be a condition for the existence of one thing solely in consideration of its essence being a condition for that thing. And the second thing can be a condition for another thing in consideration of its essence and the spirit. Both possibilities are intelligible. This should be enough for you concerning how it is that many existents emanate from the Real One. Indeed, if it is possible that the second thing can be a condition for the existence of two things, then it is possible for each of the two things to be a condition for the existence of a third and a fourth existent.

فصل ٥٨

١٢٠ الحكم بأنّه لم يتوسّط بين الواجب الحقّ وبين السماء الأولى وهو الفلك الأطلس إلّا ثلاثة من الملائكة واحد منهم روحانيّ واثنان كرويّان حكم مظنون غير مستقيم فربّما كان من الوسائط بينهما ألف أو أكثر لا بل هو الحقّ عند أرباب المعرفة. نعم لمّا لم يتمكّن العلماء في العروج إلى الأوّل من الاستدلال بحركة السماء الأولى على غير هذه الثلاثة لا جرم لم يطلبوا في نزولهم سبباً[١] لغير تلك الثلاثة وهذا مظنون قطعاً لا يجوز أن يقنع بأمثاله في العلوم النظريّة وحكمنا بأنّ الوسائط بين الواجب وبين السماء الأولى كثيرة فهو حقّ وصدق ويشاهده أهل المعرفة لا من طريق الاستدلال بل من طريق آخر. ولو كان من طريق الاستدلال أمكن ذكره فلمّا كان موقوفاً على انفتاح عين المعرفة في الباطن لم يمكن ذكره بل لمّا كان إمكانه معقولاً نُبّه عليه بقدر الوسع وممّا يعين العقل على التصديق بذلك أن يكرّر نظره في الكواكب الموجودة على السماء الثانية المعبّر عنها في لسان أهل الشرع بالكرسيّ.

فصل ٥٩

١٢١ كلّ موجود دائم الموجود فإنّه يتكرّر بالحيّ القيّوم دائماً ويتجدّد له في كلّ نفس وجود آخر شبيه بما قبله وأهل المعرفة يشاهدون ذلك صريحاً والعالم يتعذّر عليه إدراكه فكرّر نظرك فيما ذكرته من قبل فربّما تجلّى لك حقيقة هذه الأمور والله تعالى لا يجعل ذكر ذلك

---

١ ع: شيئًا.

Chapter 58: A Note on Cosmic Order

The position that the only intermediaries between the Necessary Real and the first heaven (which is the sphere of Atlas) are three angels (one being spiritual and two being cherubs) is conjectural and not properly established.[138] There might be a thousand or more intermediaries between them—indeed, that is the truth in the eyes of the masters of recognition. Since, in their upward ascent to the One, the philosophers were only able to provide demonstrative proofs for the existence of these three intermediaries by way of the motion of the first heaven, during their downward descent they undoubtedly only sought for an intermediary cause in these three entities. But this is completely conjectural, and such things do not pass muster in the theoretical sciences. My position that the intermediaries between the Necessary and the first heaven are many is right and true. The people of recognition witness this not by means of demonstrative proofs, but by another means. If this could be shown by means of demonstrative proofs, it would be possible to discuss it. But since it depends on the opening of the eye of recognition inside the self, it cannot be discussed. At the same time, since its possibility is intelligible, remarks can be made to some extent. To aid the intellect in assenting to my position, one should repeatedly gaze at the planets that exist in the eighth heaven, referred to in religious language as the "Footstool."[139] 120

Chapter 59: Witnessing Perpetual Renewal

Every existent perpetually exists and is made perpetually continuous through the Living, the Self-Abiding. In every moment, another existence similar to the one preceding it is renewed for it. The recognizers clearly witness this, whereas it is impossible for the scholar to perceive it. So reflect continuously on what I said earlier—perhaps the reality of these matters will be disclosed to you! May God 121

وبالًا عليّ وعلى من يطالعه ويجعل نفع الخلق به أكثر من الضرر. ورحم الله عبدًا طالعه بعين المعرفة وشمّر لفهمه ذيله وترك التعصّب ومراقبة الجوانب والمداهنة في المذاهب بل ينبغي أن لا يحمله على مطالعته والنظر فيه إلّا طلب الحقّ بطريق اليقين لكون سعادة النفس متعلّقة به.

١٢٢ فإنّ هذه المعاني التي ذكرتها في هذه الفصول مشاهدة بالذوق مشاهدةً لا تقصر عن مشاهدة العقل للأوّليّات إلّا أنّه لم يكن التعبير عن تلك المعاني إلّا بهذه الألفاظ والحقّ الذي لا ريب فيه أنّ من عرف الله تعالى كلّ لسانه أي لم يجد عبارة تؤدّي حقّ المعنى الذي فهمه ذوقًا إلى الأفهام.

فصل ٦٠

١٢٣ النـاظرون بعين العقل يرون للموجودات في ذواتها ترتيبًا ويرون بعضها أقرب من البعض إلى الأوّل الحقّ بالضرورة ولا يُتصوّر أن يكون إلّا كذلك ويرون مصدر الوجود واحدًا ويرون الموجودات الصادرة عنه كثيرة فلا جرم يحتاجون إلى تكلّفات باردة في بيان كيفيّة صدور الكثرة من الوحدة فأمّا الناظرون بعين المعرفة فإنّهم لا يرون للموجودات ترتيبًا أصلًا ولا يرون بعضها أقرب إلى الحقّ من البعض بل يرون هويّته مساوقة لكلّ موجود حيث مساوقتها للموجود الأوّل في نظر العلماء من غير فرق وما لم يصل الرجل إلى هذا المقام فلا يتجلّى له معنى قوله تعالى ﴿إِنَّ ٱللَّهَ يُمۡسِكُ ٱلسَّمَٰوَٰتِ وَٱلۡأَرۡضَ أَن تَزُولَاۚ وَلَئِن زَالَتَآ إِنۡ أَمۡسَكَهُمَا مِنۡ أَحَدٖ مِّنۢ بَعۡدِهِۦٓ﴾ ولا قوله ﴿فَأَيۡنَمَا تُوَلُّواْ فَثَمَّ وَجۡهُ ٱللَّهِ﴾. وإنّما يحظى من سماع أمثال هذه الآيات سماع حروف وكلمات.

not make discussing these things a tribulation for myself and my readers, and may He make it benefit people more than harm them. God bless the person who reads this discussion with the eye of recognition, immediately setting out to understand it and relinquishing bigotry, self-interest, and the artificiality usually found among the various schools of thought. Indeed, nothing should incite a person to read this discussion and reflect upon it other than the pursuit of God, being certain that attachment to Him will yield felicity for his soul.

The supra-sensory realities I have discussed in these chapters are witnessed 122
by way of tasting in a manner not less than the intellect's beholding primary concepts; it is just that it is only possible to convey these supra-sensory realities by means of these words. The indubitable truth is that "Whoever recognizes God becomes speechless."[140] That is, he has no way to convey to people's minds the meaning he has understood by way of tasting.

Chapter 60: God's Coextensiveness in the Eyes of the Recognizer

Those who look with the eye of the intellect see existents in their essences as 123
logically ordered, with some necessarily being closer than others to the Real and the One. All else is inconceivable to them. They also see the source of existence as one, and the existents that emanate from Him as multiple. In seeking to clarify how the many emanate from the One, they undoubtedly rely on inane, forced explanations. But those who look with the eye of recognition simply do not see existents as logically ordered, with some being closer to the Real than others. Rather, they see His identity as being coextensive with every existent, which is not dissimilar to the manner in which the philosophers see the coextensiveness of existents with the First Existent. As long as this station is not reached, the meanings of God's following statements will not be disclosed: «Truly God maintains the heavens and the earth so that they do not fall apart. Were they to fall apart, none could maintain them in His place»;[141] «Wherever you turn, there is the face of God».[142] Only the sounds of the letters and words will be heard.

ثمّ أهل المعرفة لا يرون مساوقته للموجودات كما يراها العلماء للعقل الأوّل ويرون أعني العارفين مصدر الموجودات كثيرًا ويرون الموجودات كلّها كالذرّة بالنسبة إلى عظمته ومن كان ينظر إلى الله عزّ وجلّ وأفعاله بهذه العين فلا يحتاج إلى العلم بكيفيّة صدور الكثرة عن الوحدة فيكون كلّ ما ذُكر في هذا المعنى عنده فضولاً مستغنى عنه فاجتهد أن تصدّق بوجود[١] عين في باطن الآدميّ إذا انفتحت كانت مدركاتها من جنس ما أُشير إليه في قولنا إنّ الهويّة الأزليّة مساوقة الوجود لوجود كلّ موجود فإنّ العقل قاصر عن إدراك ذلك فلا محالة يرى بعض الأشياء أقرب إلى الحيّ القيّوم من البعض ومهما أدركت شيئاً واستحال عندك أن تعبّر عنه إلّا بالعبارات التي يشتمل عليها هذا الفصل من مدركات العارف فاعلم يقيناً أنّ عين المعرفة قد انفتحت في باطنك وحينئذ تصير علومك المحصّلة كلّها بذوراً لثمرات المعارف. ١٢٤

فصل ٦١

لعلّ نفسك تتشوّق إلى إدراك الفرق بين العلم والمعرفة فاعلم أنّ كلّ معنى يُتصوّر أن يُعبّر عنه بعبارة تطابق ذلك المعنى حتّى إذا شرحه المعلّم للمتعلّم بتلك العبارة مرّة أو أكثر ساواه في العلم به فهو من العلوم وكلّ معنى لا يُتصوّر عنه التعبير أصلاً اللّهمّ إلّا إذا كانت الألفاظ متشابهة فهو من المعارف هذا هو اصطلاحي في هذا الكتاب وهو الغالب على أرباب القلوب وقد يُطلق لفظ العلم ويرادف به معنى المعرفة وهو كثير في القرآن قال الله عزّ وجلّ ﴿بَلْ هُوَ ءَايَٰتٌۢ بَيِّنَٰتٌ فِى صُدُورِ ٱلَّذِينَ أُوتُوا۟ ٱلْعِلْمَ﴾ . ١٢٥

[١] (أن تصدّق بوجود) في ج، ع، م؛ أ: أنّ في وجود.

Moreover, the recognizers do not see God's coextensiveness with existents in the same way that the philosophers see His coextensiveness with the First Intellect. The recognizers see the source of existents as many, and each existent thing as a speck in relation to His greatness. To see God and His actions with such an eye does not require knowledge of how it is that multiplicity emanates from oneness; in such a context, all that has been discussed on this issue is unimportant and can be done away with. Strive to assent to the existence of this inner eye. Once opened, the objects of its perception will be like what I have alluded to in my statement concerning the beginningless identity as coextensive in existence with the existence of every existent. The intellect is too limited to perceive this, for it certainly sees some things as closer to the Living, the Self-Abiding than others. So, when you perceive something that you can only convey using expressions that are exclusively perceived by the recognizer (which is the topic of this chapter), you can be certain that the eye of recognition has been opened inside you. At that time, all the knowledge you have acquired will become seeds for the fruits of recognition. 124

Chapter 61: The Difference between Knowledge and Recognition

You might yearn to perceive the difference between knowledge and recognition. 125
Knowledge pertains to any meaning that can be conveyed through expressions that conform to that meaning, even if a teacher must explain these expressions to a student one or more times so that the student can have the same knowledge of the expression as the teacher. Recognition pertains to any meaning that simply cannot be conveyed, except, of course, through ambiguous terms. This is the way these terms are used in this book, and this is mostly how the masters of the heart[143] use them. The expression "knowledge" can be used in an absolute sense and it can be used as a synonym for recognition. There are many instances of this in the Qur'an. God says, «Indeed, they are signs in the breasts of those who have been given knowledge»;[144] «God bears witness that there is no god but He,

وقال أيضاً ﴿شَهِدَ ٱللَّهُ أَنَّهُۥ لَآ إِلَٰهَ إِلَّا هُوَ وَٱلْمَلَٰٓئِكَةُ وَأُوْلُواْ ٱلْعِلْمِ﴾ . وقال أيضاً ﴿وَعَلَّمْنَٰهُ مِن لَّدُنَّا عِلْمًا﴾ . والعلوم اللدنيّة لا يُتصوّرعنها التعبير بعبارات مطابقة لها أصلاً ولذلك لمّا أراد موسى أن يحصّلها من الخضر بطريق التعليم أبى إلى أن قال ﴿فَإِنِ ٱتَّبَعْتَنِى فَلَا تَسْـَٔلْنِى عَن شَىْءٍ حَتَّىٰٓ أُحْدِثَ لَكَ مِنْهُ ذِكْرًا﴾، أي حتّى تنفتح عين المعرفة في باطنك فحينئذ تستيقن حقيقة ما رأيته من قبل وأمّا قبل انفتاح تلك العين فلا سبيل لك إلى إدراك تلك الحقائق إلّا بطريق التأويل كما قال الله حيث صمّم العزم على فراقه ﴿سَأُنَبِّئُكَ بِتَأْوِيلِ مَا لَمْ تَسْتَطِع عَّلَيْهِ صَبْرًا﴾ . ولو صبر إلى وقت انفتاح عين المعرفة لكان يحدث له ذكرًا وهو كناية عن مشاهدة حقيقة اليقين[1] بحيث لا يبقى إلى التأويل حاجة ولهذا المعنى قال النبيّ صلّى الله عليه وسلّم رحم الله أخي موسى فلو صبر مع الخضر لرأى كثيرًا من العجائب. ولعلّ الحديث من حيث اللفظ يخالفه.

فصل ٦٢

١٢٦ علوم الأنبياء لدنيّة فمن كان علمه مستفاداً من الكتب والمعلّمين فليس هو من ورثة الأنبياء في علمه ذلك إلّا من طريق التوسّع في العبارة عن لفظ علوم الميراث وعلوم الأنبياء لا تستفاد إلّا من الله عزّ وجلّ كما قال ﴿وَرَبُّكَ ٱلْأَكْرَمُ ٱلَّذِى عَلَّمَ بِٱلْقَلَمِ عَلَّمَ ٱلْإِنسَٰنَ مَا لَمْ يَعْلَمْ﴾ . لا تظننّ أنّ تعليم الحقّ يختصّ به النبيّ فقط. قال الله تعالى ﴿وَٱتَّقُواْ ٱللَّهَ وَيُعَلِّمُكُمُ ٱللَّهُ﴾ . فكلّ من وصل في سلوكه إلى حقيقة التقوى فلا بدّ أن يعلّمه الله ما لم يعلم ويكون معه كما قال الله ﴿إِنَّ ٱللَّهَ مَعَ ٱلَّذِينَ ٱتَّقَواْ وَّٱلَّذِينَ هُم

---

١ ج، ع، م: التفسير.

as do the angels, and the possessors of knowledge»;[145] «he whom We had taught knowledge from Our presence».[146] Knowledge that is God-given cannot in any way be conveyed through expressions that conform to its meaning.[147] This is why, when Moses wanted to obtain this knowledge from Khidr through instruction, Khidr refused, saying, «If you follow me, then do not question me about anything until I relate something about it to you».[148] That is to say, "Do not question me about anything until the eye of recognition is opened inside you; then you will be convinced of the reality of my earlier actions.[149] But you have no way of perceiving these realities before this eye is opened, except by way of being taken to the original meaning of my actions." This is why, when Khidr decided to part ways with Moses,[150] he said, «I will take you to the original meaning of what you could not bear with patiently».[151] Had Moses been patient until the eye of recognition opened up for him, Khidr would have "related something about it to him,"[152] which alludes to Moses witnessing the reality of certainty and having no need to be taken to the original meaning of Khidr's actions. This is why the Prophet said, "God bless my brother Moses. Had he been patient with Khidr, he would have seen many wonders."[153] The actual wording of this tradition may differ from what I have here.

Chapter 62: God-Given Knowledge

Prophetic knowledge is God-given, so anyone whose knowledge is derived 126
from books and teachers is not one of the inheritors of the Prophets in his knowledge,[154] except in the widest sense conveyed by the term "knowledge of inheritance." Prophetic knowledge is only derived from God, as He says, «And your Lord is the most generous, who taught by the pen, and taught people what they did not know».[155] Never suppose that only a Prophet is singled out for God's instruction. God says, «Be God-wary, and God will teach you».[156] Thus, those who arrive at the reality of God-wariness along their spiritual journey will inevitably learn from God what they do not know, and God will be with them: «Truly God is with the God-wary, and those who act beautifully».[157] Since

مُحۡسِنُونَ﴾ . وأمثال هذه العلوم إذا عُبّر عنها بعبارات متشابهة لم تكن فهم حقائقها من تلك العبارات إلّا لمن حصل له ذلك بطريق الذوق عن تعليم الحقّ ولذلك قال الله تعالى ﴿وَتِلۡكَ ٱلۡأَمۡثَٰلُ نَضۡرِبُهَا لِلنَّاسِ وَمَا يَعۡقِلُهَآ إِلَّا ٱلۡعَٰلِمُونَ﴾ .

١٢٧ وكلّ من لم يتعلّم القرآن من الله تعالى بغير واسطة فليس هو من العالِمين المشار إليهم في قوله تعالى ﴿وَمَا يَعۡقِلُهَآ إِلَّا ٱلۡعَٰلِمُونَ﴾ . وهذا في أمثال العامّيّ يشبه كلام العشّاق في الوصال والفراق وغيرهما من عوارض العشق وأحوال ما يتعلّق به فإنّ الأسماع إذا قُرعت بكلام العشّاق لم تفهم معناه حقّ الفهم اللّهمّ إلّا من لابس حالة العشق ذوقاً. هذا معنى قول الجنيد رضي الله عنه كلامنا إشارة ولا يُتصوّر أن يكون للعارف كلام إلّا كذلك ومن تصرّف في معانيه ببراعة عقله وعلمه زلّت قدمه. ورحم الله أبا العبّاس بن سريج حيث سأله بعض تلامذته عمّا يقول الجنيد فقال له رموز القوم لا نعرف نحن إلّا أنّ لكلام الجنيد نوراً. والغالب أنّ ابن سريج كان من أهل الذوق فإنّ كلامه هذا يعرب عن ذلك إلّا أنّه غلب عليه علم الظاهر وأمثاله كثيرة فيما بين العلماء.

فصل ٦٣

١٢٨ المسائل العقليّة تنقسم بوجه من الوجوه إلى ما لها وجهان وإلى ما لها ثلاثة أوجه وقد يُظنّ بالمسائل التي لها ثلاثة أوجه أنّها من المعارف وليست من العلوم وهو ظنّ فاسد وإنّما ذكرت هذا الفصل لتدفع أمثال هذه الظنون عن نفسك أمّا القسم الأوّل وهو الذي له وجهان أحدهما إلى نطق المعلّم المرشد والثاني إلى فهم المتعلّم المسترشد كعلم النحو والطبّ والحساب وغير ذلك أمّا القسم الثاني فهو الذي له ثلاثة أوجه أحدهما إلى نطق

knowledge like this is expressed through ambiguous terms, none can understand the realities of these terms but those who attain these realities by way of tasting the instruction that comes from God. To this effect, He says, «These are the parables we lay out for people. But none understand them except those who know».[158]

Those who do not learn the Qur'an from God without an intermediary do 127
not belong to the "knowers" alluded to in God's words, «But none understand them except those who know».[159] In terms of an everyday example, this resembles the statements of lovers about union, separation, and other such things that happen in situations of love. When people hear lovers' statements, they do not understand their meaning as they should be understood, except of course if they have tasted the state of love. This is the meaning of al-Junayd's words, "Our statements are allusions."[160] It is indeed inconceivable that a recognizer would use language in any other way. Thus, trying to penetrate such supra-sensory realities with one's own intellectual capacity and knowledge will cause you to slip. God bless Abū l-ʿAbbās ibn Surayj; when one of his disciples asked him about al-Junayd's words, he said, "We do not recognize the symbols used by the Sufis. But al-Junayd's words have light."[161] It is most likely the case that Ibn Surayj was one of the people who knew through tasting, as these words of his testify to that. It is just that he and those like him were dominated by formal knowledge, as has often been the case with scholars.

Chapter 63: Types of Knowledge and Instruction

Intellectual problems divide into two or three dimensions. It is assumed that 128
issues which have three dimensions belong to the way of recognition, not the formal sciences. This is an unsound assumption. I have written this chapter simply for you to dispel such assumptions from your mind. The first division, which has two dimensions (one being a teacher's words and the other a student's understanding), pertains to sciences such as grammar, medicine, mathematics, and the like. The second division, which has three dimensions (one being a

المفيد والثاني إلى فهم المستفيد[١] والثالث إلى ذوقه وأكثر ما يتعلّق من المسائل بالصفات هذا حكمها وكذلك ما يتعلّق بأحكام النفس كالحكم بكونها[٢] موجودة قبل البدن وأحوالها بعد الموت فهي كذلك.

١٢٩ وأمثال هذه المسائل يصعب إدراكها على العقل لاسيّما حقيقة صفة العلم الأزليّ وكيفيّة إحاطته بالجزئيّات وصفة القدرة الأزليّة وحقيقة معنى الإيجاد والاختراع في حقّ الله تعالى وكيفيّة معنى المشيئة الأزليّة والفرق بينهما وبين الإرادة وأكثر العلماء المتبحّرين يظنّون أنّهم أحاطوا علماً بمعاني هذه الصفات وإنّما حظّهم منها على الحقيقة تشبيه فقط.

فصل ٦٤

١٣٠ لعلّ الأليق[٣] بحال المستفيد في أمثال المسائل التي سبقت الإشارة أليها أن لا يستكثر فيها من حفظ الألفاظ[٤] المذكورة في الكتب إذ الغالب أنّ الاستكثار منها لا يزيده إلّا تحيّرًا وطلب الحقائق من الألفاظ المنقولة المستعارة والمتشابهة المشككة في غاية العسر بل ينبغي أن يقتصر على قدر من الألفاظ يلتقطها من أفواه العلماء ومن كتب المتأخّرين دون المتقدّمين فإذا حفظ ذلك فليصرف العناية بكلّيّتها إلى ترديد النظر فيه ولترك النظر في الكتب القديمة رأساً إلى وقت يشير عليه المعلّم بذلك.

١ (إلى فهم المتعلّم . . . إلى فهم المستفيد) في ج، ع، م؛ أ: إلى فهم المستفيد. ٢ (كالحكم بكونها) في ج، ع، م؛ أ: كالحكم الروح بكونها. ٣ (الأليق) في ج، ع، م؛ أ: الأليق. ٤ (الألفاظ) في ج، ع، م؛ أ: الأمثال.

teacher's words, the other being a student's understanding, and the third a student's tasting that understanding), pertains to most of the problems related to the divine attributes and pronouncements about them. Likewise, this division pertains to pronouncements about the human self, such as the question of its prior existence to the body and a person's state after death.

Problems such as these are difficult for the intellect to grasp, especially (1) the reality of the divine attribute of beginningless knowledge and how it encompasses particulars, (2) the divine attribute of beginningless power and the reality of the meaning of "bringing into existence" and "originating" with respect to God, and (3) the meaning of God's beginningless will and how it is distinct from God's desire. Most scholars who delve deeply into this think they know the meanings of these divine attributes, but all they really do is declare God to be similar to humans. 129

Chapter 64: Setting Out on the Path of Recognition

When it comes to these problems I have alluded to, it is probably best for the student to avoid memorizing too many of the technical terms discussed in the relevant books, for in most cases this will only increase his perplexity. Studying the realities of these metaphorical, ambiguous, and equivocal terms is extremely difficult. Thus, the student should make do with the few technical terms he can learn from contemporary scholars and the books of more recent rational theologians, not the earlier ones.[162] When the student has memorized these terms, he should devote all of his attention to their review, all the while avoiding the study of those earlier books until his teacher directs him to them. 130

فصل ٦٥

ينبغي لطالب الحقّ إذا حفظ القدر الذي يتيسّر له من تلك المسائل أن يعاود النظر إليه مرّة بعد أخرى ويجالس أهل الكمال العلميّ إن وجدهم وظفر بخدمتهم ما أمكنه ويعرض عليهم كلّ ما يسنح له من خواطر في تلك المسائل وينبغي أن يستعين على إدراك تلك الحقائق بتصفية الباطن فعساه يدركها بنفسه فليس في قوّة الواصل الكامل أن يرد به مشربه العذب ما لم يقو بنفسه على الورود وإنّما الذي إليه من أمره هو إرشاده إلى كيفيّة السلوك فقط ومهما امتثل أمره في الإرشاد لم يحرم الوصول غالباً إن كان من أهله. ١٣١

فصل ٦٦

المعين[١] للطالب على تصفية الباطن مصاحبة أهل الذوق ومجالستهم وخدمتهم من صميم القلب وأعني بأهل الذوق أقواماً طهّروا بواطنهم من رذائل الأخلاق حتّى فاضت عليها من ألطاف الحقّ ما تستحيل عنه العبارة وهذا القوم لا يشقى بهم جليسهم وقلّما تخلو بقعة من البقاع عنهم. ١٣٢

---

١ ج، ع، م: نعم المعين.

Chapter 65: The Next Step on the Path of Recognition

When the truth-seeker learns as many of these theological problems as are easy for him to understand, he should review them over and over, and spend time with those who have mastered the science of rational theology (if he can find and serve them as much as possible), expressing all of his thoughts about these problems to them. He should also seek help in grasping the realities of these problems by purifying his inner self, for he might be able to grasp them on his own. Indeed, so long as the student does not have the inner strength to reach a sweet-watered well, no consummate scholar can take him to it. All that such a scholar can do is guide the student, showing him how to travel to the well. If the student follows the scholar's guidance, he will likely reach it—if he is meant to do so. 131

Chapter 66: Spiritual Companionship

What will help the one seeking to purify his inner self is for him to wholeheartedly keep the company of people who know by way of tasting, spending time with them and serving them. By "people who know by way of tasting," I mean those who purify their inner selves from vile character traits to such an extent that, from God's generosity, such knowledge pours down on them that is impossible to attain by acts of devotion alone. These are the "people because of whom their companion will never be miserable."[163] And rarely is there a place devoid of them. 132

فصـل ٦٧

السعـادة كلّ السعادة للطالب أن يتفرّغ بكلّيّة روحه وقلبه لخدمة واصل منهم فني ١٣٣
في الله عزّ وجلّ ومشاهدته حتّى إذا أفنى عمره في خدمته أحياه الله حياةً طيّبةً ليس منها مع العلماء سوى رسم واسم فأمّا حقيقة معناها ومسماها فلا يوجد إلّا عند قوم أُرضعوا بلبان الكرم في حجر العناية.[1]

فصـل ٦٨

لولا أنّ الجود الأزليّ أخذ بضبعي ووفّقني لخدمة شيخ كبير منهم وإلّا لما يُصوّر لي ١٣٤
خلاص عن تلك الضلالات التي ترسّخت في الباطن من ممارسة العلم ولا انتفعت أيضاً بخدمة الشيخ الإمام أحمد الغزاليّ رضي الله عنه إذ لولا ملازمتي لعتبة باب ذلك الشيخ لكان يتراكم في القلب على تعاقب الأيّام والليالي صفات مذمومة يبعد[2] الخلاص عنها ويستحيل كما أراه في حقّ الأكثرين ممّن حبسه التقدير في ضيق العلم والعقل ولا تتّسع حوصلته للتصديق بما وراء ذلك من الجليّات بل[3] الغوامض من الخفيّات والله تعالى هو المشكور على إفاضته عليّ نعماً لا أحصيها ولا أستحقّها وبه اعتمادي وعليه توكّلي في إتمام تلك النعم.

---

١ زائدة في ج، ع، م: يومًا بعد يوم. ٢ ع: يتعذّر. ٣ ع: فضلاً عن؛ ج، م: بَلَه.

Chapter 67: Felicity

133 The seeker's greatest felicity lies in entirely devoting his spirit and heart to serving one of the people who have arrived,[164] who is annihilated in God and in witnessing Him. If the seeker spends his life in his service, God will cause him to live a most pleasant life[165] (which scholars only know by name). The reality of its name and meaning are only experienced by a group of people who suckle the milk of divine generosity in the lap of God's special care.

Chapter 68: God's Generosity toward Me

134 If the beginningless generosity had not guided me and granted me the success to serve one of these great masters, it would be inconceivable that I would be freed from these errors which were firmly rooted in my inner self on account of delving too deeply into the pursuit of rational theology. I surely would never have benefited from serving the master and leader Aḥmad al-Ghazālī. Had I not persisted at the door of this master, for the rest of my life my heart would have accumulated blameworthy attributes, the escape from which is hopeless and impossible. This is exactly what we see with most people destined to be imprisoned in the narrow confines of their knowledge and intelligence, never expanding their capacity to assent to the clarities beyond knowledge and intelligence, let alone to assent to obscure subtleties. I thank God for pouring down on me blessings I can never count, and do not even deserve. He is my support, and I place my trust in Him to bring these blessings to completion.

فصل ٦٩

لعـلّك تقول كيف يظفر الطالب بمثل هذا الشيخ وكيف يتيسّر للمبتدئ متابعة المنتهي ١٣٥
ومعرفته وليس يجوز للسالك أن يزن الواصلين بميزان نظره ولا أيضاً يجوز له أن يقلّد واحداً بمجرّد دعواه فبماذا يعلم أنّ الشخص الفلانيّ مثلاً مدّع وليس وراء دعواه طائل أو هو كامل منته بلغ مبلغاً يجوز أن يُقتدى به فاعلم أنّ هذا سؤال عن أمر لا يكون للخوض في جوابه عظيم فائدة فإنّ كلّ واحد من الطالبين تتسلّط عليه أسباب ما قُدر له تسليطاً لا يجد عنه محيصاً وبقدر ما قُسم لكلّ واحد من الرزق يُسلّط عليه الطالب وتيسّر له الظفر بمن يهديه الطريق وكما أنّ المتعلّم يكون طلبه ومرشده على قدر ما رزق في الأزل من العلم فكذلك ها هنا من غير فرق.

فصل ٧٠

فـإن قلت فهل من علامة يتميّز بها المدّعي عن الواصل فأقول العلامات كثيرة والتعبير ١٣٦
عنها عسير والإحاطة بجميعها متعذّرة غاية التعذّر فأمّا علامة تطرد وتنعكس فيكاد يستحيل وجودها وليس عندي من أماكنها خبر فعليك بالجدّ في الطلب فإنّه يحلّ لك كلّ مشكل ويجذب بضبعك في كلّ مسألة[1] مدلهمة وينقذك من كلّ خطب هائل ويخلّصك من كلّ داهية معضلة ومن لم يذق لم يعرف من لم يجرّب

---

[1] ج، ع، م: ملمّة.

Chapter 69: Finding a Spiritual Guide

You may ask, "How is the seeker to obtain such a master? And how can a novice easily follow someone at the end of the path, as well as his recognition, when a traveler on the path cannot, by means of the scales of his own reflection, weigh those who have arrived, nor can he just blindly imitate someone else based on his claims alone? And how, for example, is the traveler to know whether a given individual is a false claimant to spiritual guidance with no substance to his claims, or a perfect master who has reached a point on the path that he can be followed?" This is a question about a topic that will not greatly repay diving into. For each seeker is subject to causes that have been destined for him in such a way that he has no way of escaping them. Obtaining a spiritual guide who can take the seeker along the path is made easy for the seeker in accordance with the provision that has been apportioned to each person. Just as a student's seeking and his spiritual guide are given to him in accordance with his provision as dictated by God's beginningless knowledge, so too is it the case here, with no distinction between them. 135

Chapter 70: True Spiritual Guides and False Claimants

If you ask, "Is there a marker by which a false claimant can be distinguished from one who has arrived at the end of the path?," I will reply that there are many markers, but it is hard to put them into words, and comprehending all of them is absolutely impossible. It is virtually impossible to find a marker for pinning down and reining in such a one, and I do not have any information about where it would be. What you must do is strive in your search, as that will resolve all difficulties, keeping you away from every obscurity, delivering you from every terrifying danger, and releasing you from every unfortunate plight. Indeed, without tasting, there is no recognition; without your own experience, there is 136

لم تنفعه تجربة غيره ومن لم يأكل لم يشبع بمحادثة من أكل ومن لم يشرب لم يروعطشه كلام من شرب.

فصل ٧١

إيّاك وأن تغترّ بعلمك فتشتغل بالسلوك من غير قائد يقودك في الطريق فتضلّ ١٣٧
من حيث لا تدري ويكون مثالك مثال صانع تبحّر في صنعه فاشتغل بالعلوم النظريّة وتحصيلها من نفسه واستنكف من متابعة غيره من النظّار ولم يكن لذلك مستنداً إلّا عجب أثمره تبحّره في صنعته فمن الضلالات الغالبة على أهل العلم أنّهم إذا أضمروا على السلوك ظنّوا أنّهم يستغنون عن عارف بمهالك الطريق يهديهم في كلّ خطوة وقلّما ينجو أحد من النظّار والعلماء من هذا العجب الذي ثمرته الاستكبار[1] من المتابعة لأهل المعرفة إذ يبعد من العالم الذي يرى الكمال فيما حصّله من العلم أن يرى الجاهل بذلك فوق نفسه وذلك لظنّه الفاسد. الغلط بأنّ كلّ كمال فهو من المسائل التي تلقّنها وتلقّفها فلا يعلم وراء ذلك شيئاً والله الذي لا إله إلّا هو حلفة صادقة ويميناً برّة أنّ العالم وإن انتدب لخدمة بعض المشايخ فما دام يفرّق بين نفسه في الحاجة إليه وبين غيره من جهّال أقرانه فهو بعد في تضييع زمانه غير مقبل على شأنه ولا تُفهم هذه المعاني أصلاً إلّا إذا صرت لها بعد التجربة أهلا وإن ظننت أنّك تصل إليها قبل التجربة فأنت بعد ضحكة للشيطان وفي مثلك قيل [كامل]

وَإِذَا رَأَى ٱلشَّيْطَانُ[2] غُرَّةَ وَجْهِهِ   حَيَّ[3] وَقَالَ فَدَيْتُ مَنْ لَا يَفْلَحُ

---

١ ج، ع، م: الاستنكاف. ٢ (الشيطان) في ع؛ أ، ج، م: ابليس. ٣ (حيّ) في ج، ع، م؛ أ: لبى.

nothing to gain from someone else's; discussing food with someone who has just eaten will never fill your stomach; and talking about drink with someone who has just drunk will not quench your thirst.

Chapter 71: Self-Admiration and Spiritual Guidance

Be wary of being deluded by your knowledge, thus busying yourself with travel- 137
ing the path without a leader to guide you and being misguided in ways that you do not even know. You would be like a craftsman extremely proficient in his craft who busies himself with studying the rational sciences on his own, disdaining to follow the rationalist theologians, unwilling to rely on them because of his self-admiration that results from his extreme proficiency in his own craft! Thus, one of the errors that overcome the learned when they entertain the idea of traveling the path is that they think that they can do without someone who recognizes the dangers of the path and who can guide them every step of the way. How rare it is for one of the rationalist theologians and philosophers to be free from this self-admiration, which produces pride in not wanting to follow the recognizers! For a scholar who sees the perfection of the knowledge that he has acquired, it is indeed far-fetched to regard the one who is ignorant of this knowledge to be above him, on account of the corruptness of his conjecture. The error consists in the fact that his perfections all lie in the topics he has studied and acquired, but he knows nothing beyond them. By God! I truly and honestly swear that even if a scholar were to serve a master but continued to see a difference between himself and the most ignorant of his colleagues in terms of need for spiritual guidance, he would be squandering his time, wandering about aimlessly. You will simply never know these supra-sensory realities until you are worthy of experiencing them. And if you think you will attain them before experiencing them, then you would bring a smile to the Devil's face. It is said about people like you:

> When the Devil saw his noble face,
> he greeted him, "At your service, unlucky fool!"[166]

فصل ٧٢

١٣٨ اعلم أنّ هذه الفصول المعترضة في أثناء الكلام كثيرة النفع ولكن عند الأقلّين والمعجب بعقله وعلمه لا يتأثّر بها غالباً فلا ينتفع بها فإذا كان ذكرها عرضاً فأولى بي أن أقتصر على القدر المذكور.

١٣٩ وأقول قد ظهر أنّ قول القائل إنّ العالم قديم بالزمان هوس محض فنظمه في غاية الفساد وبعد ذلك فربّما يقول هبني سلّمت ذلك في السموات والأرض فما تقول في الموجود الأوّل هل كان مساوق الوجود لوجود الباري تعالى فإن قلت نعم فقد أثبتّ معه قديماً وإن قلت لا فنفرض الكلام فيه ونقول إن لم يكن موجوداً ثمّ وُجد فلما ذا لم يكن موجوداً قبله والسبب كماله موجود. وحين وُجد فهل ظهر سبب أم لا فإن قلت لا فهو محال إذ يلزم منه حدوث حادث بلا سبب وإن قلت نعم ظهر سبب فظهور سبب معدوم استمرّ في العدم على وتيرة واحدة ثمّ ظهر وجوده محال لأنّ ظهوره في ذات الواجب محال ولا موجود ثمّ غير الواجب حتّى يثبت وجوده شرطاً كما قلت ذلك في حقّ موجود يوجد بعد العدم.

١٤٠ فاعلم أنّ القبل والبعد وُجدا بعد وجود الزمن ولم يكن إذ ذاك إلّا قبليّة الشرف والذات وقولنا إذ ذاك متشابه فإنّه مشعر بوجود الزمن وقبليّة الشرف والذات بين الواجب الوجود بذاته وبين الموجودات الحادثة منه ليس لها حدّ ومنتهى فإذاً لا قول أصدق من قولنا إنّ الله كان موجوداً قبل الموجود الأوّل قبليّة لا تتناهى ولعلّ الآن يتجلّى لك حقيقة قوله عليه السلام خلق الله الأرواح قبل الأجساد بألفي ألف عام وأنّه لِمَ قدّر تلك القبليّة بمقدار متناه من الزمن وهذا سرّ عظيم فالطريق من كلّ ممكن إلى كلّ

Chapter 72: Back to the Question of Divine Priority

138 These chapters that have come up in the course of our discussion[167] are very beneficial, but only for a limited number of people. For the most part, those who admire their intelligence and knowledge will not be affected by these chapters' contents, and will derive no benefit from them. Since the discussion in these chapters was rather incidental, it is best that I confine myself to what has been said.

139 Now, it is obvious that the position to the effect that the world is eternal in time is pure foolishness, and its logical ordering is extremely corrupt. Given that, one might say, "Consider that I have conceded that the question of eternity cannot apply to the heavens and the earth; what do you say about the first existent? Can it be coextensive with the existence of the Creator? If you say yes, then you have affirmed something eternal alongside Him. But if you say no, then we will suppose the following: if the first existent was not existent and then came to exist, why was it not an existent before that, when the cause for its perfection was already existent? And, when it came to exist, did the cause appear then, or not? If you say it did not, that would be impossible since it would entail the temporal origination of something without a cause. But if you say, 'Yes, it came to exist when the cause appeared,' then a nonexistent cause that has always been nonexistent appeared in one and the same manner, which is when the first existent appeared. That too would be impossible, because the appearance of the cause in the essence of the Necessary is impossible as there cannot be an existent other than the Necessary whose existence is affirmed as a condition for that thing (as you yourself stated about an existent that comes to exist after being nonexistent)."

140 "Before" and "after" came to exist after the existence of time, when there was nothing but the priority of eminence and essence. My use of "when" here is ambiguous, for it marks the existence of time. The priority of eminence and essence between the Necessary Existent in itself and a temporally originated existent is without limits or end. Thus, I can make no truer statement than to say that God was existent before the first existent in an infinitely prior manner.[168] Perhaps now the reality of the Prophet's words will be disclosed to you, "God created spirits two million years before bodies."[169] But why did God give a finite

ممكن متناه والطريق من كلّ ممكن إلى الواجب غير متناه ولو لم يكن كذلك ألزم أن يكون ما يتناهى أكثر ممّا لا يتناهى وذلك محال وهذه القضايا من الأوّليّات التي تدركها عين المعرفة وطريق إدراكها منسدّ على عين العقل فلا تطمعنّ بعلمك وبضاعتك المزجاة منه في إدراكها.

فصل ٧٣

١٤١ فإذا تحقّق من هذا أنّه ليس موجود يساوق وجوده وجود الواجب ولا يُتصوّر أن يوجد وجود ولا غيره[١] نعم الواجب مساوق الوجود لوجود كلّ شيء ومساوقته لما لم يوجد بعد عند وجوده كمساوقته للموجود الأوّل من غير فرق وهذا هو الواجب الحقّ واعلم أنّ العارف إذا نظر بعين المعرفة أدرك لقولنا كلّ موجود فهو مساوق الوجود لوجود الواجب معنى صحيحًا ولكن العلم والعقل يمسّهما الكلال دون إدراك ذلك. وعند ذلك يقول العارف إنّ الله مع كلّ شيء وهو مع ذلك قبل كلّ شيء قبليّة لا تتناهى ويقول ليس في الوجود شيء هو مع الله ولا بعده ولا يُتصوّر أيضًا أن يكون بهذه الصفة شيء في الوجود.

١٤٢ وإيّاك أن تنكر قولنا ليس مع الله عزّ وجلّ شيء ولا بعده فتكون أعمى لا تدرك الألوان ولا تؤمن أيضًا بوجودها فإنّ ذلك حقّ وصدق وهو أجلى وأظهر لعين المعرفة من الأوّليّات لعين العقل. فاعلم أنّ العقل قد يدرك لقولنا إنّ الله مع كلّ شيء وقبل كلّ شيء معنى صحيحًا ولكن ليس ذلك المعنى في شيء ممّا يدرك بعين المعرفة فأمّا قولنا

---

١ ج، ع، م: أن يوجد أيضًا فلا الموجود الأوّل يساوق وجوده وجود الواجب ولا غيره.

measure of time to this priority? This is a great mystery. The distance from a contingent to another contingent is finite, but the distance from a contingent to the Necessary is infinite. If it were not like this, it would entail that the finite be greater than the infinite, which is impossible. These premises are primary concepts, which are perceived by the eye of recognition, but the way is blocked for the eye of the intellect. So never desire to perceive this with your formal knowledge and cheap intellectual inventory![170]

Chapter 73: God's Withness Does Not Mean Human Withness

Thus, from the foregoing it is realized that there is no existent whose existence 141
is coextensive with the existence of the Necessary, nor can it be conceived to be the case. Indeed, the Necessary is coextensive in existence with the existence of everything. And His coextensivity with what is not yet brought into existence is like His coextensivity with the first existent, with no distinction between them. This, then, is the Necessary and the Real. When the recognizer looks with the eye of recognition, he perceives as correct our statement that the existence of the Necessary is coextensive in existence with every existent. But the intellect and conventional ways of knowing grow weary before they perceive this. Thus, the recognizer says, "God is with all things, all the while being prior to all things by way of an infinite priority." And he says, "There is not a thing in existence that is with God, nor is it posterior to Him. It is also inconceivable for there to be something in existence that has this attribute."

Be wary of rejecting our statement that there is nothing with God, nor is 142
there anything posterior to Him. For you will then be like a blind man who rejects colors and even disbelieves in their existence. Indeed, our statement is true. It is clearer and more manifest to the eye of recognition than primary concepts are to the eye of the intellect! The intellect may grasp the meaning of our statement that God is with everything and is prior to everything to be correct. But that meaning is nothing like what is perceived by the eye of recognition.

ليس مع الله شيء ولا بعده شيء فذلك ممّا لا يُتصوّر للعقل أن يدرك شيئاً من معناه أصلاً والإطناب في شرح هذه القضايا لا يفيد لاستعصاء وإباء[١] على الإدراك العقليّ فالاختصار والاقتصار على القدر اليسير الذي سبق أولى ولينظر الطالب في الفصل الذي بعد هذا الفصل فإنّه كالبذر لما قبله فربّما يجتني ثمرته يوماً.

فصل ٧٤

١٤٣ القـرب والبعد ثلاثة أقسام.

١٤٤ القسم الأوّل: يوجد في الزمان والمكان كما يقال القمر أقرب إلينا من الشمس وعصر رسول الله صلّى الله عليه وسلّم أقرب إلى زماننا هذا من عصر آدم عليه الصلاة والسلام.

١٤٥ القسم الثاني: القرب العقليّ وعند وجود[٢] هذا القرب تبطل فائدة القرب الزمانيّ والمكانيّ فيقال الشافعيّ مثلاً أقرب إلى الصدّيق الأكبر من أبي جهل وإن كان هو أقرب زماناً ومكاناً من الشافعيّ وكلّ شيئين وصف أحدهما بالقرب من الآخر والبعد عنه من حيث الزمان والمكان فلا يجوز أن يكون لهما وصف من القرب والبعد العقليّ[٣] أصلاً إلّا من حيث تشابه في اللفظ والتوسّع في العبارة إذ لا يجوز أن يقال إنّ المعنى الذي كان الشافعيّ به إلى أبي بكر أقرب من غيره هو قرب من السماء والأرض أو بعد عنهما إذ ليس ذلك المعنى ممّا تسعه السماء والأرض وعند ذلك ينبغي أن تفهم أن لا نسبة لشيء من الأشياء التي توصف بالقرب الزمانيّ والمكانيّ إلى الله عزّ وجلّ في

---

١ ج: هذه الألفاظ لا يزيدها إلّا إباء واستعصاء؛ ع: هذه القضايا لا يزيدها إلّا إباء واستعصاء؛ م: هذه لا يزيدها إلّا إباء واستعصاء. ٢ (وجود) في ج، ع، م؛ أ: وجوب. ٣ (من القرب والبعد العقليّ) في ج، ع؛ أ: من القرب الأصليّ؛ م: من القرب العقليّ والبعد العقليّ.

Our statement that there is nothing with God and nothing posterior to Him is, fundamentally, one of those things whose meaning is absolutely inconceivable for the intellect to perceive. A lengthy disquisition explaining these premises will be of no benefit to the intellect, for all of its recalcitrance and refusal. So it is better for me to be concise and restrict myself to the few words that have already been stated. The seeker should also have a look at the following chapter, which is like the seed of the present one—maybe one day he will harvest its fruit.

Chapter 74: Categories of Proximity and Distance

Proximity and distance are in three categories. 143

Category 1: This pertains to time and space, as when the moon is said to be closer to us than the sun, and the Prophet's era is said to be closer to our era than Adam's era. 144

Category 2: This pertains to intelligible proximity. With the existence of this category of proximity, any benefit in talking about temporal and spatial proximity is nullified. For example, al-Shāfiʿī was closer to Abū Bakr than Abū Jahl, even though, temporally and spatially, Abū Bakr was closer to Abū Jahl than al-Shāfiʿī. When of any two things one is described as proximate to or distant from the other in time and space, they can only be described as intelligibly proximate and distant in an ambiguous manner, and in the broadest sense of these expressions. For one cannot say that the sense in which al-Shāfiʿī was closer to Abū Bakr than anyone else is the same as his proximity to or distance from the heavens and the earth, for such a meaning does not extend to them. Based on this, you should understand that there is no relation between, on the one hand, anything described as temporally and spatially proximate and, on the other, proximity and distance with respect to God. In this vein, the Prophet quoted his Lord's 145

القرب والبعد. لذلك قال صلّى الله عليه وسلّم حاكيًا عن ربّه لم تسعني سمائي ولا أرضي ووسعني قلب عبدي المؤمن الليّن الوادع.

١٤٦ والقسم الثالث: هو القرب الذي يدركه العارفون ولا يُتصوّر العلماء إدراكه أصلاً ومن الأحكام المستفادة من هذه المعرفة أن يقول العارف قرب الحقّ تعالى متساوٍ من كلّ شيء لا تفاوت فيه بوجه من الوجوه والأجسام والأرواح متساوية النسبة عليه وعند ذلك نقول كلّ موجود فهو مساوَق الوجود لوجود الحقّ لا فرق في مساوَقته[١] أصلاً واعلم أنّ الذي وصفناه من القرب والبعد من القسم الأوّل صحيح بالإضافة إلى حاسّة البصر والذي وصفناه في القسم الثاني صحيح بالإضافة إلى بصيرة العقل والذي وصفناه في القسم الثالث صحيح بالإضافة إلى بصيرة العارف والذي في القسم الثاني من علم اليقين والذي في قسم الثالث من عين اليقين[٢]. وأمّا حقّ اليقين فلم أصل بعد إليه ولا تعثّرت في طريقي عليه وأنا مؤمن به إيمان الأكمه بوجود الألوان وكما يستحيل للجامد على المحسوسات أن يدرك معنى القرب والبعد المشار إليهما في القسم الثاني فكذلك يستحيل للجامد على العقليّات أن يدرك حقيقة القرب والبعد المشار إليهما في القسم الثالث فاجتهد أن تؤمن به إيمانك بالغيب ﴿لَعَلَّ ٱللَّهَ يُحْدِثُ بَعْدَ ذَٰلِكَ أَمْرًا﴾.

فصل ٧٥

١٤٧ لعلّك تقول أين أنت من قولك إنّ هذه الفصول تشتمل على العلم بالله وبرسوله وباليوم الآخر فقد أطنبت القول في العلم بالله وبصفاته وفي الطور الذي وراء العقل وهو الذي

---

١ ع: مساوقة الموجودات؛ ج، م: مساوقتها قطعًا والبتّة. ٢ (والذي وصفناه في القسم الثاني . . . من عين اليقين) في ع، م. في ج خطأ: والذي وصفناه في قسم الثاني صحيح بالإضافة إلى عين بصيرة العقل والذي وصفناه في قسم الثالث صحيح بالإضافة إلى عين اليقين. في أ يوجد الأغلاط الواضحة في هذه الجملة: والذي وصفناه في القسم الثاني بالإضافة إلى بصيرة العارف والذي وصفناه في القسم الثاني من علم اليقين والذي في قسم الثالث من عين اليقين.

words: "Neither the heavens nor the earth can contain Me, but the heart of My faithful and humble servant can contain Me."[171]

Category 3: This is the proximity perceived by the recognizers, and it is inconceivable that scholars should perceive it. One of the judgments derived from this recognition is for the recognizer to say that God's proximity to every single thing is the same, with no trace of difference in any respect. Thus, bodies and spirits have the same relationship to Him. That is why I say that God is coextensive in existence with each existent, with absolutely no difference in His coextensivity. What I have described concerning proximity and distance in Category 1 is sound in relation to the sense of sight, and what I have described in Category 2 is sound in relation to the intellect's insight. But what I have described in the present category is sound in relation to the recognizer's insight. Category 2 pertains to the knowledge of certainty, whereas the present category pertains to the eye of certainty. As for the truth of certainty,[172] I have not arrived there yet and have not stumbled upon it on my journey, but I have faith in it, just as a man born blind has faith in the existence of colors. And, just as it is impossible for a person fixated on sensory objects to perceive the meanings of proximity and distance as indicated in Category 2, so too is it impossible for a person fixated on intelligibles to perceive the reality of proximity and distance as indicated in the present category. So strive to have faith in it, just as you have faith in the unseen! «Perhaps God will bring something new to pass thereafter».[173] 146

Chapter 75: The Last "Day"

You might say, "Why did you say that the chapters in this book deal with knowledge of God, His Messengers, and the last day, when thus far you have gone on and on about knowledge of God and His attributes, as well as the stage beyond the intellect, which itself depends on faith in prophecy? You have paid no 147

يتوقّف عليه الإيمان بالنبوّة وأمّا العلم باليوم الآخر فإنّك لم تتعرّض له أصلاً ولم تذكر في معناه فصلاً وما بالك لم تحم حول شيء من أحوال النفس وحقيقة أطوارها في عالمي الملك والملكوت.

١٤٨ فاعلم قبل كلّ شيء أنّ اليوم الآخر ليس من[١] جنس أيّامنا هذه التي تعرف بطلوع الشمس لأنّ الشمس تكون مكوّرة يوم القيامة وإنّما عُبّر عنه باليوم الآخر لضيق العبارة كما عبّر عنه رسول الله صلّى الله عليه وسلّم حيث قال ألا إنّ الزمان قد استدار كهيأة يوم خلق الله السموات والأرض. وكما عُبّر عنه في القرآن فقيل ﴿إِنَّ رَبَّكُمُ ٱللَّهُ ٱلَّذِى خَلَقَ ٱلسَّمَٰوَٰتِ وَٱلْأَرْضَ فِى سِتَّةِ أَيَّامٍ﴾. وما لم تبدّل الأرض غير الأرض والسماوات فيستحيل للسالك أن يصل إلى يوم الدين فإذا فهمت ذلك فاعلم أنّ النفس الإنسانيّة لها أطوار كثيرة وتكاد تخرج عن الحصر والتناهي فما دامت النفس في أطوار مخصوصة قيل هي في الدنيا وما دامت النفس في أطوار أُخر مخصوصة قيل هي في عرصات القيامة وما دامت في أطوار أُخر مخصوصة قيل هي في الآخرة.

فصل ٧٦

١٤٩ اعلم أنّ العقل الإنسانيّ لم يدرك حقيقة النفس إلّا ما لزم وجوده من النظر في البدن وعوارضه وذلك مثل كونها مدركة ومحرّكة وهاتان صفتان يشترك فيهما جميع الحيوان وأمّا ما أدرك من بقائها بعد انقطاع تصرّفها عن البدن فإنّما عرف ذلك من طريق النظر في الإدراك العلميّ من حيث أنّ النفس محلّ العلوم وأنّ العلوم لا تنقسم ولا يُتصوّر انقسام محلّها وأنّ كلّ ما كان كذلك فلا سبيل إليه للفناء وأمّا حكمهم بوجودها قبل البدن فلم يُقم أحد عليه برهاناً واضحاً بحيث لا يتطرّق إليه شبهة وشكّ وكان تقصير

١ (قبل كلّ شيء أنّ اليوم الآخر ليس من) في ج، ع، م: أ: قبل شيء أنّ اليوم الآخر من.

attention at all to the last day, and have not even mentioned it in any chapter. Why have you not touched on the states of the soul and the reality of its stages in both the material and spiritual realms?"

Before anything else, you should know that the last day is not the same kind of day as days are for us, known through the rising of the sun. That is because, on the day of resurrection, the sun will be folded up.[174] So it is only referred to as the last "day" because of the narrow confines of human expression, as the Prophet stated, "Time goes around just as it did the day God created the heavens and the earth,"[175] and as the Qur'an states, «Truly your Lord is God, who created the heavens and the earth in six days».[176] As long as the earth does not change to something other than the heavens and the earth,[177] it will be impossible for the traveler to arrive at a comprehension of the day of judgment. If you have understood this, then the next thing for you to understand is that the human soul has many stages, and they are almost infinite and innumerable. As long as the soul dwells in certain specific stages, it is spoken of as being in this world; as long as it dwells in certain other specific stages, it is spoken of as being on the vast plains of the day of judgment; as long as the soul dwells in certain other specific stages, it is spoken of as being in the afterlife. 148

Chapter 76: The Soul's Relationship to the Body

The human intellect can only perceive the reality of the soul as something whose existence is entailed by examining the body and its accidents, such as the soul's causing the body to perceive and to move, which are two attributes that are common to all animals. What we perceive of the soul's subsistence after the severance of its control over the body is recognized by way of examining the nature of intellectual perception insofar as the soul is the locus of knowledge. And since knowledge is indivisible, the division of its locus is inconceivable. Given this to be the case, there is no way that the soul can suffer annihilation. As for the judgment that the soul existed before the body, nobody has offered a clear demonstrative proof of it in a way that is free of obscurity and doubt. The philosophers' 149

العلماء في ذلك يرجع إلى ضيق اللفظ عن أداء حقّ ذلك المعنى وحكمهم بأنّها وجدت مع البدن وأنّ البدن كان شرطاً في وجودها من علّتها الموجبة للوجود فهو خطأ نعم تغيّر حالها عند حلول البدن معلوم.

١٥٠ والحقّ أنّ النفس كانت موجودة قبل البدن وهذا عندي واضح ولكنّني لا يمكنني التعبير عنه بحيث لا يبقى فيه إمكان شكّ ومجال اعتراض وغالب[١] أنّ كلّ من أدرك ذلك كان بهذه المنزلة في العجز عن التعبير عمّا أدركه واعتقادي هذا في النفس لم يحصل لي بكماله من النظر في البراهين العقليّة والمقدّمات العلميّة إلّا أنّ السلوك العقليّ أعانني فيه غاية الإعانة بالمقدّمات المذكورة في كتب النظّار والقدر الذي يمكن[٢] أن توشّح به هذه اللمعة أنّ سبب وجود النفس كان بكمال السببيّة موجوداً قبل وجود البدن وكان المسبَّب معه نعم تصرّفها في البدن كان موقوفاً على وجود شروط مخصوصة فلم يُوجد إلّا بعد وجود تلك الشروط.

فصل ٧٧

١٥١ معلوم أنّ النفس حادثة وباقية أبداً بعد الموت وليس ذلك إلّا أنّ سببها يبقى أبد الآباد فإذا حصل لك علم يقينيّ بوجود سببها قبل البدن حصل بالضرورة علمك بكونها موجودة قبل البدن ووجود سببها قبل البدن ظاهر في العلوم النظريّة إلّا أنّ كمال السببيّة موهوم غير مقطوع به وهذا هو القدر الذي حصل لي من طريق الذوق ولم يحصل من طريق العلم فاعلم أنّ النفس إن كان لا يُتصوّر وجودها من السبب الموجب لوجودها إلّا بشرط التصرّف في البدن لزم أن تنعدم بعد التصرّف في البدن.

---

١ ج، ع، م: غالب ظنّي. ٢ ‹يمكن› في ج، ع، م؛ ساقطة من أ.

shortcomings here go back to the limitations of technical terms in being able to properly convey its meaning. The position that the soul comes to exist with the existence of the body, as the body is a condition for the existence of the soul as a result of the cause that necessitates the soul's existence, is wrong.[178] Indeed, it is well known that the states of a soul change when it dwells in a body.

The truth of the matter is that the soul was existent before the body. This is 150
very clear to me, but I have no way of expressing it in a way that does not leave room for objections and potential doubts. Generally, to perceive this is to be incapable of expressing what has been perceived. I did not acquire the fullness of this belief in the soul by the study of intellectual proofs and logical premises, although the intellectual journey aided me greatly thanks to the premises discussed in the books of the rational theologians. This much can be stated in this book: in the perfection of its causal efficacy, the Cause of the soul's existence existed before the body, and the body is its concomitant effect.[179] Furthermore, the soul's control of the body depends on the existence of specific conditions, so this control can only be brought into existence after their existence.

Chapter 77: The Soul's Immortality

It is well known that the soul is originated and endlessly subsistent after death, 151
and that is only because its Cause subsists forever and ever. If you have certain knowledge that the Cause of the soul existed before the body, then you will of necessity know that the soul was an existent before the body. In rational theology, the existence of the soul's Cause before the body is a given, but how the perfection of its causal efficacy is realized is postulated and unconvincing. This much I have come to know by way of tasting, and not by way of formal learning. Indeed, if the soul's existence from a cause that brought it into existence is only conceivable on the condition that it must assume control of a body, then it follows that, after the soul's control of the body ceases,[180] it will become nonexistent.

فصل ٧٨

١٥٢ اعلم أنّ الله عزّ وجلّ يتعالى ويتقدّس أن يسع عظمته حضيض المكان والزمان وهذا بعينه حكم الأرواح فإنّها ليست أجساماً حتّى يتّسع الزمان والمكان للإحاطة بها ولمّا كان الأمر كذلك حكم سيّد الأوّلين والآخرين صلّى الله عليه وسلّم بأنّ الله عزّ وجلّ قبل العالم الزمانيّ والمكانيّ قبليّة إن قُدّرت بمقدار من الزمان لم يكن متناهياً وأمّا الأرواح فقدّر قبليّتها على الأجسام بمقدار ألفي ألف عام وقد أدركت هذه القبليّة بحمد الله تعالى إدراكاً أقوى وأوضح من إدراك العقل للأوّليّات وأمّا تقدير تلك القبليّة بهذا المقدار المذكور دون سائر المقادير فلم تُدرك بعد حقيقته والله عزّ وجلّ يرشّح الباطن لإدراكه بفضله وكرمه ويجعلنا ممّن يستحقّ ذلك من جوده الأزليّ.

فصل ٧٩

١٥٣ لعلّك الآن تشتهي أن تعرف السبب الموجب لوجود النفس فاعلم أنّ الحقّ الذي لا ريب فيه أصلاً عند أرباب القلوب المختصّين ببصائر تدرك المعارف التي يقصر العقل عن إدراكها بالضرورة هو أنّ النفوس مختلفة اختلافاً لا يدخل تحت الحصر درجاته وإنّ ذلك الاختلاف ليس كاختلاف الأنواع ولا كاختلاف الأجناس بل اختلاف النفوس وراء ذلك كلّه.

١٥٤ فمن النفوس ما لم يكن بينها وبين الحقّ الأوّل واسطة وهذه قضيّة يقصر العلم والعقل عن إدراكها فترى المتحذلق عند سماعها يبادر ويقول كيف يُتصوّر ذلك والنفس تتغيّر بأنواع مشهورة من التغيّرات والله عزّ وجلّ يتنزّه عن طرآن التغيّر عليه فكيف يجوز أن يكون

Chapter 78: Souls Precede Bodies

152 God is too exalted and holy for His greatness to be encompassed by the paltriness of space and time. The same judgment applies to spirits,[181] for they are not bodies that can be encompassed by time and space. Given that this is so, the Prophet, master of the first and the last,[182] stated that God existed before the temporal and spatial realms with a priority that is infinite (if you measure it with our measurement of time). The measurement of the priority of spirits to bodies is that of two million years.[183] I praise God that my perception of this priority is stronger and clearer than the intellect's perception of primary concepts. The reality of the determination of this priority with the aforementioned measurement alone cannot be perceived yet. May God, through His bounty and generosity, prepare our inner selves for its perception, including us among those who merit it from His beginningless munificence.

Chapter 79: The Diversity of Souls

153 Now, you may desire to know the cause that necessitates the soul's existence. For the masters of the heart who have been singled out with insight to perceive those realities known through recognition (but which the intellect is necessarily unable to perceive), the absolutely indubitable truth is that souls are diverse by limitless degrees. This diversity is not like the diversity among genera or species. Rather, the diversity of souls is completely beyond all of that.

154 For some souls, there is no intermediary between them and God, the First. This is a proposition that formal knowledge and the intellect are unable to perceive. You will notice that when a person who thinks he is clever hears that proposition, he is quick to retort, "How is that conceivable, seeing that the soul alters in various well-known ways, while God is far above the occurrences of change? So how can God in His essence be a direct cause for some souls without

بذاته من غير واسطة شيء سبباً لبعض النفوس وعن هذا المعنى يكنّي القرآن حيث قال ﴿مَا مَنَعَكَ أَنْ تَسْجُدَ لِمَا خَلَقْتُ بِيَدَيَّ﴾ . وإليه يشير قوله صلّى الله عليه وسلّم أنّ الله خلق آدم على صورة الرحمن وقوله صلّى الله عليه وسلّم ما خلق الله شيئاً أشبه به من آدم. ولعلّك إذا أدركت وجود الحقّ حقّ الإدراك بحيث يحيط بالأزمنة كلّها ماضيها ومستقبلها على التساوي شممت شيئاً من ذلك.[1]

١٥٥ والكلام في أمثال هذه النفوس ليس بجائز ولا يتأتّى ذلك أيضاً لأحد وكيف لا وأقلّ أحكامها ما ذكرناه وأسماع العقول تمجّها وتنبو عن إدراكها فالإعراض عن ذلك إلى ذكر ما هو مقبول عند العقلاء قاطبة أولى. واعلم أنّ النفوس إلّا قليلاً منها توسّطت بين وجودها ووجود الأوّل وسائط كثيرة وعدد الوسائط في كلّ نفس لا يحيط به إلّا علم الله عزّ وجلّ أو علم من رشّحه لذلك وهذه النفوس كلّها تشترك في كونها مسبّبة لأسباب غيبيّة ملكوتيّة.

فصل ٨٠

١٥٦ إنّما اختصّ كلّ بدن بنفس مخصوصة لكون كلّ نفس مخصوصة بصفة اقتضت ذلك مع وجود شروط أُخر متعلّقة بالحركات السماويّة والعبارة ضيّقة عن حقيقة تلك الصفة التي اختصّت بها كلّ نفس وعن تلك الشروط جميعاً ولعلّه يقلّ في الخلق من يُتصوّر إحاطة علمه بذلك لست أعني العلم الذي يستفاد من طريق التعلّم[2] فإنّ حصول ذلك من تلك الطريق يكاد يكون كالمحال ولعلّ انجذاب كلّ نفس إلى بدنها المخوض بها يشبه انجذاب الحديد إلى المغناطيس وانجذاب الذهب إلى الزيبق وانجذاب كلّ جسم إلى حيّز مخصوص وليس في شيء من ذلك عند العارفين شبهة وإذا كانت العقول عاجزة عن إدراك حقيقة

---

١ ج، ع، م: روائح ذلك. ٢ ج، ع، م: تعليم.

an intermediary?" The Qur'an alludes to this point when God says, «Iblīs! What has prevented you from prostrating to the one whom I created with My two hands?»[184] The Prophet's statements indicate this as well: "God created Adam in the form of the All-Merciful";[185] "God created nothing that resembles Him as much as Adam."[186] If you perceive God's existence as it should be perceived, as equally encompassing all past and future times, then perhaps you will catch a whiff of this!

It is not permissible to speak about these kinds of souls, nor is it manageable. 155
And how can it be otherwise, when intellectual comprehension dismisses and disagrees with the tiny amount I have said about them? It is thus best for me to shift my focus to what is accepted by each and every intelligent person. With the exception of a few souls, there are many intermediaries between their existence and the existence of the First. The number of intermediaries for each soul is only encompassed by God's knowledge or the knowledge of those prepared by Him to have it. This explains why all of these souls have something in common: they are all implicated in a causal chain that proceeds from the unseen, spiritual realm.

Chapter 80: The Relationship between the Soul and the Body

Each body is designated for a specific soul because specific to each soul is an 156
attribute that requires this relationship, in addition to the existence of other conditions connected to celestial motion.[187] Technical expressions are too limited to express the realities of both this attribute specific for each soul and all these conditions. And it is likely that there are only a few people whose range of knowledge is capable of conceiving this. By "knowledge," I do not mean what is derived by way of learning, for grasping these points in that way is nearly impossible. Perhaps each soul's attraction to the body specific for it resembles the attraction of iron to a magnet, or gold to mercury, or each body to a specific place. For the recognizers, none of this is obscure. Since the intellect is incapable of perceiving the reality of the sense in which iron is attracted to a magnet, though it is a phenomenon that can be sensed by every intelligent person, why

المعنى الذي به ينجذب الحديد إلى المغناطيس مع أنّه مشاهد محسوس للعقلاء قاطبة فأيّ عجب لو عجزت عن إدراك تلك المناسبات التي بين الأرواح والأجسام وهي خارجة عن الحصر والحدّ واعلم يقيناً أنّ العارف لا يستبعد أصلاً انجذاب كلّ نفس إلى بدنها[١] كما أنّ العقلاء لا يستبعدون أصلاً انجذاب كلّ جسم إلى حيّز مخصوص.

فصل ٨١

كما أنّ لكلّ جسم مكاناً مخصوصاً وفيه معنى يحرّكه إلى حيّزه ولا يقف به دونه فكذلك كلّ نفس خرجت من معدن مخصوص واختلاف النفوس من اختلاف معادنها والناس معادن كمعادن الذهب والفضّة كما أخبر عنه سيّد الأنبياء صلّى الله عليه وسلّم وقد خلق الله تعالى في كلّ نفس معنى مخصوصاً يحرّكها إلى معدنها الأصليّ ولا يقف بها دونه هذا هو الحقّ المشاهد الذي لا ريب فيه أصلاً للعارف. ١٥٧

وعن مثل هذا المعنى يترجم القرآن حيث يقول ﴿قَدْ عَلِمَ كُلُّ أُنَاسٍ مَّشْرَبَهُمْ﴾. ١٥٨
وحركات الجوارح آثار تلك المعاني التي عبّأتها القدرة الأزليّة في النفوس إتماماً للحكمة وإظهاراً لكمال اللطف والخبرة فالنفوس التي لا يكون بينها وبين الأوّل واسطة تنجذب إلى جنابه طبعاً كانجذاب الحديد إلى المغناطيس وهذه النفوس هي العارفة بالله عزّ وجلّ حقّاً وقوله تعالى ﴿يُحِبُّهُمْ وَيُحِبُّونَهُ﴾، كناية عن أهل هذه المعرفة. وإنّما عرفه هؤلاء معرفة حقيقيّة لأنّه تعالى تعرّف لهم في تجلّيه من غير واسطة فاستغرقوا بكلّيّتهم في معرفته فقوله تعالى ﴿أَلَسْتُ بِرَبِّكُمْ﴾ عبارة عن تعرّفه وتجلّيه لهم. وقولهم ﴿بَلَىٰ﴾ عبارة عن استغراقهم في مشاهدة ذلك الجمال.

١ (كلّ نفس إلى بدنها) في ع؛ أ، ج، م: الحديد إلى المغناطيس.

would it be surprising if the intellect is incapable of perceiving the relationships between spirits and bodies, which are innumerable and unlimited? You should know with total certainty that the recognizer does not at all consider how the soul is attracted to a body to be far-fetched, much in the same way that intelligent people do not at all consider how a body is attracted to a specific place to be far-fetched.

Chapter 81: God's Self-Disclosure

Just as each body has a specific space within which there is a supra-sensory real- 157
ity that moves the body to its ambit, not causing it to stop short, so too does each soul emerge from a specific source. Thus, the diversity of souls comes from the diversity of the sources from which they have emerged. For "People are sources, like gold and silver mines,"[188] as the master of the Prophets is reported to have said.[189] God has created a specific supra-sensory reality in each soul, which moves it to its original source, not causing it to stop short. This is the indubitable truth that is observed by the recognizer.

The Qur'an alludes to the likes of this supra-sensory reality: «each group 158
knew now their drinking place».[190] The movements of the body's limbs are the effects of this supra-sensory reality, which the beginningless power has placed within the soul as a way of bringing God's wisdom to completion, and manifesting the perfection of His gentleness and awareness. Thus, those souls that do not have an intermediary between themselves and the First are naturally attracted to Him, just as iron is attracted to a magnet. These souls truly recognize God. His words, «He loves them, and they love Him»,[191] allude to those who are worthy of this recognition. Such souls truly recognize God because He makes Himself recognizable to them in His self-disclosure, without any intermediary. In recognizing God, they are therefore immersed in their entirety. The question «Am I not your Lord?»[192] is an expression of His making Himself recognizable to them in His self-disclosure, and their reply, «Yes indeed!»,[193] is an expression of their immersion in witnessing His beauty.

١٥٩ ورحم الله شيخ الإسلام عبد الله الأنصاريّ لقد أفصح عن هذا المعنى غاية الإفصاح حيث قال في بعض كلامه الحقّ أراد في امتناع نعوته وعلوّ عزّته أن يُعرف فيعرّف فيُعرف لا بعلم فيُعبّر عنه ولا بسبب فيُشار إليه ولا بنعت فيثبت به بل معرفة وقعت قهراً فأوجبت منعاً[1] فلم تدع رسماً فصارت في الرسم جحداً وقامت في الحقيقة حقّاً. إلٰهي تلطّفتَ لأوليائك فعرفوك ولو تلطّفت لأعدائك لما جحدوك. فهذا حكم النفوس التي لم يكن بينها وبين الأوّل واسطة فعرفته حقّ المعرفة لأنّه تعرّف لها بلا حجاب وأمّا النفوس التي كانت بينها وبين الأوّل الحقّ واسطة فإنّما تعرّف لها من وراء حجاب فكانت هذه المعرفة قاصرة عن معرفة المصطفَين في الصفة الأولى.

فصل ٨٢

١٦٠ لمّا بلغتُ هذا الفصل أشرقت سلطنة الجلالة الأزليّة فتلاشى العلم والعقل وبقي الكاتب بلا هو لا بل غشيته الهويّة الحقيقيّة فاستغرقت هويّته المجازيّة فلمّا ردّ جمال الأزل عقله وعلمه ونفسه عليه كان لسانه يتلجلج بقول الشاعر [بسيط]

وَكَانَ مَا كَانَ مِمَّا لَسْتُ أَذْكُرُهُ ... فَظُنَّ خَيْرًا وَلَا تَسْأَلْ عَنِ ٱلْخَبَرِ

[1] ج، ع، م: جمعًا.

God have mercy on the Shaykh of Islam ʿAbd Allāh al-Anṣārī, who spoke most eloquently on this. In one of his sermons, he said, "In His utter inaccessibility and complete transcendence, God desires to be recognized and so He makes Himself recognizable. He is then recognized, but neither by knowledge that can express Him, nor by any cause that can point to Him, nor by any description through which He can be affirmed. Rather, it is through a recognition that overpowers and forbids, leaving no room for opposition; for all that remains in reality is the Real. My Lord! You are generous to Your Friends, and so they recognize You. But if You are generous to Your enemies, they would not oppose You!"[194] This, then, is the situation of those souls that do not have a barrier between themselves and the First. They recognize God as He should be recognized precisely because He makes Himself recognizable to them without a veil. God makes Himself recognizable to those souls that have an intermediary between themselves and Him, but from behind a veil. The recognition of this latter class of souls falls short of the recognition of those souls standing in the former class. 159

Chapter 82: The Annihilation of My Metaphorical Identity

When I got to writing this chapter, the splendor of majestic beginninglessness shone forth: knowledge and intellect became naught, and there remained only the writer, but without himself. Rather, the real identity enveloped me and drowned my metaphorical identity. When the beginningless beauty returned my intellect, knowledge, and self, my tongue began to ring with the words of the poet: 160

> What happened, I will not mention.
> Think well, and ask no more![195]

فصل ٨٣

كانت الدموع ملأت المحاجر والقلوب بلغت الحناجر وبرّحت بالعاشق صبوته وعظمت حسرته وقال إلى متى الهذيان الفارغ وأنّى ينفع ذكر المعشوق والعاشق في سجن الفراق. فلمّا اشتدّ بالمسكين حرصه[١] واتّفق إلى وطنه الأصليّ رجوعه بقي القلم[٢] وقد أعوزه الكاتب. ١٦١

فصل ٨٤

وردّ عليه من حضرة السلطان أمر جازم بالدخول عليه فطار الطائر إلى عشّه الأصليّ ومعدنه الفطريّ وترك القفص وجرى بينه وبين السلطان وهو على يده ما لا يُتصوّر ذكره فلمّا أذن له في الانصراف استأذن في حكاية حاله للمساكين[٣] في حضيض الزمان والمكان فأذن له في ذلك. فلمّا عاود مستقرّه من السجن راجع ما كان بصدده وكتب هذه الفصول المشتملة على حكاية حاله وما جرى عليه. ١٦٢

١ ج، م: جوعه؛ ع: حرّة روعه. ٢ (القلم) في ج، ع، م؛ أ: العلم. ٣ ج، ع: للسالكين؛ م: للساكنين.

Chapter 83: My Yearning to Return Home

My eyes were filled with tears and death was knocking at my door; troubled by the fervor of my love and in the depths of despair, I exclaimed, "How long will this empty madness last? What good can there be in remembering the Beloved when the lover is trapped in the prison of separation?" As the desire in my wretched self grew stronger, I was given a way back to my original home. Now the pen remains, but the writer is gone. 161

Chapter 84: In the Divine Presence

When the command came to enter into the presence of the King, the bird of my soul flew back to its original nest and primordial home, leaving the cage of this world behind. Then something happened between myself and the King that cannot be put into words. When He allowed me to leave, I asked for permission to relate this tale to those poor souls still confined by time and space, and He allowed me to do so. Returning to my lodging in this worldly prison, I returned to the task at hand and wrote these chapters that tell my tale. 162

فصـل ٨٥

إن خطر ببالك أنّه ما الذي جرى نوديت من وراء حجب الغيب تأدّب. ما للعميان والسؤال عن حقيقة الألوان فوالذي بيده الملك والملكوت وتحت سلطانه الجبروت لو ظهرت ممّا جرى بيننا ذرّة في عالمكم هذا لتلاشى العرش والكرسيّ فضلاً عن السموات والأرضين. ١٦٣

فصـل ٨٦

إيّاك ثمّ إيّاك أن تستشرف للطمع في إدراك تلك المعاني من هذه الألفاظ فتتصرّف فيها بعقلك المزخرف وفطنتك البتراء واقبل منّي هذه النصيحة مجّانًا ولا أراك تقبل وعذرك عندي واضح فلقد شاهدت من ممارسة العلم عجائب لا أستنكرمعها ذلك لا منك ولا من غيرك من أهل النظر. نعم إن شئت أن تصل إلى حقيقة ذلك الطريق[1] فدع الدنيا النجسة بما فيها من القاذورات للمقبلين إليها والمتوجّهين بهممهم الدنيّة إليها. وأمّا الآخرة فلا تعجّ فيها عبثاً[2] والعاشق يكفيه بالوقوف درك[3] الوصول إلى معشوقه عارًا وشيناً لعمري ﴿مِنكُم مَّن يُرِيدُ ٱلدُّنْيَا وَمِنكُم مَّن يُرِيدُ ٱلْأَخِرَةَ﴾. ولكن أين أنت من قوم نبذوها من وراء ظهورهم فأثنى عليهم القرآن الكريم وقال ﴿يُرِيدُونَ وَجْهَهُۥ﴾. فإنّك إذا فعلت ذلك ألحقك الجود الأزليّ والكرم السرمديّ بقلب لا يتعلّق بشيء من الأرض والسموات ولا يشفي غليل صدرك[4] إلّا حال الذلّ[5] وهو ماء الحياة. ١٦٤

١ ج،ع،م: بطريق الذوق. ٢ ج،ع: غبنًا. ٣ ج،ع،م: الوقوف دون. ٤ (صدرك) في ج،ع،م؛أ: صداه. ٥ ج،ع: جمال الأزل؛ م: جمال الأزليّ.

Chapter 85: A Final Word about My Journey

If the thought occurs to you, "What is it that happened when you were called from behind the veil of the unseen?," I would say, "Have etiquette! Why should a blind man ask about the reality of colors?" I swear by Him who holds the earthly and spiritual realms in His hands, and whose power rules the invincible realm,[196] if even a speck of what took place between us were to appear in this world of yours, the Throne and the Footstool would come to naught, let alone the heavens and the earth! 163

Chapter 86: Fleeing from This World

Be extremely wary of the desire to try to perceive these supra-sensory realities by means of human expressions, poring over them with your vain intelligence and defective acumen. Take this advice for free, although I do not see you accepting it. And your reasons are plain for me to see. Indeed, in pursuing rational theology I have beheld some marvels, so I do not wish to discourage you or any other thinker from them. But if you want to reach the reality of this path, leave this impure world and its defilements to those in pursuit of it, those with lowly aspirations who are preoccupied with it. As for the afterlife, do not think it is a game! The lover is content to stop short of union with his Beloved, shamed and disgraced. By my life! «Among you are those who desire this world, and among you are those who desire the afterlife».[197] But you are still very far from those people who have cast this world aside, and whom the Qur'an praises when it says, «they desire His face».[198] If you also cast this world aside, God's beginningless munificence and everlasting generosity will join you to a heart that has no attachment to anything in the heavens and the earth;[199] for nothing will quench your thirsty heart but the state of lowliness,[200] which is the water of life. 164

فصل ٨٧

١٦٥ ما أصدق المثل السائر الكلام يجرّ الكلام فقد انتهى بنا الكلام في النفوس وأحوالها إلى عوالم لا نهاية لعجائبها وبحار لا قيمة لجواهرها فنرجع الآن إلى المطلب المقصود ونستوعب في بيانه غاية المجهود.

١٦٦ ونقول كما أنّ الجسم إذا تحرّك بطبعه إلى حيّز مخصوص فلا بدّ وأن تكون حركته إليه من أقرب الطرق وهو الخطّ المستقيم والذي لا يُتصوّر فيه انحراف أصلاً وهذا معلوم قطعاً بالبرهان اليقينيّ ومشهور عند من[1] يتصفّح أمثال ذلك فكذلك كلّ نفس من هذه النفوس فإنّها تتحرّك إلى حيّزها الأصليّ وهو المعدن الذي خرجت منه من أقرب الطرق ولا تلتفتنّ إلى عوائق تعوقها في الطريق عن الحركة وتمنعها عن الانجذاب فإنّ ذلك غير قادح في غرضنا هذا.

١٦٧ فأشرف النفوس إذا ما يتحرّك إلى الله عزّ وجلّ طبعاً لا تكلّف فيه على الصراط المستقيم الذي هو أقرب الطرق فإن وقف القدر ببعض النفوس في الطريق على شيء فذلك خارج عن طبيعتها الأصليّة ولا اكتراث[2] بأمثاله. وهؤلاء ما داموا في الطريق فتجدهم أخفّاء الألسنة بقوله ﴿ٱهۡدِنَا ٱلصِّرَٰطَ ٱلۡمُسۡتَقِيمَ﴾ كما أخبر عنه في حقّ الخليل خاصّة في القرآن حكاية عنه أنّه قال ﴿إِنِّي ذَاهِبٌ إِلَىٰ رَبِّي سَيَهۡدِينِ﴾. ولا شكّ عندك أنّ المغناطيس إذا كان يجذب الحديد إلى نفسه من أقرب الطرق فقد هداه الصراط المستقيم ولمّا كانت هذه النفوس أشرف النفوس كلّها قال الله تعالى في كتابه ﴿وَمَنۡ أَحۡسَنُ دِينٗا مِّمَّنۡ أَسۡلَمَ وَجۡهَهُۥ لِلَّهِ وَهُوَ مُحۡسِنٞ وَٱتَّبَعَ مِلَّةَ إِبۡرَٰهِيمَ حَنِيفٗاۗ وَٱتَّخَذَ ٱللَّهُ إِبۡرَٰهِيمَ خَلِيلٗا﴾.

---

١ م: اليقينيّ لمن. ٢ (اكتراث) في ج، ع، م؛ أ: الإكرار.

Chapter 87: Unhindered Souls

165 How true is the proverb, "Words draw out more words." In discussing souls and their states, I have been taken to worlds replete with endless wonders and into oceans filled with priceless jewels. I will now return to my intended goal, dedicating all of my efforts to it.

166 Just as a body naturally moves to a specific place and must do so by way of the most proximate of paths (namely, a straight line, the deviation from which is inconceivable, as can certainly be shown through demonstration and is well known to anyone who has examined similar things), so too is the case with each soul. It moves to its original place (which is the source from which it has been brought forth) by way of the most proximate of paths, its motion being unimpeded by obstacles that would bar it from attraction to its source. But this point should not detract me from my goal.

167 When the noblest of souls naturally move to God, they are unburdened along the straight path, which is the most proximate of paths. Indeed, some souls will pay no attention to some burden or other that they may encounter along the way: these burdens are external to their original nature. For as long as these souls travel the path, you will find them whispering God's words, «Guide us upon the straight path».[201] It is just as the Qur'an has reported specifically about Abraham, relating his words, «I am indeed going to my Lord. He will guide me».[202] Likewise, you would never doubt that when a magnet attracts iron by way of the most proximate path, it has guided it to the straight path. Since the souls that are attracted in this way are the noblest of all souls, God says in His book, «And who is more beautiful in religion than one who submits his face to God, acting beautifully and following the creed of Abraham, unswerving? And God did take Abraham as an intimate friend».[203]

فصل ٨٨

هذه المعاني التي أُودعت في هذه الألفاظ بعيدة جدّاً عن ظواهر مفهوماتها فإنّها وُضعت للدلالة على معان غير هذه المعاني المقصودة بها فمن سمعها فلا بدّ وأن تسبق إلى فهمه عند سماعها مفهوماتها الحاصلة[١] بها بالضرورة وإنّما يشمّ مبادئ روائحها قليل من فحول العلماء الناظرين.[٢] ١٦٨

وعذري في ذلك واضح فمن أراد أن يُفهِم الأكمه كيفيّة إدراك الألوان أو العنّين حقيقة لذّة الواقع[٣] لم يكن له بدّ من أن يقول إنّ للإنسان معنى يدرك به الأشياء كما يدرك سائر الحواسّ ومع ذلك فتلك المدركات لا تناسب المذوقات والمشمومات والمعقولات والمسموعات وهذا يعسر على الأكمه التصديق به وإن اعترف بلسانه وقال اعتقدت ذلك اعتقاداً يقينياً علمنا أنّ اعترافه ذلك إيمان بالغيب وأنّ اعترافه لا بدّ وأن يكون مركّباً من خيالات فاسدة قد عشّشت في دماغه. ١٦٩

فكذلك إذا قيل لنا إنّ في الآخرة أموراً لا تناسب المحسوسات ولا المعقولات عسر علينا التصديق بذلك إلّا أن نؤمن بالغيب إيمان الأكمه بالألوان إلى أن يصل إليها ذوقاً. ولهذا المعنى رأيت الاختصار في ذكر أحوال النفوس وأطوارها أولى ولعلّ القدر اليسير الذي ذكرته كان الأولى أيضاً تركه فإنّ الأكثرين يستبعدون ذلك فينكرونه ويتضرّرون بإنكاره. ١٧٠

---

١ ج، ع، م: الخاصّة. ٢ ج، ع: في العلوم الحقيقيّة. ٣ (لذّة الوقاع) في ج، ع، م؛ أ: الوقاع.

Chapter 88: Faith in the Afterlife

The supra-sensory realities that have been placed in these words are very far off from the apparent sense of these words. Indeed, these words are conventionally used to denote meanings quite different from the supra-sensory realities in question. When these words are heard, they will inevitably be understood in the sense they have acquired. To be sure, there are but a few stalwart rationalists who can even catch a whiff from where it is that the fragrances of these words emanate! 168

My excuse for employing linguistic expressions to convey these supra-sensory realities is clear: if you want to make a person who is born blind understand how to perceive color, or to make an impotent person understand the reality of sexual pleasure, you have no other recourse than to tell them that people have a certain sense, much like other senses, through which things can be perceived. However, this sense's objects of perception do not correspond to what is normally tasted, smelled, understood, or heard. This is very difficult for the person born blind to assent to, even if he were to acknowledge it verbally, saying, "I believe in this with utter certainty." But I know that his acknowledgment of this other sense would be tantamount to having faith in the unseen, and that it would inevitably be made up of corrupt images caught up in his mind. 169

In the same vein, when we are told that things in the afterlife will not correspond to what is sensory or intelligible, it is difficult for us to assent to this except by having faith in the unseen in the same way the person born blind has faith in colors—until, of course, we taste these things. This is why it is best for me to be brief in discussing the states and stages of the soul. Perhaps it is also best to put aside the little that I have said, for most people will deem it far-fetched and reject it, harming themselves in the process. 170

فصل ٨٩

١٧١ كأنّك بعقلك الضعيف تبادر إلى التكذيب بقولنا أمور الآخرة لا تناسب المعقول ولا المحسوس وتقول كفى ببطلان هذا القول شاهداً حكم العقل بطريق يقينيّ حاصر أنّ الموجود ينقسم إلى المعقول والمحسوس وإن كانت أمور الآخرة موجودة[١] فكيف لقائل أن يقول بأنّها لا تناسب المحسوس ولا المعقول. وعليك الآن أن تصبر صبراً جميلاً حتّى أبيّن لك موضع الخلل في ذلك ثمّ عليك بعد ذلك أن تراجع نفسك وتطالبها بالإنصاف حتّى لا يستولي[٢] عليك في اعتراضها جهل بما تسمع.

١٧٢ فاعلم أنّ الأكمه أيضاً ينحصر عنده الموجودات كلّها في المعقول والمحسوس وكذلك ينحصر عنده من وجوه كثيرة كانحصارها في القديم والحادث والسبب والمسبّب والناقص والكامل ومع ذلك فإذا قيل له إنّ الألوان لا يناسب المعقول ولا المحسوس كانت هذه القضيّة صادقة إذا أردنا بالمحسوس ما يدركه بحواسّه الأربع والأكمه قد يكذّب بها ويقول[٣] إذا كان الوجود بكلّيّته منحصراً في المعقول والمحسوس فكيف يجوز أن لا تكون الألوان محسوسة ولا معقولة مع أنّها موجودة وليس لتكذيبه هذا مستند إلّا أنّه حصر المحسوسات في مدركات الحواسّ الأربع.

١٧٣ فكذلك إذا قلنا أمور الآخرة لا تناسب المحسوس ولا المعقول فكذّب به الجاحدون لم يكن لتكذيبهم مستند أصلاً إلّا أنّهم حصروا المحسوسات في مدركات الحواسّ الخمس وليس ذلك بلازم البتّة وحصر الموجودات كلّها فيما يدرك بالحسّ والعقل أيضاً ليس بلازم فكم من شيء يعجز العقل إدراكه ويكون كالوهم إذا عجز عن إدراك كثير من العقليّات الصرفة الغامضة وذلك لا يدلّ على أنّ كلّ ما يدركه الوهم غير صادق وكذلك البصر يدرك المحسوسات ويكون حكمه فيها ينقسم إلى الصادق والكاذب فحكمه بأنّ هذا الجزء مثلاً مقداره كذا حكم صادق وحكمه بأنّ الشمس مقدارها مقدار مجنّ

١ (موجودة) في ج، ع، م؛ أ: موجلة. ٢ (لا يستولى) في ع؛ أ: لا فصول تستولى؛ ج، م: حتّى لا تستولى. ٣ (بها ويقول) في ج، ع، م؛ أ: بها.

Chapter 89: The Intellect and the Afterlife

With your weak mind, you will probably be quick to reject my statement that things in the afterlife will correspond to neither the sensory nor the intelligible: "The intellect's certainty that existents divide into the sensory and the intelligible is alone sufficient proof of the falsehood of your statement. For, if the things in the afterlife are existent, then how can one say that they will correspond to neither the sensory nor the intelligible?" Now you must patiently bear with me until I explain the flaw in your position. Then, when I am done, you should go back and in all fairness examine yourself so that your ignorance regarding what you have heard does not get the better of you. 171

The person born blind confines all existents to what is intelligible and sensory, and confines them further in many other ways, such as eternal and originated, cause and effect, and perfect and deficient. Nevertheless, when he is told that colors correspond to neither the intelligible nor the sensory, which would be a true proposition if by "sensory" we mean what the blind person's four senses can grasp, he would reject that statement, saying, "Since all of existence is confined to the intelligible and the sensory, how can colors be neither sensory nor intelligible given that colors are existents?" But this denial of his has no basis but the fact that he confines what is sensory to objects that can be perceived by his four senses. 172

Likewise, if I were to say that the things in the afterlife correspond to neither the sensory nor the intelligible, and the naysayers were to reject it, their rejection would have no basis but the fact that they confine the sensory to what can be perceived by the five senses. Of course, this conclusion is not logically necessary. This is because it is not logically necessary that every existent should be confined to what can be perceived through the senses and the intellect. Indeed, how many things there are that the intellect is simply incapable of perceiving! And when the intellect cannot perceive the many obscure, purely intellectual matters that are out there, it functions more like the imaginal faculty. But this does not indicate that all of the things the imaginal faculty perceives are unreal. In the same vein, sight perceives sensory objects, and judgments about them are divided into either true or false. So the judgment is true that a part of something, for example, has a certain size, but the judgment is false that the sun is the size 173

وأنّ الكواكب مقدارها مقدار دينار حكم كاذب وليس لذلك مستند إلّا أنّه لا يدرك البعيد كما يدرك القريب.

١٧٤ فكذلك فاعلم يقيناً أنّ حكم العقل بأنّ الله تعالى موجود وواحد وقديم وخالق حكم صادق قطعاً وحكمه بأنّ كلّ موجود فلا بدّ وأن يدركه كأمور الآخرة حكم كاذب قطعاً واعلم بعد ذلك أنّ الله عزّ وجلّ أبعد عن بصيرة العقل من الشمس عن بصيرة الحسّ بدرجات لا تتناهى فلغاية بُعده وكمال إشراقه يستحيل للعقل إدراكه فبصيرة العقل بالإضافة إلى إدراكه كالخفّاش بالإضافة إلى إدراك نور الشمس[١] حيث الشمس فلا يُتصوّر وجود الخفّاش ولا وجود الإنسان من حيث الحقيقة.

فصل ٩٠

١٧٥ الحقّ[٢] أنّ علم الساعة مردود إلى الله كما قال تعالى ﴿إِلَيْهِ يُرَدُّ عِلْمُ ٱلسَّاعَةِ﴾. وليس لك أن تؤمن بشيء من أسرارها أصلاً إلّا إيمان الأكمه بالألوان فتأمّل أوّلاً أنّه كيف ينبغي للأكمه إذا آمن بالألوان من طريق الغيب أن يقطع نظره عن الحواسّ الأربع ومدركاتها حتّى يُتصوّر له أن يؤمن بالغيب من غير تشبيه وتمثيل وطالب بعد ذلك نفسك[٣] بالإيمان حتّى تكون مؤمناً بالغيب وموقناً بالآخرة كما قال تعالى ﴿يُؤْمِنُونَ بِٱلْغَيْبِ وَيُقِيمُونَ ٱلصَّلَوٰةَ وَمِمَّا رَزَقْنَٰهُمْ يُنفِقُونَ﴾ ﴿وَبِٱلْأَخِرَةِ هُمْ يُوقِنُونَ﴾. فإن لم تجد نفسك متحلّية بمثل هذا الإيمان فاعلم أنّ الشيطان قد جوّلك[٤] ودلّاك بحبل غروره.

١ زائدة في ع، م: وبصيرة العارف بالإضافة إلى إدراكه كالإنسان بالإضافة إلى إدراك قرص الشمس. أضاف ج هناك: وكالإنسان بالإضافة إلى قرص الشمس. ٢ زائدة في ج، ع، م: الذي لا شكّ فيه. ٣ زائدة في ج، ع، م: بمثل هذا. ٤ (جوّلك) في ج؛ أ: حولق؛ ع: حولقك؛ م: جولقك.

of a plate, or that the planets are the size of gold coins. Yet the basis for this kind of false judgment is simply the fact that sight cannot perceive what is far away as well as it can what is near.

In the same vein, the intellect's judgment that God exists, is one, eternal, and 174
the creator, is absolutely true; but the intellect's judgment that it must be able to perceive every existent (for instance, the matters of the afterlife) is absolutely false. After all, God is infinitely further away to the insight of the intellect than the sun is to the sense of sight! It is thus impossible for the intellect to perceive God's utter distance and the perfection of His luminosity. In relation to perceiving God, the insight of the intellect is like that of bats in relation to perceiving the light of the sun. The sun in itself cannot be perceived by bats, and Reality in itself cannot be perceived by humans.

Chapter 90: Faith in the Unseen

The truth is that knowledge of the Hour goes back to God, as He says, «Knowl- 175
edge of the Hour goes back to Him».[204] You basically have no way to believe in any of its mysteries other than to have the faith that a person born blind has in colors. First, think about how when a person born blind believes in colors as an unseen reality he turns away from his four senses and objects of perception so that he can have faith in what is unseen, with no resemblance or likeness in his mind. Then, search within yourself for this kind of faith until you come to have faith in the unseen and come to be certain of the afterlife. As God says, «Those who believe in the unseen, perform the prayer, and spend from what We have provided them . . . and who are certain of the afterlife».[205] If you do not find your soul adorned with this kind of faith, you should know that Satan has encircled you, pulling you along with the rope of his delusion.

فصل ٩١

١٧٦ ينبغي لك أن تتأمّل تأمّلاً شافياً إن كنت من أهل الطلب فيما وظّفته عليك من شروط الإيمان بالغيب وتكرّر فيه نظرك مرّة بعد أخرى حتّى يصير التصديق بالغيب لك طبعاً بحيث لا تحتاج معه إلى النظر في المقدّمات وحينئذ يصير باطنك شديد الاستعداد لأن يفيض عليه من الله عزّ وجلّ نور يثمر انشراح الصدر وسعة الحوصلة كما قال تعالى ﴿أَفَمَن شَرَحَ ٱللَّهُ صَدۡرَهُۥ لِلۡإِسۡلَٰمِ فَهُوَ عَلَىٰ نُورٖ مِّن رَّبِّهِۦ﴾ . ومهما انشرح صدرك للإيمان بالغيب فاض على باطنك نور لم تكن شاهدتَ مثله قبل ذلك فاعلم أنّ ذلك أثر من آثار الطور الذي يظهر[١] بعد طور العقل فاستوعب جهدك في الطلب فإنّه يكفيك في الوجدان فمن طلب وجدّ وجد وأوحى الله تعالى إلى داود عليه السلام يا داود من طلبني وجدني ومن يطلب غيري لم يجدني. وهذا يلزم منه بطريق البرهان أنّ من طلبه لا يُتصوّر منه طلب غيره. وإلى مثل ذلك يشير قوله عليه السلام من أدمن قرع الباب يوشك أن يُفتح له.

فصل ٩٢

١٧٧ مدركات هذا الطور تنقسم بوجه من الوجوه إلى ما نسبته إليه نسبة الأوّليّات إلى العقل وإلى ما نسبته إليه نسبة الغوامض النظريّة التي لا تدرك إلّا بتوسّط إليه أعني العقل وهذه القضيّة عسير إدراكها صعب منالها فلا تطمع في الوصول إليها

١ (الطور الذي يظهر) في ج، ع، م؛ أ: الظهور الذي.

Chapter 91: Searching for God

If you are a true seeker, you should carefully think about the conditions of faith in the unseen that I have put in your charge, scrutinizing them over and over until belief in the truth of the unseen becomes natural to you so that you no longer need to reflect on logical premises. At that time, your inner self will very much be prepared for God to cause a light to pour forth, resulting in an expansion of your heart and a widening of your spiritual capacity; as God says, «What of one whose heart God has expanded for submission so that he follows a light from his Lord?»[206] When your heart has expanded for faith in the unseen, God will cause a light to pour into your inner self, the likes of which you have not witnessed before. This is one of the traces of that stage that appears after the stage of the intellect. So intensify your search, for that alone is what you need in order to attain awareness! Because "the one who fervently searches will find what he is after."[207] God inspired David: "O David, whoever searches for Me will find Me, but whoever searches for anything else will never find Me."[208] A logical conclusion necessarily follows: it is inconceivable that a person in search of God would search for anything else. Something similar has been alluded to in the Prophet's words: "If you keep knocking at the door, it is likely to be opened."[209] 176

Chapter 92: Striving for Understanding

What is perceived in the stage beyond the intellect is in one respect divided into those things whose relationship to this stage is like the relationship of primary concepts to the intellect, and those things whose relationship to it is like the relationship of theoretical obscurities that can only be perceived through an intermediary—namely, the intellect. These issues are easy to perceive, but 177

واجتهد أن تصدّق بها تصديقك بالغيب لعلّ الله يرزقك بالوصول إليها فتستغني بالذوق عن السماع.

فصل ٩٣

مدركات هذا الطور أسرار على العلم التميزيّ وعلى العقل الإنسانيّ كما أنّ مدركات ١٧٨
البصر أسرار على حاسّة الشمّ ومدركات الوهم أسرار على قوّة الخيال والحفظ ومدركات اللمس أسرار على قوّة السمع والذوق والأوّليّات أسرار على الحواسّ كلّها والتحقيق في ذلك أنّ السرّ والعلانية اسمان إضافيّان فربّ شيء هو سرّ على مدرك وهو علانية بالإضافة إلى مدرك آخر فالأوّليّات علانية عند العقل وأسرار عند الحواسّ وأكثر ما يطلق عليه اسم السرّ في لسان الشرع وعلى ألسنة الصوفيّة فهو سرّ عند العقل الإنسانيّ وسرّ على الحروف والأصوات وكلّ ما لا يُتصوّر عنه العبارة فهو سرّ على العبارة. ولهذا المعنى قال عليه السلام إذا ذُكر القدر فأمسكوا يعني أنّ القدر سرّ على الكلام البشريّ والنطق الإنسانيّ فلا يُتصوّر عنه العبارة أصلاً. ولذلك قال سهل التستريّ رحمة الله عليه الكلام في القدر عند المخالف بدعة. وتحقّق هذا الفصل فإنّك تحتاج إليه فيما بعد.

difficult to obtain. So do not desire to attain them, but rather strive to assent to them just as you assent to the unseen. Perhaps God will grant them to you, and tasting them will free you from the need of hearsay.

Chapter 93: The Evident and the Mysterious

What is perceived in the stage beyond the intellect is a mystery to knowledge 178
based on distinctions and to the human intellect, just as what is perceived by eyesight is a mystery to the sense of smell, what is perceived by the faculty of estimation is a mystery to the faculties of imagination and memory, what is perceived by the sense of touch is a mystery to the faculties of hearing and taste, and what is perceived by primary concepts is a mystery to all the five senses. The fact is that "mystery" and "evident" are relative terms, for there are many things that are a mystery to one perceiver but evident to another. Primary concepts, for instance, are evident to the intelligence but a mystery to the senses. Indeed, most of what is called a mystery in the language of the revealed law and by the Sufis is a mystery to both the human intellect and to language. And whatever cannot be conceived of through expressions will remain a mystery to expressions, which is why the Prophet said, "When destiny is discussed, desist from it!"[210] In other words, destiny is a mystery to human speech and language, and we simply cannot conceive of an expression for it. This explains why Sahl al-Tustarī said, "Discussing destiny in a contentious manner is a reprehensible innovation in religion."[211] Now verify what is in this chapter, as you will need it for what will come next.

فصل ٩٤

١٧٩ أمور القيامة كلّها أسرار على العلم الإنسانيّ فلا يُتصوّر أن يحيط بها أحد ما دام في الدنيا ولم يتخلّص عن أسر الوهم وتغليط الخيال. وقول الكفّار ﴿مَتَىٰ هَٰذَا ٱلْوَعْدُ إِن كُنتُمْ صَٰدِقِينَ﴾ سؤال عن شيء يستحيل الجواب عنه على موجبه فإنّ أمر الساعة إذا كان ﴿كَلَمْحِ ٱلْبَصَرِ أَوْ هُوَ أَقْرَبُ﴾ وكان متى سؤالاً عن الزمان استحال جواب السائل عنه وهو كقول الأكمه إذا وصفنا له المبصرات المتلوّنة فقال كيف تُذاق هذه المبصرات أو كيف تُشمّ هذه المبصرات فالجواب الحقّ في ذلك أن نقول العلم بالمبصرات عند البصير فإن تخيّل شيئاً في معنى ما وصفناه وحكيناه له على سبيل المقايسة أخطأ فيه بالضرورة.

١٨٠ فإذاً الجواب الحقّ مع الكفّار إذا قالوا ﴿مَتَىٰ هَٰذَا ٱلْوَعْدُ﴾ أن يقال لهم العلم في ذلك عند الله. فمن رجع إلى الله تعالى وحُشر إليه كان عنده فلا بدّ وأن يعرف حينئذ حقيقة الساعة بالضرورة لأنّه ﴿وَعِندَهُۥ عِلْمُ ٱلسَّاعَةِ﴾. فإذاً بالضرورة لا تقوم الساعة وعلى وجه الأرض من يقول لا إله إلا الله كما أخبر عنه سيّد الأوّلين والآخرين صلوات الله وسلامه عليه. فإنّ من كان بعد على وجه الأرض لم يُحشر بعد إلى الله عزّ وجلّ فإذا من كان ﴿فِى مَقْعَدِ صِدْقٍ عِندَ مَلِيكٍ مُّقْتَدِرٍ﴾، فقد قامت له القيامة. وكذلك المجرمون وإن كانوا ﴿نَاكِسُو رُءُوسِهِمْ﴾، فإنّ القيامة في حقّهم قائمة لأنّهم عند ربّهم. ولعلّ من يقول أبيت عند ربّي يطعمني ويسقيني يصدّق منه أن يقول بُعثتُ والساعة كهاتين إن كادت لتسبقني فسبقتها أنا.

١٨١ واعلم أنّ الساعة من داخل حجب السماوات والأرض ومنزلتها من تلك الحجب منزلة الجنين من رحم أمّه ولذلك لا تقوم إلّا ﴿إِذَا زُلْزِلَتِ ٱلْأَرْضُ زِلْزَالَهَا﴾ وانشقّت السماء وانتثرت الكواكب وكُوّرت الشمس وسُيّرت الجبال وعُطلت العشار و﴿بُعْثِرَ مَا فِى ٱلْقُبُورِ وَحُصِّلَ مَا فِى ٱلصُّدُورِ﴾. وعلى الجملة ﴿تُبَدَّلُ ٱلْأَرْضُ

Chapter 94: The Coming of the Hour

179 Everything that will happen on the Day of Resurrection is a mystery to human knowledge. It is inconceivable for anyone to encompass it while he remains in this world and is not free from the bonds of fantasy and the error of imagination. The statement of the disbelievers, «When will this promise come to pass, if you are truthful?»,[212] is a question that is impossible to properly answer. Since the coming of the Hour «is like the blinking of an eye, or even closer»,[213] and the question "when?" is one that pertains to time, it is impossible to answer it. It is like the question posed by a person born blind when we describe colorful objects to him: "How can these objects be tasted or smelled?" The correct response to this would be for us to say, "The person who can see can know these objects." So if, by means of analogy, you try to imagine a fraction of the meaning of what we have described and related to you, it will necessarily be incorrect.

180 Therefore, the correct response to the disbelievers' question, «When will this promise come to pass?»,[214] is to say that its knowledge lies with God. Whoever returns to God and is mustered from the grave and brought before Him will inevitably come to know the reality of the Hour at that time, since «Knowledge of the Hour lies with Him».[215] The Prophet, master of the first and the last, said, "The Hour will not come so long as there is someone on the earth who says, 'There is no god but God.'"[216] Those who are still on the earth will not yet be brought before God, whereas the Resurrection has already come for those who are «upon a firm seat before an omnipotent King».[217] The same applies to the guilty. When they «bend their heads low»,[218] the Resurrection has effectively come for them, since they will be with their Lord. Perhaps the one who said, "I spend the night with my Lord who feeds me and gives me to drink"[219] confirmed this point when he also said, "I have been sent while the coming of the Hour is as short as the distance between my two fingers; even if it is almost before me, I have come before it."[220]

181 The Hour is within the veils of the heavens and the earth like a fetus in the womb of its mother, which is why the Hour will only come «When the earth is violently shaken»,[221] the sky is split apart,[222] the stars are dispersed,[223] the sun is enfolded,[224] the mountains are set in motion,[225] pregnant camels are abandoned,[226] and «when what lies in the graves is turned inside out, and what lies

غَيۡرَ ٱلۡأَرۡضِ وَٱلسَّمَٰوَٰتُ﴾ . فما دام السالك خارج حجب الأرض والسموات فلا تقوم له القيامة وإنّما كانت القيامة داخل الحجب لأنّ الله عزّ وجلّ داخل الحجب ﴿وَعِندَهُۥ عِلۡمُ ٱلسَّاعَةِ﴾ .

١٨٢ فقوله عليه السلام لا تقوم الساعة وعلى وجه الأرض من يقول لا إله إلّا الله معناه أنّ الرجل ما دام خارج الحجب فالقيامة سرّ على علمه فإذا قطع في سلوكه تلك الحجب وتبجح في حضرة العنديّة صار سرّ القيامة عنده علانية ولهذا السبب لم يجز أن يرى الله عزّ وجلّ في الدنيا أحد أصلاً لا نبيّ ولا وليّ وأمّا رسول الله صلّى الله عليه وسلّم فإنّما رآه بعد أن قطع الحجب ليلة المعراج. ولمّا قيل لموسى عليه السلام ﴿أَنَّ ٱلسَّاعَةَ ءَاتِيَةٌ﴾ لا جرم لمّا طلب الرؤية قيل ﴿لَن تَرَىٰنِي﴾ . واعلم أنّ محمّدًا صلّى الله عليه وسلّم إنّما كانت القيامة عنده علانية حين قطع حجب السماوات والأرض ونفذ من أقطارها فلمّا رجع إلى مستقرّه من خارج الحجب كان ذلك العلم عنده سرًّا كما كان قبل ذلك وإنّما كانت علانية له من وراء الحجب.

١٨٣ وعلى الجملة فالسرّ سرّ أبدًا حيث هو سرّ والعلانية علانية أبدًا حيث هي علانية لا يتغيّران إلّا بتغيّر أحوال السالكين. وإلى مثل ذلك أشير بقوله تعالى ﴿يَسۡـَٔلُونَكَ عَنِ ٱلسَّاعَةِ أَيَّانَ مُرۡسَىٰهَا فِيمَ أَنتَ مِن ذِكۡرَىٰهَآ﴾ . أي إن كان سرّ القيامة علانية لك ليلة المعراج فما الذي بقي على ذكرك وعلى علمك ومن تصرّف ببضاعة العقل في هذه الألفاظ فقد ظلم نفسه. وإيّاك يا مسكين أن تدع خاطرك يحوم حول التكذيب بذلك أو التشكّك فيه فتكفر بما أنزل الله على أنبيائه فلولا أنت وأمثالك من العميان لما خُوطب رسول الله صلّى الله عليه وسلّم بقوله ﴿وَكَذَّبَ بِهِۦ قَوۡمُكَ وَهُوَ ٱلۡحَقُّ﴾ .

in hearts is made known».[227] In short, the Hour will come when «the earth will be changed into something other than the earth, and the heavens as well».[228] So long as the traveler is outside of the veils of the earth and the heavens, the Resurrection will not happen for him, for the Resurrection is only within the veils because God is within the veils: «Knowledge of the Hour lies with Him».[229]

Therefore, the Prophet's statement, "The Hour will not come so long as there 182
is someone on the earth who says, 'There is no god but God,'" means that so long as a person remains outside of the veils, the Resurrection will be a mystery to him. But when he cuts through these veils on his journey, delighting in the presence of divine proximity, the mystery of the Resurrection will come into the open for him. It is for this reason that absolutely nobody (not even a Prophet or a Friend of God) is allowed to see God in this world. The Messenger of God only saw God in this world after he had cut through the veils on the night of the Ascension.[230] When it was said to Moses that «the Hour is coming»,[231] he asked to see God,[232] but was told, «You shall never see Me».[233] You should thus know that the Resurrection only came into the open for Muḥammad when he cut through the veils of the heavens and the earth and penetrated their regions.[234] When he settled back down in this world outside of the veils, knowledge of the Resurrection was a mystery for him just as it had been before the Ascension, yet this time it was out in the open for him, and thus beyond any veils.

A mystery is always a mystery as such, and what is out in the open is always 183
out in the open as such. Both "change" only as the states of the travelers change. God alludes to this when He says, «They ask you about the Hour: "When will it set in?" But what have you to do with its mention?»[235] In other words, "If the mystery of the Resurrection came into the open for you on the night of the Ascension, what is left for you to know and say?" To try to make do with the intellect alone in understanding these words is to have wronged oneself. Be careful, wretch, not to be led by your thoughts, rejecting or doubting these things and thereby coming to disbelieve in what God has revealed to His Prophets. Were it not for you and those blind like you, God would not have addressed the Prophet with these words: «Your people have denied it, though it is the truth».[236]

فصل ٩٥

١٨٤ فإن قلت فهل تقول إنّ كلّ عاقل فلا بدّ وأن يصل إلى الطور الذي وراء العقل كما أنّ كلّ طفل رضيع فلا بدّ وأن يصل إلى طور التمييز إذا كان وقته فاعلم أنّ الأطوار كثيرة ولا بدّ أن يصل كلّ واحد إلى طور ما وراء العقل وإن كان بعد الموت فأمّا أن يصل الكلّ إلى الأطوار الممكنة في حقّ البعض فلا يجوز لا بل الواجب الحقّ أن يصل واحد من الخلق إلى أطوار كثيرة وراء العقل وهو بعد في دنياه غير متجرّد عن جلباب قالبه ولا يُتصوّر لغيره الوصول إلى أكثرها لا في الدنيا ولا في الآخرة وهذا حقّ وصدق يشاهده العارفون ببصائرهم[1] كما يشاهد العقل أنّ العشرة أكثر من الواحد. والغالب على من لم يُقدّر له الوصول إلى الطور المشار إليه أن يصرّ على التكذيب بوجوده ويموت عليه إلى أن ينكشف عنه الغطاء كما أشار إليه القرآن في حقّ الكفّار حيث قال ﴿فَوَيْلٌ لِّلَّذِينَ كَفَرُوا مِن مَّشْهَدِ يَوْمٍ عَظِيمٍ أَسْمِعْ بِهِمْ وَأَبْصِرْ يَوْمَ يَأْتُونَنَا﴾ . ومن كان حاله التصديق بأمثال ما حكيناه طبعاً من غير تكلّف فلا بدّ وأن يكون رُزق من ذلك شيئاً.

فصل ٩٦

١٨٥ لا شكّ أنّ العاقل يستدلّ بمشاهدة كلّ بدن على نفسه كما يستدلّ بمشاهدة بدن الفرس والحمار والقرد والبعير والإنسان على تفاوت الأنفس المتصرّفة في تلك الأبدان ويسهل عليه إدراك الفرق بين الأبدان التي هي بعد في تصرّف نفوسها وبين الأبدان التي

١ (أكثرها لا في الدنيا ولا في الآخرة وهذا حقّ وصدق يشاهده العارفون ببصائرهم) في ج، ع، م؛ أ: أكثرها لأبصارهم.

Chapter 95: The Stage beyond the Intellect Is Accessible to All

184 You might ask, "Do you hold that every intelligent person will inevitably reach the stage beyond the intellect, just as every nursing child will inevitably reach the stage of discretion at its proper time?" Well, there are many stages, and every single person will inevitably reach the stage beyond the intellect, even if it is after death. But it is impossible for everyone to reach the stages that are only possible for a few. Rather, it is true and necessary that, without shedding the bodily frame he is clothed in, a person can reach many stages beyond the intellect (which are beyond this world); but it is inconceivable that others can reach most of these stages, whether in this world or in the afterlife. This is the truth that the recognizers witness by means of their insight, just as the intellect beholds the fact that ten is greater than one. For the most part, a person who is not destined to reach the stage alluded to will persistently deny its existence, and may even die in his denial, until the covering is lifted from his eyes, as is indicated by the Qur'an with reference to the disbelievers: «Woe to those who disbelieve at the witnessing of a momentous day! How well they will hear and how well they will see on the day they come to Us.»[237] Whoever naturally and unforcedly assents to the truth of the kind of thing I have related here will inevitably be granted some of it.

Chapter 96: The Intellect and the Stage beyond It

185 In beholding bodies, an intelligent person will undoubtedly infer the existence of their respective souls, just as in beholding the bodies of horses, donkeys, monkeys, camels, and humans he will infer the differences between the souls that control these bodies. And it would be easy for him to perceive the distinction between those bodies that are still under the control of their souls and those

فارقتها نفوسها بالموت فكذلك فاعلم يقيناً أنّ العقل الإنسانيّ للصور التي[1] وراءه بمنزلة البدن للنفس والعارفون الكاملون في المعرفة يستدلّون بمشاهدة قوالب العقول على تفاوت أرواح الأطوار الكامنة فيها كمون النار في الحجر ويسهل عليهم إدراك الفرق بين عقل عبيّ فيه أطوار كثيرة وبين عقل لا شيء فيه من تلك الأطوار بل هو كقالب انقطع عنه تصرّف النفس.

فصل ٩٧

١٨٦ إذا أخذ في وداعك الطمع البارد الذي يستولي على النظّار العلماء في الوقوف على حقائق جميع الأشياء تجلّى لك حقيقة قوله عليه السلام عليكم بدين العجائز. فاعلم أنّ صبح هذا الطور[2] قد تنفّس كما أنّ ابن المهد إذا صار بحيث يدرك الأوّليّات العقليّة فقد طلع له صبح عقله. واعلم أنّ مثل العلماء في طمعهم ذلك مثل رجل شهد الميزان الذي يُوزن به الذهب فطمع في أن يزن به جبلاً مثلاً وذلك محال وهذا لا يدلّ على أنّ الميزان ليس بصادق في أحواله وأحكامه.

١٨٧ واعلم أنّ العقل ميزان صحيح وأحكامه صادقة يقينيّة لا كذب فيها وهو عادل لا يُتصوّر عنه جور أبداً ومع ذلك فإذا طمع العاقل أن يزن به كلّ شيء حتّى أمور الآخرة وحقيقة النبوّة وحقائق الصفات الأزليّة كان ذلك طمعاً منه في محال.

١٨٨ واعلم أنّ هذا الطمع ينمحق قليلاً قليلاً عند إشراق نور الطور الذي وراء العقل كما أنّ نور الكواكب ينمحق قليلاً قليلاً عند طلوع الصبح. وفرق بين أن يودّعك[3] الطمع

---

١ ج،ع،م: للطور الذي. ٢ (الطور) في ج،ع،م؛أ: الصبح. ٣ (يودّعك) في ج،ع؛أ،م: يودّ عليك.

bodies whose souls have separated from them upon death. Likewise, you should know with certainty that, in relation to the forms beyond it, the human intellect is like a body in relation to a soul. For, by beholding the frame of the intellect, the recognizers who are complete in their recognition can infer the difference between the frame of the intellect and the spirits of the stages latent within it like fire's latency in a stone. Thus, it is easy for them to perceive the distinction between an intellect that has many stages within it and one that has no stages within it. Indeed, the latter is like a bodily frame from which the soul's control has been severed.

Chapter 97: Overcoming the Desire to Know

When the silly desire that has overcome the rationalist theologians to know the 186
realities of all things bids you farewell, the reality of the Prophet's words will be disclosed to you: "Follow the religion of old women."[238] That is when the dawn of this stage will break through,[239] just as when the dawn of a baby's intellect is signaled by his coming to perceive primary concepts. The rationalist theologian who desires such knowledge is like a man who sees a scale in which gold is being weighed and desires that a mountain, for example, be weighed with it. But that is impossible. However, it does not mean that the scale is untrue in what it can weigh and measure.

The intellect is a valid scale and its measurements are certain and true, with 187
no falsehood in it; and it is a just scale: it is inconceivable that it can ever be unjust. Having said that, when an intelligent person desires to weigh everything with the intellect—even the matters of the afterlife, the reality of prophecy, and the realities of the beginningless divine attributes—that is a desire for the impossible.

With the illumination of the light of the stage beyond the intellect, this 188
desire will diminish bit by bit, just as the light of the planets diminishes bit by bit at the crack of dawn. There is a distinction between a desire bidding you

اضطراراً وبين أن تودّعه أنت[١] اختياراً وهذا مزلّة القدم فخذ منها حذرك فوداع هذا الطمع ليس إلى اختيارك حتّى تودّعه متى شئت بل هو موقوف على طلوع الصبح المشار إليه وأنت مضطرّ فيه شئت أم أبيت فانمحاق هذا الطمع بالكلّيّة موقوف على إشراق نور الشمس.

فصل ٩٨

إذا صرت بحيث يقلّ الشكّ[٢] بإدراك الغوامض العقليّة من طرق البراهين الصادقة ١٨٩
القطعيّة حتّى يكون أنسك به أنس النظّار مثلاً المتبحّرين في حقائق العلوم بإدراك المسائل المظنونة فلعلّ وقتك هذا وقت الإسفار فلازم سلوك الطريق فلعلّ الشمس تطلع لك فتشاهد جمال الفطرة المذكورة في قوله تعالى ﴿فِطْرَتَ ٱللَّهِ ٱلَّتِى فَطَرَ ٱلنَّاسَ عَلَيْهَا﴾ . وحينئذ تنفكّ رقبتك من أسر الزمان والمكان ويصير تحت قدمك كلّ ما كان عليه وَضَر الحدثان وعند ذلك تبذل لك خلعة الاجتباء ويكون ذهابك إلى الله طبعاً لا تكلّف فيه كما قال عليه السلام أنا وأتقياء أمّتي براء من التكلّف.

١ (يودّعك) في ج،ع؛ أ،م: يودّ عليك. ٢ ج،ع،م: أنسك.

farewell through compulsion, and your bidding farewell to a desire through choice. This is a pitfall, so be wary of it. Indeed, bidding farewell to this desire is not your choice so that you cast it aside whenever you choose. Rather, it is dependent upon the emergence of the aforementioned dawn, which is when you are compelled, irrespective of whether you want it or reject it. Thus, the complete obliteration of this desire is dependent upon the illumination of the Sun's light.

Chapter 98: Freedom from Time and Space

When you have next to no doubt in perceiving intellectually recondite matters 189
by way of true and unequivocal proofs so that you enjoy the same kind of intimate familiarity, for example, as do the rationalist theologians (who are adept in the intellectual sciences through grasping its supposed problems), then perhaps it is time for you to set out on your journey. You must take the spiritual path, so that the Sun may rise for you and you can witness the beauty of the primordial nature mentioned in God's statement, «the primordial nature from God, upon which He originated people».[240] This is when you will be set free from the captivity of time and space, leaving every kind of worldly defilement behind you in exchange for the robe of divine selection. You will thus naturally go to God, without any difficulty, as the Prophet said, "The God-wary among my people and I are free from difficulty."[241]

فصل ۹۹

۱۹۰ إذا أُوتيت رشدك وبرزت لك الأمانة من خدرها وهي الخزانة النبويّة فنفذت ﴿مِنْ أَقْطَارِ ٱلسَّمَٰوَٰتِ وَٱلْأَرْضِ﴾ واستدار لك الزمان كهيأة يوم لا يوم بعده فحينئذ تطلع شمسك ويحسد غدك أمسك وتوجّه وجهك لفاطر السماوات والأرض وتُقبل في مناهل الحيّ القيّوم على شرب ماء الحياة وتخرق الآن من قلبك خرقًا إلى ربّك وهو طريق طيرانك إلى الأزل فلا تزال شموس الأزليّة تشرق عليك متى شئت.

۱۹۱ وأقلّ علامات الإشراق أن تتلاشى فيه إذ يستحيل للعاشق أن يصل إلى معشوقه إلّا بعد تلاشيه فلا تظنّنّ أنّ الوصول يحتمل زحمة وجودك[۱] وهذا لا يُتصوّر بيانه فإنّه يجاوز حدود العلم والعقل.

فصل ۱۰۰

۱۹۲ فهذه تسعة وتسعون فصلاً وقد أكملتها بهذا الفصل المائة ونعمت عُدّة للطالب إذا سلك طريق العلم وحصل منها مقصوده فلم تقف به همّته العليّة بل طالبته بالطلب لما وراء ذلك نفسه الزكيّة فهذا هو القدر الذي أمكنني العبارة عنه ممّا انكشف لي بعد الفراغ من تحصيل العلم.[۲]

۱ ع: زحمة الوجود. ۲ زائدة في ج: بالله وبما سواه هَذا جِنَايَ وَخِيَارُهُ فِيهِ إِذْ كُلُّ جَانٍ يَدُهُ إِلَى فِيهِ؛ زائدة في ع، م البيت فقط.

Chapter 99: Reaching God

When you are guided and the Trust[242] emerges from her domicile (namely, the Prophetic treasury) so that you penetrate «the regions of the heavens and the earth»,[243] and time moves for you as if there were no days to come, then your sun will rise and your future will be the envy of your past. You will turn your face toward the originator of the heavens and the earth,[244] drawing near to the living and self-subsisting springs and imbibing the water of life. At that moment, they will pierce your heart, opening up a way to your Lord; this is the path of your flight to the Beginningless. And the beginningless Sun will illuminate you as long as you wish. 190

The least sign of this illumination is that you will come to naught, as it is only possible for a lover to reach his beloved after his having come to naught. So do not in any way suppose that your existence can get in the way of reaching God! Any explanation of this is inconceivable, for it passes beyond the limits of knowledge and the intellect. 191

Chapter 100: An Invitation

With this hundredth chapter, I hereby complete the foregoing ninety-nine. How fine a provision it is for a seeker on the path of knowledge who obtains his goal, and whose lofty aspiration does not stop there, but whose pure soul incites him to press on in search of what is beyond this knowledge. This, then, is as much as I could convey about what was disclosed to me after I had disposed of formal learning. 192

الخاتمة

١٩٣ اعلم أنّ هذا الكتاب قليل الجدوى إلّا لمن أطال نظره في الحقائق وكثر تعبه في طلبها حتّى تبحرّ فيها ثمّ لا يكفيه ذلك إن لم يجد نفسه متشوّقة إلى شيء آخر وراء العلم والعقل فمن لم يكن في باطنه هذا التشوّق فليعاود مطالعة هذا الكتاب مرّة بعد أخرى فالغالب أنّه يظهر ذلك فيه. وإن شغلته صفة مذمومة عن التكرار في مطالعته لم يظفر به والصفات المانعة عن ذلك كثيرة والوقت لا يتّسع لشرحها فقد غشيني الملال.

١٩٤ وهذا عذري في كلّ فصل لم أوفّه حقّه في استيفاء المقدّمات التي يتعلّق النظر في ذلك الفصل بها فقد صدّني عن ذلك انجذاب القلب إلى ما هو أهمّ منه بكثير نعم وقد أمليت ذلك لجماعة لم أر بهم حاجة إلى ما وراء ذلك من المقدّمات فأوجزت القول لهذين المعنيين.

١٩٥ ومن طمع أن يحيط حقّ الإحاطة بحقائق المعاني المذكورة في هذه الفصول بمجرّد مطالعته مرّة أو مرّتين أو أكثر فقد طمع في محال إنّما وحقّ لمن يتصفّحها أن يكبّ طول الليل والنهار على ترديد هذا النظر وتكرير التأمّل فيها حتّى تعلق كلّ كلمة على خيالها بحفظه ثمّ يصير ما يتفهّمه منها بذرًا لفهمه الحقيقيّ ولا يتأتّى ذلك إلّا بكثرة الممارسة والصبر عليها على تعاقب الليل والنهار ومهما لم تكن أرض القلب سبخة فلا بدّ وأن يقع وقوع هذه المعاني وقوع البذر في الأرض الطيّبة النقيّة ويثمر له ذلك عن قريب إن أحسن القيام على تعهّده بسقي الماء في وقته وحفظه عن الآفات العارضة لأمثاله وغير ذلك فمن وجد في نفسه[1] نفرة عن الصبر على ذلك أو لم يكن بالصفة المذكورة في العلم النظريّ فليهجر مطالعة هذا الكتاب فلكلّ عمل رجال وكلّ ميسّر لما خلق له وما أنصف القائل حيث قال [وافر]

---

١ (نفسه) في ج، ع، م؛ أ: صبره.

Conclusion: On Yearning

This book is practically useless except for those who assiduously reflect on intellectual realities, exhausting themselves a great deal in their pursuit until they become adept. But such learning is not enough if they do not experience yearning for something beyond knowledge and the intellect. Therefore, those who do not have this yearning inside themselves should study this book over and over, since it is very likely that this yearning will appear within them. But if blameworthy attributes distract them from constant study of this book, they will get nothing from it. There are many attributes that will block this yearning. But there is no time to elaborate, and I am fatigued. 193

This is my excuse for any chapter whose topic I did not do justice to in terms of fully laying out those premises that pertain to the study of that chapter. I was ultimately prevented from doing so because of my heart's attraction to what is much more important. Moreover, I dictated this book to a group of people whom I did not think were in need of more premises than those I laid out. I thus condensed my statements for these two reasons. 194

To desire to properly encompass the reality of the meanings mentioned in these chapters simply by studying this book once, twice, or even more, is to desire the impossible. The only way it can properly be studied is by dedicating days and nights to reviewing it, repeatedly reflecting upon its contents until the image of each word becomes imprinted in the mind. Whatever has been understood will then become seeds for proper understanding. This can only be achieved through regular practice and patient perseverance in that practice, day and night. As long as a person's heart is not infertile, the meanings contained in this book will inevitably be planted in it as seeds are planted in rich and healthy soil, quickly bearing fruit (on condition that the seeds are maintained and cared for through being watered at the right time and protected from the kinds of damage that affect vegetation). Those who find that they are averse to this kind of patient pursuit or that they do not have the abovementioned attributes for theoretical knowledge should not study this book. After all, "There is always a right man for the job"[245] and "What each person is created for is made easy for him."[246] How fairly has the poet spoken with these words: 195

إِذَا لَمْ تَسْتَطِعْ أَمْرًا[1] فَدَعْهُ وَجَاوِزْهُ إِلَى مَا تَسْتَطِيعُ

١٩٦ فقوّة كلّ طائر على قدر حوصلته ﴿قَدْ عَلِمَ كُلُّ أُنَاسٍ مَّشْرَبَهُمْ﴾ . وهل رأيت الكنّاس قطّ يزاحم الملوك في سلطانهم[2] [متقارب]

فَكُلُّ طَرِيقٍ أَتَاهُ ٱلْفَتَى عَلَى قَدْرِ ٱلرِّجْلِ فِيهِ ٱلْخُطَى

١٩٧ والحمد لله الذي تتمّ الحاجات الصالحات[3] بنعمه وتدلّ[4] ذرّات الوجود[5] على علمه وقدرته وحكمته[6] والصلاة على رسوله الذي طلعت شمسه على الآفاق فأشرقت بنورها غاية الإشراق محمّد خير الخلائق المستمرّ على أحمد الطرائق وعلى آله مصابيح[7] الهدى وينابيع الجود والندى[8] وعلى أصحابه[9] الذين هم كالنجوم الزاهرات وأزواجه الطيّبات الطاهرات.

١ (أمرًا) في ج، ع، م؛ أ: شيئًا. ٢ زائدة في ج، ع، م: هيهات هيهات. ٣ ج: تتمّ الصالحات؛ ع، م: يتمّ الصالحات.
٤ (تدلّ) في ع؛ أ، ج، م: تتمّ. ٥ م: الموجودات. ٦ ساقطة من م. ٧ م: وأصحابه. ٨ ع: الذرى. ٩ (وعلى أصحابه) ساقطة من م.

If you cannot do something, leave it
and move on to what you can do.[247]

The strength of every bird's power accords with its given capacity: «each group knew now their drinking place».[248] Have you ever seen street cleaners contend with kings for their kingship? 196

The path that a man tries to travel
accords with the steps his feet can take.[249]

Praise be to God, who fulfills every righteous need with His blessings and whose knowledge, power, and wisdom are pointed to by the merest specks of existence. Blessings be upon His Messenger Muḥammad, the best of creatures, who unceasingly walked the most praiseworthy of paths and whose sun rose over the horizon, illuminating it entirely. And blessings be upon his progeny, lamps of guidance and springs of munificence and magnanimity; his companions, like resplendent stars; and his goodly and pure wives. 197

Notes

1 The reference here is to an eschatological hadith where the Prophet says that he will be the leader of humankind on the Day of Resurrection, and will be given "the banner of praise" (*liwā' al-ḥamd*). See al-Tirmidhī, *Sunan*, no. 3975.

2 The Abode of Peace is a reference to Paradise. See Q Yūnus 10:25 and the commentary in *Study Quran*, 551.

3 That is, God's oneness (*tawḥīd*), prophecy (*nubuwwah*), and eschatology (*maʿād*).

4 The knowledge of certainty alludes to Q Takāthur 102:5. The Qur'an outlines the process of attaining certainty in three steps. First there is the knowledge of certainty, which is followed by the eye of certainty (Q Takāthur 102:7). Last comes the truth of certainty (Q Wāqiʿah 56:95 and Ḥāqqah 69:51). The Sufis offer a number of metaphors to concretely illustrate how these ascending stages of certainty function. The most famous of these draws on imagery from Moses's meeting with God on Mt. Horeb, recounted in the Bible and the Qur'an. First, one learns of the existence of a fire (knowledge of certainty) and then sets out toward it, whereupon he sees the fire (eye of certainty). Finally, he enters into the presence of the fire and is consumed by it (truth of certainty). For more on these three modes of certainty in the Qur'an, see *Study Quran*, 929 and 1329. As ʿAyn al-Quḍāt states here, the *Essence* is primarily concerned with taking its readers to the knowledge of certainty.

5 A no longer extant Arabic theological treatise, which ʿAyn al-Quḍāt dedicated to an important Seljuq state official (for whom, see Safi, *Politics of Knowledge in Premodern Islam*, 190). In *Nāmah-hā*, 2:483, ʿAyn al-Quḍāt says that he wrote the treatise in order to refute erroneous positions in matters of creed. He also mentions this work in *Shakwā*, 40.

6 Namely, *al-salaf al-ṣāliḥūn*, a term deployed especially by Sunnis to affirm the probity of the first three generations of the Muslim community.

7 The reference is to a special kind of prayer known as the *istikhārah*. See *Study Quran*, xxxix.

8 For this hadith, see al-Ḥusaynī, *al-Tanwīr: Sharḥ al-Jāmiʿ al-ṣaghīr*, 9:388.

9 Q Āl ʿImrān 3:173.

10 Another no longer extant theological treatise in Arabic. ʿAyn al-Quḍāt makes a passing reference to it in *Shakwā*, 40.

11 Alluding to Q Takāthur 102:5. See n. 4 above.

12 In Islamic cosmology, the material realm (*ʿālam al-mulk*) and the spiritual realm (*ʿālam al-malakūt*) generically refer to two distinct "worlds." The former is characterized by bodies, visibility, and darkness (namely, the entire cosmos), and the latter by spirits, invisibility, and light (namely, the entire domain of the unseen). See Murata, *The Tao of Islam: A Sourcebook on Gender Relationships in Islamic Thought*, 60–61.

13 "Those who have arrived" (*al-wāṣilūn*) refers to people who have reached the end of the Sufi path and now find themselves perpetually in the divine presence, in union with God. The Sufis most commonly convey this notion by employing two nouns that are etymologically related to *wāṣilūn*: *wuṣūl*, which denotes "arrival," and *wiṣāl*, which denotes "union." See Chittick, *Divine Love*, index s.v. "union (*wiṣāl*)."

14 An allusion to Q Fātiḥah 1:6.

15 Q Fuṣṣilat 41:39 and Aḥqāf 46:33.

16 Q Āl ʿImrān 3:103.

17 A reference to part of a statement that goes back to al-Shiblī. See Chittick, *Divine Love*, 294.

18 I have been unable to identify the author of this poem, although it goes back to at least the late third/ninth century, since a version of the second hemistich was cited by a Sufi figure from that era at the moment of his death. See Ibn ʿAsākir, *Tārīkh madīnat Dimashq*, 66:148.

19 This "thing" is the presence of God. For a related discussion, see Rustom, *Inrushes of the Heart*, chapter 1.

20 An allusion to Q Baqarah 2:144 and 149–50.

21 In Q ʿAnkabūt 29:14, Noah is said to have lived 950 years.

22 Al-Ḥamdānī, *Dīwān Abī Firās al-Ḥamdānī bi-riwāyat Ḥusayn ibn Aḥmad ibn Khālawayh*, 2:214.

23 Cited in al-Thaʿālibī, *Yatīmat al-dahr*, 5:74.

24 Al-Mutanabbī, *Dīwān*, 479.

25 Al-Mūsawī is al-Sharīf al-Raḍī: *Dīwān*, 2:151.

26 Abū l-ʿAtāhiyah, *Dīwān*, 407.

27 By virtue of their proximity to the Prophet, ʿAyn al-Quḍāt says that a select group of individuals can come to enjoy this special kind of brotherhood with him. See Rustom, *Inrushes of the Heart*, chapter 7.

28 Al-Marzūqī, *Sharḥ Dīwān al-Ḥamāsah*, 1413.

29 Abū Nuwās, *Dīwān*, 1:127. The lines appear here in reverse order. ʿAyn al-Quḍāt's use of these verses is a fine example of how he spiritualizes a poem written in a different context and for a different purpose. The "Muḥammad" referred to in the poem by Abū Nuwās is the sixth Abbasid caliph, al-Amīn, whose first name was Muḥammad, and the

"camels" seem to refer to actual camels. Based on his prefatory remarks to the citation, ʿAyn al-Quḍāt understands these camels to refer to the Sufi concept of aspiration, and the Muḥammad in question is of course the Prophet. ʿAyn al-Quḍāt thus takes the verses to mean that, when the Sufi has entered into the presence of the Prophet (and thus proximity to him) by virtue of his high aspiration, it becomes entirely forbidden to him to direct his aspiration elsewhere, since that would naturally remove him from his state of proximity with the Prophet.

30 Felicity (*saʿādah*) specifically refers to the soul's ultimate deliverance and its permanent state of joy in the afterlife. Its antonym is misery (*shaqāwah*).

31 ʿAyn al-Quḍāt gives us here a juxtaposition between two kinds of scholars, which became standard fare in Sufi culture after his time: there are those who are given to the formal aspects of learning, but are not transformed by their knowledge—in the *Essence*, they are the "rationalists." In contrast to this group are those who put their learning into action until it transforms their entire being. They are the ones who verify the truth (*al-muḥaqqiqūn*). What this latter group verifies is the reality of God and the situation of their souls vis-à-vis God and the cosmic order.

32 Q Qaṣaṣ 28:77.

33 Q Ṣād 38:24.

34 Al-Rāghib al-Iṣfahānī, *Muḥāḍarāt al-udabāʾ wa-muḥāwarāt al-shuʿarāʾ wa-l-bulaghāʾ*, 1:426.

35 For the problem of God's knowledge of particulars, see Avicenna, *The Metaphysics of the Healing*, 283ff., and al-Ghazālī, *The Incoherence of the Philosophers*, 134–43.

36 That is, *al-qadīm*, which conveys the sense in which God is logically prior to not only time, but eternity itself.

37 An allusion to a phrase that occurs in the singular in Q Baqarah 2:108 et passim.

38 An allusion to a phrase that occurs in the singular in Q Aḥqāf 46:30.

39 See al-Ghazālī, *Moderation in Belief*, 41–45.

40 An allusion to Q Ḥāqqah 69:51. See also n. 4.

41 That is, *wājib al-wujūd*, or that which necessarily exists by virtue of itself and thus cannot not be (namely, God); see Adamson, "From the Necessary Existent to God," and Benevich, "The Necessary Existent (*wājib al-wujūd*): From Avicenna to Fakhr al-Dīn al-Rāzī."

42 This is a kind of hypothetical proposition (*al-qaḍiyyah al-sharṭiyyah*), which takes the form "if *x*, then *y*." See El-Rouayheb, *Relational Syllogisms and the History of Arabic Logic, 900–1900*, 263–64.

43 In this section, ʿAyn al-Quḍāt's exposition is in some ways indebted to the corresponding discussion in al-Ghazālī, *Moderation in Belief*, 41–45.

44 ʿAyn al-Quḍāt has in mind the well-known Sufi teaching that "none knows God but God." See Rustom, *Inrushes of the Heart*, chapter 7.

45 Q Naḥl 16:60.

46 An allusion to Q Fuṣṣilat 41:37.

47 Q Shūrā 42:11.

48 Q Fatḥ 48:6.

49 Q Ṣāffāt 37:180.

50 Q Ikhlāṣ 112:3.

51 Q Jinn 72:3.

52 This famous line goes back to al-Mutanabbī, having first made its appearance in anthologies of Arabic poetry and then been incorporated into the commentarial tradition. See al-Yāzijī, *Al-ʿArf al-ṭayyib fī Sharḥ Dīwān Abī l-Ṭayyib*, 351.

53 For an extensive treatment of the divine names written in the same generation as ʿAyn al-Quḍāt and which in many ways mirrors his overall concerns, see Samʿānī, *The Repose of the Spirits: A Sufi Commentary on the Divine Names* (the two names featured in the present context are discussed on pp. 457–61). A standard theological exposition of the divine names can be found in al-Ghazālī's popular work *The Ninety-Nine Beautiful Names of God*.

54 As will be clear at the end of the paragraph, by *min ḥayth al-ḥaqīqah* ʿAyn al-Quḍāt means "from the perspective of the intellect" (*min ḥayth al-ʿaql*).

55 Q Aʿrāf 7:180.

56 That is, the *malakūt*, which is juxtaposed with the earthly realm or *mulk*.

57 This is to say that God is called Living because all else is dead, and He is called Real because all else is unreal.

58 That is, God (*Allāh*).

59 Q Aḥzāb 33:62.

60 Which is to say that it will not become a contingent existent in actuality.

61 ʿAyn al-Quḍāt entertains the possibility here that the universe came about by virtue of God's nature, which would imply that God's existence necessarily entails ontological production (i.e., that all things come from God by virtue of a necessity in the divine nature).

62 This is a noncanonical *ḥadīth qudsī* (an extra-Qur'anic statement made by God) used by Sufis of various persuasions throughout the centuries to explain the origin and goal of the cosmos. For ʿAyn al-Quḍāt's use of this tradition, see Rustom, *Inrushes of the Heart*, chapters 5 and 10. See also Maghsoudlou, "La pensée de ʿAyn al-Quḍāt al-Hamadānī," 381n929. For the *ḥadīth qudsī* genre, see Graham, *Divine Word and Prophetic Word in Early Islam*.

63 In other words, they wrongly think that any change in particulars—all of which God knows—also spells a change in God's knowledge; this is untenable since it would introduce change in the divine nature itself.

64 Q A'rāf 7:7.

65 Q Ṭā Hā 20:98.

66 Q Ṭalāq 65:12.

67 An allusion to Q Isrā' 17:43.

68 Q Nisā' 4:116 and 136.

69 That is, the *ūlū l-albāb*. For this special class of people mentioned in the Qur'an on many occasions, see *Study Quran*, 78 and 1121.

70 Q Ṭā Hā 20:98.

71 By "sensory image" (*al-mithāl al-maḥsūs*), 'Ayn al-Quḍāt has in mind things like drawings and paintings.

72 'Ayn al-Quḍāt is alluding to an important saying in the Islamic tradition, "The incapacity to perceive is perception," to which he will return in Chapter 29.

73 Q Baqarah 2:117 and An'ām 6:101.

74 That is, the question of how the human intellect can fathom God's knowledge.

75 Al-Ṣūlī, *Akhbār al-Buḥturī*, 160.

76 Q Baqarah 2:115.

77 Q Baqarah 2:115.

78 In Arabic logic, primary concepts (*al-awwaliyyāt*) are more commonly referred to as "primary intelligibles" (*al-ma'qūlāt al-ūlā*). They refer to the basic building blocks of all logical propositions, and are thus simply givens to the mind. A common example of a primary concept is the notion that the whole is greater than the part.

79 One would not qualify since it is the basis of all numerical multiplicity and is thus not a number per se.

80 Q Baqarah 2:17.

81 For the phenomenon of friendship with God (*walāyah*) and the revered status of God's Friends (*awliyā'*) in the Sufi tradition, see Renard, *Friends of God: Images of Piety, Commitment, and Servanthood.*

82 Q 'Ankabūt 29:6.

83 Q Zumar 39:47.

84 'Ayn al-Quḍāt is employing imagery from the ritual pilgrimage to Mecca in a way that is difficult to capture in translation. The pilgrims consecrate themselves by wearing a ritual garb (*iḥrām*), which places certain restrictions on their physical person, thus allowing them to fully turn themselves to God. Throughout the rites of the pilgrimage, they chant the *talbiyah* ("At your service, O God, at your service . . ."), a response to God's invitation

to them to make the pilgrimage. The Kaaba, the Muslim direction of prayer, plays a major role in the pilgrimage as well. ʿAyn al-Quḍāt sees the Kaaba here as a symbol for the face of God. At the same time, he is alluding to Q Baqarah 2:115, which, as we have seen in §59, speaks of God's face being wherever one may turn.

85 Q Āl ʿImrān 3:20.

86 Q Āl ʿImrān 3:19.

87 Q Rūm 30:30.

88 Q Zumar 39:3.

89 Q Baqarah 2:256.

90 Q Balad 90:11.

91 The term used here is *ṭāmmāt* (derived from Q Nāziʿāt 79:34), and is a synonym for the better-known Sufi expression *shaṭaḥāt* or "ecstatic utterances" (for which, see Ernst, *Words of Ecstasy in Sufism*).

92 ʿAyn al-Quḍāt clearly thinks that at least some people who uttered these ecstatic utterances were blameworthy. At the same time, he has the highest respect for two early Sufi figures known for such statements—namely, al-Ḥallāj and Basṭāmī; see Rustom, *Inrushes of the Heart*, passim. For al-Ḥallāj and Basṭāmī's *shaṭaḥāt*, see Ernst, *Words of Ecstasy*; a recent study that focuses on Basṭāmī in this regard can be found in Keeler, "Wisdom in Controversy: Paradox and the Paradoxical in Sayings of Abū Yazīd al-Bisṭāmī (d. 234/848 or 261/875)."

93 Q Aḥqāf 46:11.

94 Q Yūnus 10:39.

95 ʿAyn al-Quḍāt is referring to a famous prayer of the Prophet in which he declares his inability to fully praise God as He should be praised. See Rustom, *Inrushes of the Heart*, chapter 5.

96 For which, see n. 98.

97 I.e., *al-ṣiddīq al-akbar* (literally "the greatest truthful one"), which is a special title of Abū Bakr.

98 This famous saying goes back to Abū Bakr. See Aḥmad al-Ghazālī, *Sawāniḥ*, 26 and 41–42, as well as Baqlī, *Sharḥ-i shaṭḥiyyāt*, 86–87.

99 This saying is not listed in the traditional Hadith sources. See al-Ḥaddād, *Takhrīj aḥādīth Iḥyāʾ ʿulūm al-dīn*, 4:1758, and Forouzanfar, *Aḥādīth-i Mathnawī*, 231.

100 For the background to the problem of the relationship between God's essence and attributes, to which ʿAyn al-Quḍāt will now turn more fully, see al-Ghazālī, *Moderation in Belief*, 129–55.

101 Q Raḥmān 55:26.

102 The standard Hadith sources all have "poet" or "poets" in place of "Arabs." See, for example, al-Bukhārī, *Ṣaḥīḥ*, no. 6568.

103 For ʿAyn al-Quḍāt's refutation of dualism, see Rustom, "Devil's Advocate," 74–75, and Rustom, *Inrushes of the Heart*, chapter 4.

104 Q Nūr 24:45.

105 Q Insān 76:30.

106 Q Āl ʿImrān 3:26.

107 Q Shūrā 42:11.

108 Q Mu'minūn 23:80.

109 Q Mu'minūn 23:80.

110 Q Shūrā 42:11.

111 Abū Dāwūd, *Sunan*, no. 5077.

112 Q Mā'idah 5:120.

113 Meaning the two would in fact be one.

114 If this were the case, then the two necessary beings would still stand in need of something above them.

115 See, for example, the discussion in al-Ghazālī, *Incoherence of the Philosophers*, 92ff.

116 On the problem of the world's eternity and its defense, see Avicenna, *al-Ishārāt wa-l-tanbīhāt*, 3:57–117. On the problem of the world's eternity and its refutation, see al-Ghazālī, *Incoherence of the Philosophers*, 12–54. See also Davidson, *Proofs for Eternity, Creation, and the Existence of God in Medieval Islamic and Jewish Philosophy*.

117 The referent in question is a well-known Islamic philosophical principle (inspired by but distinct from a Neoplatonic doctrine), which states that "Only one emanates from the One." In Islamic philosophy, the one that emanates from God is the First Intellect (*al-ʿaql al-awwal*), the first of ten intellects, which emanate successively until there arises the realm of matter. See Avicenna, *Metaphysics of the Healing*, 328–30 (defense) and al-Ghazālī, *Incoherence of the Philosophers*, 65ff. (rejection), as well as the helpful discussions in Amin, "'From the One, Only One Proceeds': The Post-Classical Reception of a Key Principle of Avicenna's Metaphysics," and Dadikhuda, "Rule of the One: Avicenna, Bahmanyār, and al-Rāzī on the Argument from the *Mubāḥathāt*."

118 Q Ḥadīd 57:25.

119 Q Rūm 30:27.

120 Q Qaṣaṣ 28:88.

121 For this tradition and its attribution and uses in Islamic philosophical and mystical literature, see Rustom, "Psychology, Eschatology, and Imagination in Mullā Ṣadrā Shīrāzī's Commentary on the *Ḥadīth* of Awakening," 10nn1–2.

122 Q Qaṣaṣ 28:88.

123 Q Ghāfir 40:16.

124 In the language of Islamic philosophy, things are contingent in themselves, and necessary through others. This stands in stark contrast to God, the Necessary Existent, who is simply necessary in Himself and is the ground of all contingent, existential necessity.

125 ʿAyn al-Quḍāt is being rhetorical here, since a thing's existing through itself is always impossible.

126 Namely, earth, air, fire, and water.

127 For the First Intellect, see n. 117. ʿAyn al-Quḍāt is not against the notion of existence being coextensive (*taswīq al-wujūd*) per se. What he is opposed to is that anything should be seen as coextensive with God, even if the coextensivity in question entails God's logical priority (which is surely the case with the view he is refuting here). As ʿAyn al-Quḍāt will go on to argue in §116, God is coextensive with everything, but nothing is coextensive with Him; and He is "with" everything, but nothing is "with" Him.

128 These two sentences (1) allude to a famous Prophetic saying recorded in al-Bukhārī, *Ṣaḥīḥ*, no. 3227, which ʿAyn al-Quḍāt quotes in §108, and (2) a qualification of this hadith attributed to al-Junayd; see Chittick, *The Self-Disclosure of God: Principles of Ibn al-ʿArabī's Cosmology*, 70, 180, and 182.

129 That is, if we look at any one moment in time *x*, that moment can be split up into many sub-moments (*y*). This means that the specific relationship between the sun and the earth will be different at every *y*; thus, no two rays in *x* will ever be the same.

130 In other words, the various relationships in question obtain amid the sub-moments that run across any given moment in time.

131 Q Zumar 39:68.

132 Ṣād 38:24.

133 "Withness" translates *maʿiyyah*, which is a concrete synonym for *taswīq al-wujūd* (see n. 127).

134 Informing this position is ʿAyn al-Quḍāt's disagreement with the view that God is the "causer of causes" (*musabbib al-asbāb*), since, for him, God is the only real cause. See Izutsu, "Mysticism and the Linguistic Problem of Equivocation," 167–68. Cf. Maghsoudlou, "La pensée de ʿAyn al-Quḍāt al-Hamadānī," 245–65.

135 The two types of proximity being referred to are proximity in time and space, and intelligible proximity. See §§143–44.

136 Here, ʿAyn al-Quḍāt subscribes to the position that sees the First Intellect as the first descent from the Godhead, since in Islamic philosophy the Intellects are identified with angels. See Corbin, *Avicenna and the Visionary Recital.*

137 Q Nabaʾ 78:38.

138 For the complex structure of classical Islamic cosmology, see Nasr, *An Introduction to Islamic Cosmological Doctrines.*

139 In Islamic cosmological teachings, God's Throne (*ʿarsh*) is in the ninth heaven, and situated below it is His Footstool (*kursī*) in the eighth. For more on the Throne and the Footstool, see *Study Quran*, 111, and Murata, *Tao of Islam*, 156.

140 See n. 99.

141 Q Fāṭir 35:41.

142 Q Baqarah 2:115.

143 Masters of the heart (*arbāb al-qulūb*) is a synonym for the recognizers.

144 Q ʿAnkabūt 29:49.

145 Q Āl ʿImrān 3:18.

146 Q Kahf 18:65.

147 That is, *al-ʿilm al-ladunī*, which is contrasted with *al-ʿilm al-muktasab* or knowledge that is acquired by human effort.

148 Q Kahf 18:70. The meeting between Moses and the mysterious Khidr (whose image is central to Sufi teachings) is recounted in Q Kahf 18:65–82. In Kahf 18:65, Khidr is singled out as having that God-given knowledge which ʿAyn al-Quḍāt is discussing in this chapter.

149 These actions refer to three things Khidr does that perplex Moses, leading him to question Khidr about each of them. See *Study Quran*, 751–56.

150 Moses's last question served as the catalyst for Khidr's parting with him.

151 Q Kahf 18:78.

152 The allusion here is to Khidr's statement to Moses in Q Kahf 18:70, which was cited several lines earlier.

153 Cf. al-ʿAsqalānī, *Fatḥ al-Bārī fī sharḥ Ṣaḥīḥ al-Bukhārī*, 6:337.

154 This is an allusion to a famous hadith to the effect that the knowers (*al-ʿulamāʾ*) are the ones who inherit from the Prophets. See Ibn Mājah, *Sunan*, no. 228. In *Nāmah-hā*, 1:47, ʿAyn al-Quḍāt understands the knowers in this tradition to be a reference to spiritual masters in particular.

155 Q ʿAlaq 96:3–5.

156 Q Baqarah 2:282.

157 Q Naḥl 16:128.

158 Q ʿAnkabūt 29:43.

159 Q ʿAnkabūt 29:43.

160 See Aḥmad al-Ghazālī, *Sawāniḥ*, 3–4.

161 Cf. al-Sīrjānī, *Sufism, Black and White: A Critical Edition of Kitāb al-Bayāḍ wa-l-Sawād of Abū l-Ḥasan al-Sīrjānī (d. ca. 470/1077)*, 30.

162 ʿAyn al-Quḍāt distinguishes between the first generations of rationalist theologians who discussed technical terms in their books and the later generations, the most eminent of the latter category in his eyes being al-Ghazālī. ʿAyn al-Quḍāt's position is informed by the practical fact that the technical expressions employed in later books of rational theology are more likely to be precise and refined, drawing as they do on the cumulative tradition that preceded them.

163 Muslim, *Ṣaḥīḥ*, no. 7015.

164 For an extended analysis of ʿAyn al-Quḍāt's teachings on the master-disciple relationship, see Rustom, *Inrushes of the Heart*, chapter 6.

165 An allusion to Q Naḥl 16:97.

166 Al-Qurṭubī, *Bahjat al-majālis wa-uns al-mujālis*, 1:341.

167 That is, Chapters 64–71.

168 See also the helpful discussion in al-Ghazālī, *Moderation in Belief*, 41–45.

169 Al-ʿAjlūnī, *Kashf al-khafā'*, 315 and 704. It is important to note that in the *Essence*, ʿAyn al-Quḍāt will occasionally use the term "spirits" (*arwāḥ*) as a synonym for souls (*nufūs*). Elsewhere, he explains that the "subtle human reality" (*laṭīfat ḥaqīqat al-insāniyyah*) consists of three distinct levels: soul (*nafs*), heart (*qalb*), and spirit (*rūḥ*); see Rustom, *Inrushes of the Heart*, chapter 5. ʿAyn al-Quḍāt departs in this regard from al-Ghazālī, who sees human personhood as comprised of four levels (namely, spirit, heart, soul, and intellect); see al-Ghazālī, *The Marvels of the Heart*, chapter 1.

170 The wording, "cheap inventory," is an allusion to Q Yūsuf 12:88.

171 This hadith is considered to be a *ḥadīth qudsī* by many Sufis, although it is not found in the standard sources. See the inquiry in Nasr, "The Heart of the Faithful Is the Throne of the All-Merciful."

172 For these levels of certainty, see n. 4.

173 Q Ṭalāq 65:1.

174 For the eschatological picture that ʿAyn al-Quḍāt takes for granted in this and the following related chapters, see Rustom, "Qur'anic Eschatology."

175 Al-Bukhārī, *Ṣaḥīḥ*, no. 4708.

176 Q Aʿrāf 7:54 and Yūnus 10:3.

177 An allusion to Q Ibrāhīm 14:48.

178 ʿAyn al-Quḍāt is responding to Avicenna's position concerning the manner in which a body's specific constitution acts as an accidental cause for a particular soul's emergence into the sublunary realm. See Maghsoudlou, "La pensée de ʿAyn al-Quḍāt al-Hamadānī," 307.

179 In the following chapter, ʿAyn al-Quḍāt will clarify this statement.

180 Which is to say, after the death of the body.

181 By "spirits" here ʿAyn al-Quḍāt intends what he has been calling "souls" throughout the book. See also n. 169.

182 *Sayyid al-awwalīn wa-l-ākhirīn* is a famous title of the Prophet.

183 ʿAyn al-Quḍāt is referring to the hadith that he cited in §140.

184 Q Ṣād 38:75.

185 ʿAyn al-Quḍāt cites this hadith in *Tamhīdāt*, 323; a slight variant is in al-Ṭabarānī, *al-Muʿjam al-kabīr*, 12:430. Another popular version can be found in al-Bukhārī, *Ṣaḥīḥ*, no. 6299.

186 This hadith is untraced, but cf. the related discussion in ʿAyn al-Quḍāt, *Tamhīdāt*, 323.

187 For ʿAyn al-Quḍāt's appropriation of this Avicennan position, see the fine discussion in Maghsoudlou, "La pensée de ʿAyn al-Quḍāt al-Hamadānī," 311–12.

188 Muslim, *Ṣaḥīḥ*, no. 6877.

189 Another title of the Prophet Muḥammad.

190 Q Baqarah 2:60.

191 Q Māʾidah 5:54.

192 Q Aʿrāf 7:172.

193 Q Aʿrāf 7:172.

194 This statement is not to be found in al-Anṣārī's extant writings. Cf. the report of his interpretation of this verse in Maybudī, *The Unveiling of the Mysteries and the Provision of the Pious*, 213.

195 Ibn al-Muʿtazz, *Dīwān*, 247.

196 "Invincible realm" translates *jabarūt*, which is the highest spiritual world.

197 Q Āl ʿImrān 3:152.

198 Q Anʿām 6:52.

199 Namely, a spiritual master.

200 Dedication to the spiritual path under the guidance of a master requires one to become nothing, hence the reference here to the "state of lowliness" (*ḥāl al-dhull*). This is why the realized Sufi is called a *faqīr*, or one who is poor. For the important role of the *faqīr* in ʿAyn al-Quḍāt's writings, see Rustom, *Inrushes of the Heart*, chapter 10.

201 Q Fātiḥah 1:6.

202 Q Ṣāffāt 37:99.

203 Q Nisāʾ 4:125.

204 Q Fuṣṣilat 41:47. For the Hour (*al-sāʿah*) in Islamic eschatological teachings, see Rustom, "Qur'anic Eschatology."

205 Q Baqarah 2:3 and conclusion of verse 4.

206 Q Zumar 39:22.

207 A well-known Arabic proverb.

208 Cf. Matthew 7:7 and Luke 11:9. See al-Ghazālī, *Iḥyā' 'ulūm al-dīn*, 8:459, where Abū l-Dardā' attributes this saying to the Prophet Muḥammad. Among other Sufi texts, a shorter version is anonymously cited in Sam'ānī, *Repose of the Spirits*, 210 and 342.

209 This saying is not found in the standard Hadith collections, and is attributed to various individuals in the Islamic tradition. After the Prophet, Abū l-Dardā' is one of the earliest figures to whom a version of this saying is ascribed. See Ibn Abī Shaybah, *al-Muṣannaf*, 10:16.

210 Al-Ḥaddād, *Takhrīj*, 1:112–13. 'Ayn al-Quḍāt discusses this tradition in *Nāmah-hā*, 2:292–93.

211 Cf. al-Tustarī, *Tafsīr al-Tustarī*, 143.

212 Q Yūnus 10:48.

213 Q Naḥl 16:77.

214 Q Yūnus 10:48.

215 Q Zukhruf 43:85.

216 Cf. Aḥmad, *Musnad*, no. 14041.

217 Q Qamar 54:55. The allusion before the verse is to a hadith: "Whoever dies, his Resurrection has already happened." See 'Ayn al-Quḍāt, *Tamhīdāt*, 177 and 322. On occasion, the saying is attributed to Ziyād al-Namarī. See al-Iṣfahānī, *Ḥilyat al-awliyā'*, 6:268.

218 Q Sajdah 32:12. This verse relates the debased state of, and the statements made by, the guilty sinners at the time of their individual deaths. See *Study Quran*, 1012.

219 Al-Bazzār, *al-Baḥr al-zakhkhār*, 15:391.

220 Al-Bukhārī, *Ṣaḥīḥ*, no. 4986 (with a slight variation). Since 'Ayn al-Quḍāt is saying that the Resurrection happens for any person who is "with" God, this equally applies to those who have undergone physical death, as well as those who have died to themselves, been resurrected in the divine presence, and are with God even during their earthly lives, as was the case with the Prophet. 'Ayn al-Quḍāt's understanding of these two types of death is discussed in Rustom, *Inrushes of the Heart*, chapter 5. See also Lewisohn, "In Quest of Annihilation: Imaginalization and Mystical Death in the *Tamhīdāt* of 'Ayn al-Quḍāt Hamadhānī."

221 Q Zalzalah 99:1.

222 An allusion to Q Inshiqāq 84:1.

223 An allusion to Q Infiṭār 82:2.

224 An allusion to Q Takwīr 81:1.

225 An allusion to Q Takwīr 81:3.

226 An allusion to Q Takwīr 81:4.

227 Q 'Ādiyāt 100:9–10.

228 Q Ibrāhīm 14:48.

229 Q Zukhruf 43:85.

230 That is, *laylat al-miʿrāj*, which refers to the Prophet's famous ascension to the divine presence. See *Study Quran*, 694–95 and 1290–92.

231 Q Ḥajj 22:7.

232 An allusion to Q Aʿrāf 7:143.

233 Q Aʿrāf 7:143.

234 An allusion to Q Raḥmān 55:33, which ʿAyn al-Quḍāt will cite toward the end of the book.

235 Q Nāziʿāt 79:42–43.

236 Q Anʿām 6:66.

237 Q Maryam 19:37–38.

238 Al-Ḥaddād, *Takhrīj*, 4:1590–91. ʿAyn al-Quḍāt discusses this saying in *Tamhīdāt*, 111.

239 A subtle reference to Q Takwīr 81:8.

240 Q Rūm 30:30.

241 Cf. al-Bukhārī, *Ṣaḥīḥ*, no. 7379.

242 A discussion on the significance of the Trust (*amānah*), which is mentioned in Q Aḥzāb 33:72, can be found in *Study Quran*, 1040–41. For ʿAyn al-Quḍāt's understanding of the Trust and its relationship to the pact (*mīthāq*) between God and humankind (mentioned in Q Aʿrāf 7:172), see Rustom, *Inrushes of the Heart*, chapter 8.

243 Q Raḥmān 55:33.

244 An allusion to Q Anʿām 6:79.

245 Part of an Arabic proverb, the full version of which is, "There is always a right man for the job, and there is always a right word for the occasion."

246 Al-Bukhārī, *Ṣaḥīḥ*, no. 7646.

247 Cited in Ibn ʿAbd Rabbihi, *al-ʿIqd al-farīd*, 3:406.

248 Q Baqarah 2:60.

249 This poem is attributed to al-Mutanabbī. See Yāqūt al-Ḥamawī, *Muʿjam al-buldān*, 3:109.

Glossary of Names

ʿAbd Allāh al-Anṣārī (d. 481/1089) mystic and theologian whose intimate prayers in Persian are particularly popular in Sufism and Islamic oral culture.

ʿAbd al-Ghanī al-Nābulusī (d. 1143/1731) important Arab theologian and Sufi follower of Ibn al-ʿArabī.

Abū l-ʿAbbās ibn Surayj (d. 306/918) jurist in the early Shāfiʿī school of Islamic law responsible for its widespread popularity.

Abū Bakr (r. 11–13/632–34) father-in-law and close friend of the Prophet who became the first caliph of Islam.

Abū l-Dardāʾ (d. 32/653) companion of the Prophet best remembered for his renunciation of the world and dedication to worship.

Abū Ḥāmid al-Ghazālī (d. 505/1111) one of the most revered authors in Islam in the fields of legal theory, philosophy, theology, and mysticism.

Abū Nuwās (d. 200/815) court poet of the early Abbasid era generally seen as the popularizer of the wine song.

Abū Firās al-Ḥamdānī (d. 357/968) member of the ruling family of the Hamdanid dynasty and poetic rival of al-Mutanabbī.

Abū l-ʿAtāhiyah (d. 211/826) contemplative bard whose poetry deals with the themes of renunciation and asceticism.

Abū Jahl (d. 2/624) one of the Prophet's main enemies, killed at the battle of Badr.

Aḥmad al-Ghazālī (d. 520/1126) younger brother of Abū Ḥāmid al-Ghazālī, spiritual master of ʿAyn al-Quḍāt, and author of profound works on love and beauty.

al-Amīn, Muḥammad (r. 193–98/809–13) son of Hārūn al-Rashīd and Abbasid caliph who was deposed and killed by his half brother al-Maʾmūn.

Avicenna (d. 428/1037) highly innovative philosopher and towering figure in the Islamic intellectual tradition whose writings were also influential in the medieval Latin West.

Barakah Hamadānī (d. 520/1126) early spiritual teacher of ʿAyn al-Quḍāt distinguished by his charismatic personality, sagacity, and clairvoyant powers.

Basṭāmī, Abū Yazīd (d. ca. 260/874) widely venerated Sufi figure legendary for his ecstatic utterances and esoteric knowledge.

Dargazīnī, Abū l-Qāsim (d. 527/1133) ruthless Seljuq vizier responsible for the execution of ʿAyn al-Quḍāt.

Fakhr al-Dīn al-Rāzī (d. 606/1210) preeminent philosopher and theologian whose writings include a voluminous and penetrating commentary on the Qurʾan.

al-Fārābī, Abū Naṣr (d. 339/950) founder of Neoplatonic Islamic philosophy who wrote widely on a variety of subjects, from metaphysics and political theory to music and logic.

al-Ḥallāj (d. 309/922) celebrated mystic and martyr known for his ecstatic utterance "I am the Real!" and his defense of Satan's monotheism.

Hārūn al-Rashīd (r. 170–93/787–809) fifth Abbasid caliph, whose reign is characterized as a golden age of prosperity and imperial expansion.

Hülegü Khan (d. 663/1265) grandson of Genghis Khan and founder of the Ilkhanid dynasty who patronized Naṣīr al-Dīn al-Ṭūsī's observatory in Marāghah.

Ibn al-ʿArabī (d. 638/1240) profound Andalusian mystic whose teachings left an indelible mark upon the later Islamic intellectual tradition from North Africa to China.

Ibn al-Muʿtazz (d. 296/908) poet and Abbasid caliph who was murdered after ruling for a day.

Ismailism significant branch of Shīʿī Islam, which played an important role in the development of classical Islamic thought.

al-Junayd (d. 298/910) universally respected early Sufi master who trained a number of illustrious figures, such as al-Shiblī and al-Ḥallāj.

Labīd ibn Rabīʿah (d. ca. 40/660) poet of the Kilab tribe and one of the composers of the classics of early Arabic poetry known as the *Muʿallaqāt* or the "Suspended" Odes.

Maḥmūd II (d. 525/1131) Seljuq sultan who ordered ʿAyn al-Quḍāt's execution.

al-Mutanabbī (d. 354/965) itinerant poet noted for his panegyric verse and innovations in the qasida genre.

Naṣīr al-Dīn al-Ṭūsī (d. 672/1274) Shīʿī polymath who authored widely acclaimed works in philosophy, logic, theology, political theory, astronomy, and ethics.

Seljuqs major Turko-Persian Sunni empire that came to prominence during the Abbasid era. They were bitter enemies of Ismailism. At the peak of their power during the fifth–sixth/eleventh–twelfth centuries, they ruled over a large area of Asia from Anatolia, Syria, and the Hejaz in the west to Transoxania in the east.

Sahl al-Tustarī (d. 283/896) influential early Sufi master and esoteric commentator on the Qur'an.

al-Shāfiʿī, Muḥammad ibn Idrīs (d. 204/820) eponymous founder of the Shāfiʿī legal school and pioneer of Islamic legal theory.

al-Sharīf al-Raḍī (d. 406/1015) Shīʿī nobleman from Baghdad skilled in Arabic rhetoric and panegyric poetry.

Shihāb al-Dīn al-Suhrawardī (d. 587/1191) philosopher and mystic of the first magnitude and founder of the School of Illumination who was put to death at the order of Saladin.

al-Shiblī, Abū Bakr (d. 334/946) close friend of al-Ḥallāj and disciple of al-Junayd admired by Sufis for his single-minded devotion to God.

ʿUmar ibn Sahlān al-Sāwī (d. after 537/1143) key logician and philosopher known for his reevaluation of Aristotle's *Organon*.

ʿUmar Khayyām (d. ca. 517/1124) poet, philosopher, and mathematician whose quatrains were well received in the literary circles of nineteenth-century England.

Ziyād al-Namarī (d. ca. 279/892) Basran scholar of Prophetic traditions who taught some famous masters of Hadith.

Bibliography

Abū l-ʿAtāhiyah. *Dīwān*. Edited by Karam al-Bustānī. Beirut: Dār Bayrūt, 1986.

Adamson, Peter. "From the Necessary Existent to God." In *Interpreting Avicenna: Critical Essays*, edited by Peter Adamson, 170–89. Cambridge: Cambridge University Press, 2013.

———. *A History of Philosophy without Any Gaps*. Vol. 3, *Philosophy in the Islamic World*. Oxford: Oxford University Press, 2016.

Abū Dāwūd. *Sunan*. Vol. 5 of *Jamʿ jawāmiʿ al-aḥādīth*.

Abū Nuwās. *Dīwān*. Edited by Ewald Wagner (vols. 1–3 and 5) and Gregor Schoeler (vol. 4). 5 vols. 2nd ed. Stuttgart: Franz Steiner, 2003–06.

Aḥmad ibn Ḥanbal. *Musnad*. Vol. 12 of *Jamʿ jawāmiʿ al-aḥādīth*.

Aladdin, Bakri. "Aspects of Mystical Hermeneutics and the Theory of the Oneness of Being (*waḥdat al-wujūd*) in the Work of ʿAbd al-Ghanī al-Nābulusī (1143/1731)." In *The Spirit and the Letter: Approaches to the Esoteric Interpretation of the Qur'an*, edited by Annabel Keeler and Sajjad Rizvi, 395–413. Oxford: Oxford University Press in association with The Institute of Ismaili Studies, 2016.

Al-ʿAjlūnī, Ismāʿīl ibn Muḥammad. *Kashf al-khafāʾ*. 2 vols. Cairo: Maktabat al-Qudsī, 1932–33.

Ali, Mukhtar H. *The Horizons of Being: The Metaphysics of Ibn al-ʿArabī in the Muqaddimat al-Qayṣarī*. Leiden: Brill, 2020.

Amin, Wahid. "'From the One, Only One Proceeds': The Post-Classical Reception of a Key Principle of Avicenna's Metaphysics." *Oriens* 48, nos. 1–2 (2020): 123–55.

Aminrazavi, Mehdi. *The Wine of Wisdom: The Life, Poetry and Philosophy of Omar Khayyam*. Oxford: Oneworld, 2005.

Andani, Khalil. "The Merits of the Bāṭiniyya: Al-Ghazālī's Appropriation of Ismaʿili Cosmology." *Oxford Journal of Islamic Studies* 29, no. 2 (2018): 189–229.

Arif, Hassan. "Defending Sufi Metaphysics in British India: Faḍl-i Ḥaqq Khayrābādī's (d. 1277/1861) Treatise on *waḥdat al-wujūd*." PhD diss., McGill University, Institute of Islamic Studies, in progress.

Asghari, Seyed Amir Hossein. "Ontology and Cosmology of the *ʿaql* in Ṣadrā's Commentary on *Uṣūl al-kāfī*." *Journal of Shīʿa Islamic Studies* 10, no. 2 (2017): 157–82.

Al-ʿAsqalānī, Ibn Ḥajar. *Fatḥ al-Bārī fī sharḥ Ṣaḥīḥ al-Bukhārī*. Edited by ʿAbd al-Raḥmān Muḥammad. 14 vols. Beirut: Dār al-Turāth al-ʿArabī, 1985.

Avicenna. *Ibn Sīnā on Mysticism: Remarks and Admonitions*. Part 4. Translated by Shams Inati. London: Kegan Paul, 1996.

———. *Al-Ishārāt wa-l-tanbīhāt*. Edited by Sulaymān Dunyā. 4 vols. Cairo: Dār al-Maʿārif, 1957–60.

———. *The Metaphysics of the Healing*. Translated by Michael Marmura. Provo, UT: Brigham Young University Press, 2005.

ʿAyn al-Quḍāt. *Nāmah-hā*. Edited by ʿAlī Naqī Munzawī (vols. 1–3) and ʿAfīf ʿUsayrān (vols. 1–2). 3 vols. Tehran: Intishārāt-i Asāṭīr, 1998.

———. *Shakwā l-gharīb*. In part 3 of ʿAyn al-Quḍāt, *Muṣannafāt-i ʿAyn al-Quḍāt*, 1–51. Edited by ʿAfīf ʿUsayrān. Tehran: Intishārāt-i Dānishgāh-i Tihrān, 1962. English translation by A. J. Arberry as *A Sufi Martyr: The "Apologia" of ʿAin al-Quḍāt al-Hamadhānī*. London: Kegan Paul, 1969.

———. *Tamhīdāt*. Edited by ʿAfīf ʿUsayrān. Reprint, Tehran: Intishārāt-i Manūchihrī, 1994.

———. *Zubdat al-ḥaqāʾiq*. In part 1 of ʿAyn al-Quḍāt, *Muṣannafāt-i ʿAyn al-Quḍāt*, 1–131. English translation by Omar Jah as *The Zubdat al-Ḥaqāʾiq of ʿAyn al-Quḍāh al-Hamadānī*. Kuala Lumpur: ISTAC, 2000. French translation by Salimeh Maghsoudlou as "La quintessence des vérités." In Maghsoudlou, *La pensée de ʿAyn al-Qudāt al-Hamadānī*, 367–444.

Baqlī, Ruzbihān. *Sharḥ-i shaṭḥiyyāt*. Edited by Henry Corbin. Reprint, Tehran: Intishārāt-i Ṭahūrī, 2010.

Al-Bazzār, Abū Bakr. *Al-Baḥr al-zakhkhār*. Edited by Maḥfūẓ al-Raḥmān Zayn al-Dīn et al. 20 vols. Medina: Maktabat al-ʿUlūm wa-l-Ḥikam, 2006.

Benevich, Fedor. "The Necessary Existent (*wājib al-wujūd*): From Avicenna to Fakhr al-Dīn al-Rāzī." In *Philosophical Theology in Islam: Later Ashʿarism East and West*, edited by Ayman Shihadeh and Jan Thiele, 123–55. Leiden: Brill, 2020.

Boylston, Nicholas. "Islam from the Inside Out: ʿAyn al-Quḍāt Hamadānī's Reconception of Islam as Vector." *Oxford Journal of Islamic Studies* 32, no. 2 (2021): 161–202.

———. "Writing the Kaleidoscope of Reality, the Significance of Diversity in 6th/12th Century Persian Metaphysical Literature: Sanāʾī, ʿAyn al-Quḍāt and ʿAṭṭār." PhD diss., Georgetown University, 2017.

Al-Bukhārī. *Ṣaḥīḥ*. Vol. 2 of *Jamʿ jawāmiʿ al-aḥādīth*.

Chittick, William. *Divine Love: Islamic Literature and the Path to God*. New Haven, CT: Yale University Press, 2013.

———. *In Search of the Lost Heart: Explorations in Islamic Thought*. Edited by Mohammed Rustom, Atif Khalil, and Kazuyo Murata. Albany, NY: SUNY Press, 2012.

———. *The Self-Disclosure of God: Principles of Ibn al-ʿArabī's Cosmology*. Albany, NY: SUNY Press, 1998.

———. *The Sufi Path of Knowledge: Ibn al-ʿArabī's Metaphysics of Imagination*. Albany, NY: SUNY Press, 1989.

———. "The Translator's Dilemmas." In Chittick, *Self-Disclosure of God*, xxxv–xl.

Coomaraswamy, Ananda. *Time and Eternity*. New Delhi: Munshiran Manoharlal Publishers, 2001.

Corbin, Henry. *Avicenna and the Visionary Recital*. Translated by Willard Trask. Irving, TX: Spring Publications, 1980.

Dadikhuda, Davlat. "Rule of the One: Avicenna, Bahmanyār, and al-Rāzī on the Argument from the *Mubāḥathāt*." *Nazariyat* 6, no. 2 (2020): 69–97.

Davidson, Herbert. *Proofs for Eternity, Creation, and the Existence of God in Medieval Islamic and Jewish Philosophy*. New York: Oxford University Press, 1989.

Ebstein, Michael. "The Human Intellect: Liberation or Limitation? Some Notes on *ʿAql* in Classical Islamic Mysticism." *Journal of Sufi Studies* 8, no. 2 (2019): 198–233.

El-Rouayheb, Khaled. *Relational Syllogisms and the History of Arabic Logic, 900–1900*. Leiden: Brill, 2010.

Encyclopaedia Islamica. Edited by Wilferd Madelung and Farhad Daftary. Leiden: Brill in association with The Institute of Ismaili Studies, 2008–.

Encyclopaedia of Islam. Edited by Gudrun Krämer, Denis Matringe, John Nawas, and Everett Rowson. 3rd ed. Leiden: Brill Online, 2014–.

Ernst, Carl. *Words of Ecstasy in Sufism*. Albany, NY: SUNY Press, 1985.

Faruque, Muhammad. "Sufi Metaphysical Literature." In *Brill Handbook of Sufi Literature*, edited by Alexander Knysh and Bilal Orfali. Leiden: Brill, forthcoming.

Forouzanfar, Badiozzaman, ed. *Aḥādīth-i Mathnawī*. Tehran: Intishārāt-i Dānishgāh-i Tihrān, 1955.

Al-Ghazālī, Abū Ḥāmid Muḥammad. *The Condemnation of Pride and Self-Admiration*. Translated by Mohammed Rustom. Cambridge: The Islamic Texts Society, 2018.

———. *Iḥyāʾ ʿulūm al-dīn*. 10 vols. Jeddah: Dār al-Minhāj, 2011.

———. *The Incoherence of the Philosophers*. 2nd ed. Translated by Michael Marmura. Provo, UT: Brigham Young University Press, 2000.

———. *Maqāṣid al-falāsifah*. Edited by Muḥyī al-Dīn al-Kurdī. Cairo: al-Maṭbaʿah al-Maḥmūdiyyah, 1936.

———. *The Marvels of the Heart*. Translated by Walter Skellie. Louisville, KY: Fons Vitae, 2010.

———. *Moderation in Belief*. Translated by Aladdin Yaqub. Chicago: University of Chicago Press, 2013.

———. *Al-Munqidh min al-ḍalāl*. Edited by Kāmil ʿAyyād and Jamīl Ṣalībā. Beirut: Dār al-Andalus, 1967.

———. *The Niche of Lights*. Translated by David Buchman. Provo, UT: Brigham Young University Press, 1998.

———. *The Ninety-Nine Beautiful Names of God*. Translated by David Burrell and Nazih Daher. Cambridge, UK: The Islamic Texts Society, 1992.

Al-Ghazālī, Aḥmad. *Mukātabāt-i Khwājah Aḥmad Ghazālī bā ʿAyn al-Quḍāt Hamadānī*. Edited by Nasrollah Pourjavady. Tehran: Khānaqāh-i Niʿmatullāhī, 1977.

———. *Sawāniḥ*. Edited by Nasrollah Pourjavady. Tehran: Intishārāt-i Bunyād-i Farhang-i Īrān, 1980.

Graham, William. *Divine Word and Prophetic Word in Early Islam*. The Hague: Mouton, 1977.

Gramlich, Richard. *Alte Vorbilder des Sufitums*. 2 vols. Wiesbaden, Germany: Harrassowitz, 1995–96.

Griffel, Frank. *The Formation of Post-Classical Philosophy in Islam*. New York: Oxford University Press, 2021.

———. *Al-Ghazālī's Philosophical Theology*. New York: Oxford University Press, 2009.

Al-Ḥaddād, ʿAbd Allāh ibn Muḥammad, ed. *Takhrīj aḥādīth Iḥyāʾ ʿulūm al-dīn*. 7 vols. Riyadh: Dār al-ʿĀṣimah, 1987.

Halman, Hugh Talat. *Where the Two Seas Meet: The Qurʾānic Story of al-Khiḍr and Moses in Sufi Commentaries as a Model for Spiritual Guidance*. Louisville, KY: Fons Vitae, 2013.

Al-Ḥamdānī, Abū Firās. *Dīwān Abī Firās al-Ḥamdānī bi-riwāyat Ḥusayn ibn Aḥmad ibn Khālawayh*. Edited by Sāmī Dahhān. 3 vols. printed in 2. Beirut: al-Maʿhad al-Faransī bi-Dimashq li-l-Dirāsāt al-ʿArabiyyah, 1944.

Harawī, Aḥmad ibn Muḥammad. *Al-Gharībayn fī l-Qurʾān wa-l-ḥadīth*. Edited by Aḥmad Farīd al-Mizyadī. 6 vols. Riyadh: Maktabat Nizār Muṣṭafā l-Bāz, 1999.

Hawking, Stephen. *A Brief History of Time*. New York: Bantam, 1998.

Hirtenstein, Stephen. "*Dhawq*." In *Encyclopaedia Islamica*.

Al-Ḥusaynī, Muḥammad ibn Muḥammad. *Al-Tanwīr: Sharḥ al-Jāmiʿ al-ṣaghīr*. Edited by Muḥammad Ibrāhīm. 11 vols. Riyadh: Maktabat Dār al-Salām, 2011.

Ibn ʿAbd Rabbihi. *Al-ʿIqd al-farīd*. Edited by Aḥmad Amīn, Aḥmad al-Zayn, and Ibrāhīm al-Abyārī. 7 vols. Beirut: Dār al-Kitāb al-ʿArabī, 1990–91.

Ibn Abī Shaybah. *Al-Muṣannaf*. Edited by Ḥamad ibn ʿAbd Allāh al-Jumuʿah and Muḥammad ibn Ibrāhīm al-Luḥaydān. 16 vols. Riyadh: Maktabat al-Rushd, 2004.

Ibn ʿAsākir. *Tārīkh madīnat Dimashq*. Edited by ʿUmar ibn Gharāmah al-ʿUmrawī. 80 vols. Beirut: Dār al-Fikr, 1995–98.

Ibn Mājah. *Sunan*. Vol. 8 of *Jamʿ jawāmiʿ al-aḥādīth*.

Ibn al-Muʿtazz. *Dīwān*. Edited by Karam al-Bustānī. Beirut: Dār Ṣādir, 1961.

Al-Iṣfahānī, Abū l-Faraj. *Kitāb al-Aghānī*. Edited by ʿAbd al-Karīm al-ʿAzbāwī et al. 24 vols. Cairo: Dār-Kutub al-Miṣriyyah, 1927–38.

Al-Iṣfahānī, Abū Nuʿaym. *Ḥilyat al-awliyāʾ*. 11 vols. Beirut: Dār al-Fikr, 1996.

Al-Iṣfahānī, al-Rāghib. *Muḥāḍarāt al-udabāʾ wa-muḥāwarāt al-shuʿarāʾ wa-l-bulaghāʾ*. Edited by Sajīʿ al-Jubaylī. 4 vols. Beirut: Dār al-Kutub al-ʿIlmiyyah, 2009.

Izutsu, Toshihiko. "Creation and the Timeless Order of Things: A Study in the Mystical Philosophy of ʿAyn al-Qudat Hamadani." *The Philosophical Forum* 4, no. 1 (1972): 124–40.

———. "Mysticism and the Linguistic Problem of Equivocation in the Thought of ʿAyn al-Qudat Hamadani." *Studia Islamica* 31 (1970): 153–70.

Jamʿ jawāmiʿ al-aḥādīth wa-l-asānīd wa-maknaz al-siḥāḥ wa-l-sunan wa-l-masānīd. Vaduz, Liechtenstein: Jamʿiyyat al-Maknaz al-Islāmī, 2000.

Al-Kindī, Abū Yaʿqūb. *Al-Kindi's Metaphysics*. Translated by Alfred Ivry. Albany, NY: SUNY Press, 1974.

Kaukua, Jari. "Post-Classical Islamic Philosophy—A Contradiction in Terms?" *Nazariyat* 6, no. 2 (2020): 1–21.

Keeler, Annabel. "Wisdom in Controversy: Paradox and the Paradoxical in Sayings of Abū Yazīd al-Bisṭāmī (d. 234/848 or 261/875)." *Journal of Sufi Studies* 7, nos. 1–2 (2018): 1–26.

Labīd ibn Rabīʿah. *Dīwān*. Beirut: Dār Ṣādir, n.d.

Landolt, Hermann. "ʿAyn al-Quḍāt al-Hamadhānī 1: Life and Work." In *Encyclopaedia of Islam*, 3rd ed.

———. "Early Evidence for Nāṣir-i Khusraw's Poetry in Sufism: ʿAyn al-Quḍāt's Letter on the Taʿlīmīs." In *Fortresses of the Intellect: Ismaili and Other Islamic Studies in Honour of Farhad Daftary*, edited by Omar Alí-de-Unzaga, 369–86. London: I. B. Tauris in association with The Institute of Ismaili Studies, 2011.

———. "Ghazālī and 'Religionswissenschaft': Some Notes on the *Mishkāt al-Anwār* for Professor Charles J. Adams." *Asiatische Studien* 45, no. 1 (1991): 19–72.

Lewisohn, Leonard. "In Quest of Annihilation: Imaginalization and Mystical Death in the *Tamhīdāt* of ʿAyn al-Quḍāt Hamadhānī." In *The Heritage of Sufism*, edited by Leonard Lewisohn (vols. 1–3) and David Morgan (vol. 3), 1:285–336. 3 vols. Oxford: Oneworld, 2001.

Lumbard, Joseph. *Aḥmad al-Ghazālī, Remembrance, and the Metaphysics of Love*. Albany, NY: SUNY Press, 2016.

Maghsoudlou, Salimeh. "Étude des doctrines du nom dans *al-Maqṣad al-asnā* d'al-Ghazālī et de leur origine théologique et grammaticale." *Studia Islamica* 112, no. 1 (2017): 29–75.

———. "La pensée de ʿAyn al-Quḍāt al-Hamadānī (m. 525/1131), entre avicennisme et héritage ġazālien." PhD diss., École Pratique des Hautes Études, 2016.

Al-Marzūqī, Abū ʿAlī Aḥmad ibn Muḥammad. *Sharḥ Dīwān al-Ḥamāsah*. Edited by Aḥmad Amīn. 2 vols. Beirut: Dār al-Jīl, 1991.

Maybudī, Rashīd al-Dīn. *The Unveiling of the Mysteries and the Provision of the Pious*. Partial English translation by William Chittick. Louisville, KY: Fons Vitae, 2015.

McGinnis, Jon. *Avicenna*. New York: Oxford University Press, 2010.

Murata, Sachiko. *The Tao of Islam: A Sourcebook on Gender Relationships in Islamic Thought*. Albany, NY: SUNY Press, 1992.

Muslim. *Ṣaḥīḥ*. Vol. 4 of *Jamʿ jawāmiʿ al-aḥādīth*.

Al-Mutanabbī, *Dīwān*. Edited by Karam al-Bustānī. Beirut: Dār Bayrūt, 1983.

Nasr, Seyyed Hossein. "The Heart of the Faithful Is the Throne of the All-Merciful." In *Paths to the Heart: Sufism and the Christian East*, edited by James Cutsinger, 32–45. Bloomington, IN: World Wisdom, 2002.

———. *An Introduction to Islamic Cosmological Doctrines*. Albany, NY: SUNY Press, 1993.

———. "Mystical Philosophy in Islam." In *Routledge Encyclopedia of Philosophy*.

———, Caner Dagli, Maria Dakake, Joseph Lumbard, and Mohammed Rustom, eds. *The Study Quran: A New Translation and Commentary*. New York: HarperOne, 2015.

Ormsby, Eric. "The Taste of Truth: The Structure of Experience in al-Ghazālī's *al-Munqidh min al-ḍalāl*." In *Islamic Studies Presented to Charles J. Adams*, edited by Wael Hallaq and Donald Little, 133–52. Leiden: Brill, 1991.

Pourjavady, Nasrollah, *ʿAyn al-Quḍāt wa-ustādān-i ū*. Tehran: Intishārāt-i Asāṭīr, 1995.

———. "Introduction," iii–xii. In Pourjavady, ed., *Majmūʿah-yi falsafī-yi Marāghah*.

———, ed. *Majmūʿah-yi falsafī-yi Marāghah*. Tehran: Markaz-i Nashr-i Dānishgāhī, 2002.

Pūrnāmdāryān, Taqī and Mīnā Ḥafīẓī. "Nigāhī ba-taṣḥīḥ-i Tamhīdāt pas az nīm qarn." *Nāmah-yi farhangistān* 16, no. 2 (2010): 118–32.

Al-Qurṭubī, Abū ʿUmar Yūsuf. *Bahjat al-majālis wa-uns al-mujālis*. Edited by Muḥammad Mursī al-Khūlī. 2 vols. Beirut: Dār al-Kutub al-ʿIlmiyyah, 1982.

Al-Qushayrī, Abū l-Qāsim. *Al-Risālah al-Qushayriyyah*. Edited by Anas Muḥammad ʿAdnān al-Sharafāwī. Jeddah: Dār al-Minhāj, 2017.

Renard, John. *Friends of God: Images of Piety, Commitment, and Servanthood*. Berkeley, CA: University of California Press, 2008.

Routledge Encyclopedia of Philosophy. Edited by Edward Craig. New York: Routledge, 1998.

Rustom, Mohammed. "ʿAyn al-Quḍāt." In *Stanford Encyclopedia of Philosophy*.

———. "ʿAyn al-Quḍāt between Divine Jealousy and Political Intrigue." *Journal of Sufi Studies* 7, nos. 1–2 (2018): 47–73.

———. "Devil's Advocate: ʿAyn al-Quḍāt's Defence of Iblis in Context." *Studia Islamica* 115, no. 1 (2020): 65–100.

———. "Ibn ʿArabī's Letter to Fakhr al-Dīn al-Rāzī: A Study and Translation." *Oxford Journal of Islamic Studies* 25, no. 2 (2014): 113–37.

———. *Inrushes of the Heart: The Sufi Philosophy of ʿAyn al-Quḍāt*. Albany, NY: SUNY Press, in press.

———. "Philosophical Sufism." In *The Routledge Companion to Islamic Philosophy*, edited by Richard Taylor and Luis Xavier López-Farjeat, 399–411. New York: Routledge, 2016.

———. "Psychology, Eschatology, and Imagination in Mullā Ṣadrā Shīrāzī's Commentary on the *Ḥadīth* of Awakening." *Islam and Science* 5, no. 1 (2007): 9–22.

———. "Qur'anic Eschatology." In *The Routledge Companion to the Qur'an*, edited by George Archer, Maria Dakake, and Daniel Madigan, 69–79. New York: Routledge, 2022.

Safi, Omid. *The Politics of Knowledge in Premodern Islam: Negotiating Ideology and Religious Inquiry*. Chapel Hill: University of North Carolina Press, 2006.

———. "The Sufi Path of Love in Iran and India." In *A Pearl in Wine: Essays on the Life, Music and Sufism of Hazrat Inayat Khan*, edited by Pirzade Zia Inayat Khan, 221–66. New Lebanon, NY: Omega, 2001.

Samʿānī, Aḥmad. *The Repose of the Spirits: A Sufi Commentary on the Divine Names*. Translated by William Chittick. Albany, NY: SUNY Press, 2019.

Al-Sarrāj, Abū Naṣr. *Kitāb al-Lumaʿ fī l-taṣawwuf*. Edited by R. A. Nicholson. London: Luzac, 1914.

Schimmel, Annemarie. *Mystical Dimensions of Islam*. Chapel Hill: University of North Carolina Press, 1975.

Shajjārī, Murtaḍā. "Maʿrifat az dīdgāh-i ʿAyn al-Quḍāt." *Faṣl-nāmah-yi adabiyyāt-i ʿirfānī wa-usṭūrah-shinākhtī* 6, no. 20 (2010): 85–112.

Al-Sharīf al-Raḍī. *Dīwān*. Edited by Yūsuf Shukrī Farḥāt. 2 vols. Beirut: Dār al-Jīl, 1995.

Shihadeh, Ayman. "Classical Ashʿarī Anthropology: Body, Life, and Spirit." *Muslim World* 102, nos. 3–4 (2012): 433–77.

Shushtarī, Nūr Allāh. *Majālis al-muʾminīn*. Edited by Ibrāhīm ʿArabpūr. Mashhad, Iran: Bunyād-i Pizhūhish-hā-yi Islāmī, 2013–14.

Al-Sīrjānī, Abū l-Ḥasan. *Sufism, Black and White: A Critical Edition of Kitāb al-Bayāḍ wa-l-Sawād of Abū l-Ḥasan al-Sīrjānī (d. ca. 470/1077)*. Edited by Bilal Orfali and Nada Saab. Leiden: Brill: 2012.

Stanford Encyclopedia of Philosophy. Edited by Edward Zalta. http://plato.stanford.edu.

Al-Suhrawardī, Shihāb al-Dīn. *The Philosophy of Illumination*. Translated by John Walbridge and Hossein Ziai. Provo, UT: Brigham Young University Press, 1999.

Al-Ṣūlī, Abū Bakr. *Akhbār al-Buḥturī*. Edited by Ṣāliḥ al-Ashtar. Damascus: Maṭbūʿāt al-Majmaʿ al-ʿIlmī al-ʿArabī, 1958.

Al-Ṭabarānī, Sulaymān ibn Aḥmad. *Al-Muʿjam al-kabīr*. Edited by ʿAbd al-Majīd al-Salafī. 25 vols. Cairo: Maktabat Ibn Taymiyyah, 1994.

Al-Thaʿālibī, Abū Manṣūr. *Yatīmat al-dahr*. Edited by Mufīd Muḥammad Qumayḥah. 5 vols. Beirut: Dār al-Kutub al-ʿIlmiyyah, 2000.

Tirmidhī. *Sunan*. Vol. 6 of *Jamʿ jawāmiʿ al-aḥādīth*.

Turner, Denys. *Faith, Reason and the Existence of God.* New York: Cambridge University Press, 2004.

Al-Tustarī, Sahl ibn ʿAbd Allāh. *Tafsīr al-Tustarī.* Translated by Annabel and Ali Keeler. Louisville, KY: Fons Vitae, 2011.

ʿUsayrān, ʿAfīf. "Muqaddimah-yi muṣaḥḥiḥ." In ʿAyn al-Quḍāt, *Tamhīdāt,* 1–192.

———. "Muqaddimat al-muṣaḥḥiḥ." In ʿAyn al-Quḍāt, *Zubdat al-ḥaqāʾiq*, 1–73.

Wakelnig, Elvira, ed. and trans. *A Philosophy Reader from the Circle of Miskawayh.* Cambridge: Cambridge University Press, 2014.

Wisnovsky, Robert. "Essence and Existence in the Eleventh- and Twelfth-Century Islamic East (*Mašriq*): A Sketch." In *The Arabic, Hebrew and Latin Reception of Avicenna's Metaphysics*, edited by Dag Nikolaus Hasse and Amos Bertolacci, 27–50. Berlin: De Gruyter, 2012.

Wolfson, Harry. *The Philosophy of the Kalam.* Cambridge, MA: Harvard University Press, 1976.

Yāqūt al-Ḥamawī. *Muʿjam al-buldān.* 5 vols. Beirut: Dār Ṣādir, 1977–93.

Al-Yāzijī, Naṣīf. *Al-ʿArf al-ṭayyib fī Sharḥ Dīwān Abī l-Ṭayyib.* Edited by ʿUmar Fārūq al-Ṭabbāʿ. Beirut: Dār al-Arqam, 1995.

Yūsuf-i Thānī, Maḥmūd and Ḥasan Mahdīpūr. "Tabyīn-i kathrat wa-waḥdat-i wujūd dar andīshah-yi ʿAyn al-Quḍāt Hamadānī bar asās-i ṭawr-i ʿaql wa-ṭawr-i warā-yi ʿaql." *Jāwīdān khirad* 21, no. 4 (2012): 135–64.

Further Reading

Ali, Mukhtar H. *Philosophical Sufism: An Introduction to the School of Ibn al-ʿArabī*. London: Routledge, 2021.

Chittick, William. *The Heart of Islamic Philosophy: The Quest for Self-Knowledge in the Writings of Afḍal al-Dīn Kāshānī*. New York: Oxford University Press, 2001.

Dagli, Caner. *Ibn al-ʿArabī and Islamic Intellectual Culture: From Mysticism to Philosophy*. New York: Routledge, 2016.

Corbin, Henry. *En islam iranien*. 4 vols. Paris: Gallimard, 1971–72.

Faruque, Muhammad. *Sculpting the Self: Islam, Selfhood, and Human Flourishing*. Ann Arbor: University of Michigan Press, 2021.

Ha'iri Yazdi, Mahdi. *Universal Science: An Introduction to Islamic Metaphysics*. Translated by John Cooper. Edited by Saiyad Nizamuddin Ahmad. Leiden: Brill, 2017.

Izutsu, Toshihiko. *Creation and the Timeless Order of Things: Essays in Mystical Philosophy*. Ashland, OR: White Cloud Press, 1994.

Kaukua, Jari. *Self-Awareness in Islamic Philosophy: Avicenna and Beyond*. Cambridge: Cambridge University Press, 2015.

Koca, Özgür. *Islam, Causality, and Freedom: From the Medieval to the Modern Era*. New York: Cambridge University Press, 2020.

Landolt, Hermann. *Recherches en spiritualité iranienne*. Tehran: University of Tehran Press, 2005.

Nasr, Seyyed Hossein. *Knowledge and the Sacred*. Albany, NY: SUNY Press, 1989.

Nasr, Seyyed Hossein and Mehdi Aminrazavi, eds. *An Anthology of Philosophy in Persia*. Vol. 4, *From the School of Illumination to Philosophical Mysticism*. London: I. B. Tauris in association with The Institute of Ismaili Studies, 2012.

Orfali, Bilal, Atif Khalil, and Mohammed Rustom, eds. *Mysticism and Ethics in Islam*. Beirut: American University of Beirut Press, 2022.

Rustom, Mohammed. "The Great Chain of Consciousness: Do All Things Possess Awareness?" *Renovatio* 1, no. 1 (2017): 49–60.

Shah-Kazemi, Reza. *Paths to Transcendence*. Bloomington, IN: World Wisdom, 2006.

Shihadeh, Ayman, ed. *Sufism and Theology*. Edinburgh: Edinburgh University Press, 2007.

Tabataba'i, Sayyid Muhammad Husayn. *The Elements of Islamic Metaphysics*. 2nd ed. Translated by Sayyid 'Ali Quli Qara'i. London: ICAS Press, 2018.

Todd, Richard. *The Sufi Doctrine of Man: The Metaphysical Anthropology of Ṣadr al-Dīn al-Qūnawī*. Leiden: Brill, 2014.

Zargar, Cyrus. *The Polished Mirror: Storytelling and the Pursuit of Virtue in Islamic Philosophy and Sufism*. London: Oneworld, 2017.

Index of Qur’anic Verses

Paragraph numbers marked with * indicate the reference is a paraphrase or allusion rather than a literal quotaion.

Index

About the NYU Abu Dhabi Institute

The Library of Arabic Literature is supported by a grant from the NYU Abu Dhabi Institute, a major hub of intellectual and creative activity and advanced research. The Institute hosts academic conferences, workshops, lectures, film series, performances, and other public programs directed both to audiences within the UAE and to the worldwide academic and research community. It is a center of the scholarly community for Abu Dhabi, bringing together faculty and researchers from institutions of higher learning throughout the region.

NYU Abu Dhabi, through the NYU Abu Dhabi Institute, is a world-class center of cutting-edge research, scholarship, and cultural activity. The Institute creates singular opportunities for leading researchers from across the arts, humanities, social sciences, sciences, engineering, and the professions to carry out creative scholarship and conduct research on issues of major disciplinary, multidisciplinary, and global significance.

About the Typefaces

The Arabic body text is set in DecoType Naskh, designed by Thomas Milo and Mirjam Somers, based on an analysis of five centuries of Ottoman manuscript practice. The exceptionally legible result is the first and only typeface in a style that fully implements the principles of script grammar (*qawāʿid al-khaṭṭ*).

The Arabic footnote text is set in DecoType Emiri, drawn by Mirjam Somers, based on the metal typeface in the naskh style that was cut for the 1924 Cairo edition of the Qur'an.

Both Arabic typefaces in this series are controlled by a dedicated font layout engine. ACE, the Arabic Calligraphic Engine, invented by Peter Somers, Thomas Milo, and Mirjam Somers of DecoType, first operational in 1985, pioneered the principle followed by later smart font layout technologies such as OpenType, which is used for all other typefaces in this series.

The Arabic text was set with WinSoft Tasmeem, a sophisticated user interface for DecoType ACE inside Adobe InDesign. Tasmeem was conceived and created by Thomas Milo (DecoType) and Pascal Rubini (WinSoft) in 2005.

The English text is set in Adobe Text, a new and versatile text typeface family designed by Robert Slimbach for Western (Latin, Greek, Cyrillic) typesetting. Its workhorse qualities make it perfect for a wide variety of applications, especially for longer passages of text where legibility and economy are important. Adobe Text bridges the gap between calligraphic Renaissance types of the 15th and 16th centuries and high-contrast Modern styles of the 18th century, taking many of its design cues from early post-Renaissance Baroque transitional types cut by designers such as Christoffel van Dijck, Nicolaus Kis, and William Caslon. While grounded in classical form, Adobe Text is also a statement of contemporary utilitarian design, well suited to a wide variety of print and on-screen applications.

Titles Published by the Library of Arabic Literature

For more details on individual titles, visit www.libraryofarabicliterature.org

Classical Arabic Literature: A Library of Arabic Literature Anthology
Selected and translated by Geert Jan van Gelder **(2012)**

A Treasury of Virtues: Sayings, Sermons, and Teachings of ʿAlī, by al-Qāḍī al-Quḍāʿī, with the **One Hundred Proverbs** attributed to al-Jāḥiẓ
Edited and translated by Tahera Qutbuddin **(2013)**

The Epistle on Legal Theory, by al-Shāfiʿī
Edited and translated by Joseph E. Lowry **(2013)**

Leg over Leg, by Aḥmad Fāris al-Shidyāq
Edited and translated by Humphrey Davies **(4 volumes; 2013–14)**

Virtues of the Imām Aḥmad ibn Ḥanbal, by Ibn al-Jawzī
Edited and translated by Michael Cooperson **(2 volumes; 2013–15)**

The Epistle of Forgiveness, by Abū l-ʿAlāʾ al-Maʿarrī
Edited and translated by Geert Jan van Gelder and Gregor Schoeler **(2 volumes; 2013–14)**

The Principles of Sufism, by ʿĀʾishah al-Bāʿūniyyah
Edited and translated by Th. Emil Homerin **(2014)**

The Expeditions: An Early Biography of Muḥammad, by Maʿmar ibn Rāshid
Edited and translated by Sean W. Anthony **(2014)**

Two Arabic Travel Books
Accounts of China and India, by Abū Zayd al-Sīrāfī
Edited and translated by Tim Mackintosh-Smith **(2014)**
Mission to the Volga, by Aḥmad ibn Faḍlān
Edited and translated by James Montgomery **(2014)**

Disagreements of the Jurists: A Manual of Islamic Legal Theory, by al-Qāḍī al-Nuʿmān
Edited and translated by Devin J. Stewart **(2015)**

Consorts of the Caliphs: Women and the Court of Baghdad, by Ibn al-Sāʿī
Edited by Shawkat M. Toorawa and translated by the Editors of the Library of Arabic Literature **(2015)**

What ʿĪsā ibn Hishām Told Us, by Muḥammad al-Muwayliḥī
Edited and translated by Roger Allen **(2 volumes; 2015)**

The Life and Times of Abū Tammām, by Abū Bakr Muḥammad ibn Yaḥyā al-Ṣūlī
Edited and translated by Beatrice Gruendler **(2015)**

The Sword of Ambition: Bureaucratic Rivalry in Medieval Egypt, by ʿUthmān ibn Ibrāhīm al-Nābulusī
Edited and translated by Luke Yarbrough **(2016)**

Brains Confounded by the Ode of Abū Shādūf Expounded, by Yūsuf al-Shirbīnī
Edited and translated by Humphrey Davies **(2 volumes; 2016)**

Light in the Heavens: Sayings of the Prophet Muḥammad, by al-Qāḍī al-Quḍāʿī
Edited and translated by Tahera Qutbuddin **(2016)**

Risible Rhymes, by Muḥammad ibn Maḥfūẓ al-Sanhūrī
Edited and translated by Humphrey Davies **(2016)**

A Hundred and One Nights
Edited and translated by Bruce Fudge **(2016)**

The Excellence of the Arabs, by Ibn Qutaybah
Edited by James E. Montgomery and Peter Webb
Translated by Sarah Bowen Savant and Peter Webb **(2017)**

Scents and Flavors: A Syrian Cookbook
Edited and translated by Charles Perry **(2017)**

Arabian Satire: Poetry from 18th-Century Najd, by Ḥmēdān al-Shwēʿir
Edited and translated by Marcel Kurpershoek **(2017)**

In Darfur: An Account of the Sultanate and Its People, by Muḥammad ibn ʿUmar al-Tūnisī
Edited and translated by Humphrey Davies **(2 volumes; 2018)**

War Songs, by ʿAntarah ibn Shaddād
Edited by James E. Montgomery
Translated by James E. Montgomery with Richard Sieburth **(2018)**

Arabian Romantic: Poems on Bedouin Life and Love, by ʿAbdallāh ibn Sbayyil
Edited and translated by Marcel Kurpershoek **(2018)**

Dīwān ʿAntarah ibn Shaddād: A Literary-Historical Study
By James E. Montgomery **(2018)**

Stories of Piety and Prayer: Deliverance Follows Adversity, by al-Muḥassin ibn ʿAlī al-Tanūkhī
Edited and translated by Julia Bray **(2019)**

The Philosopher Responds: An Intellectual Correspondence from the Tenth Century, by Abū Ḥayyān al-Tawḥīdī and Abū ʿAlī Miskawayh
Edited by Bilal Orfali and Maurice A. Pomerantz
Translated by Sophia Vasalou and James E. Montgomery **(2 volumes; 2019)**

Tajrīd sayf al-himmah li-stikhrāj mā fī dhimmat al-dhimmah: A Scholarly Edition of ʿUthmān ibn Ibrāhīm al-Nābulusī's Text
By Luke Yarbrough **(2020)**

The Discourses: Reflections on History, Sufism, Theology, and Literature—Volume One, by al-Ḥasan al-Yūsī
Edited and translated by Justin Stearns **(2020)**

Impostures, by al-Ḥarīrī
Translated by Michael Cooperson **(2020)**

Maqāmāt Abī Zayd al-Sarūjī, by al-Ḥarīrī
Edited by Michael Cooperson **(2020)**

The Yoga Sutras of Patañjali, by Abū Rayḥān al-Bīrūnī
Edited and translated by Mario Kozah **(2020)**

The Book of Charlatans, by Jamāl al-Dīn ʿAbd al-Raḥīm al-Jawbarī
Edited by Manuela Dengler
Translated by Humphrey Davies **(2020)**

A Physician on the Nile, by ʿAbd al-Laṭīf al-Baghdādī
Edited and translated by Tim Mackintosh-Smith **(2021)**

The Book of Travels, by Ḥannā Diyāb
Edited by Johannes Stephan
Translated by Elias Muhanna **(2 volumes; 2021)**

Kalīlah and Dimnah: Fables of Virtue and Vice, by Ibn al-Muqaffaʿ
Edited by Michael Fishbein
Translated by Michael Fishbein and James E. Montgomery **(2021)**

Love, Death, Fame: Poetry and Lore from the Emirati Oral Tradition, by al-Māyidī ibn Ẓāhir
Edited and translated by Marcel Kurpershoek **(2022)**

The Essence of Reality: A Defense of Philosophical Sufism, by ʿAyn al-Quḍāt
Edited and translated by Mohammed Rustom **(2022)**

English-only Paperbacks

Leg over Leg, by Aḥmad Fāris al-Shidyāq **(2 volumes; 2015)**
The Expeditions: An Early Biography of Muḥammad, by Maʿmar ibn Rāshid **(2015)**
The Epistle on Legal Theory: A Translation of al-Shāfiʿī's *Risālah*, by al-Shāfiʿī **(2015)**
The Epistle of Forgiveness, by Abū l-ʿAlāʾ al-Maʿarrī **(2016)**
The Principles of Sufism, by ʿĀʾishah al-Bāʿūniyyah **(2016)**
A Treasury of Virtues: Sayings, Sermons, and Teachings of ʿAlī, by al-Qāḍī al-Quḍāʿī, with the **One Hundred Proverbs** attributed to al-Jāḥiẓ **(2016)**
The Life of Ibn Ḥanbal, by Ibn al-Jawzī **(2016)**
Mission to the Volga, by Ibn Faḍlān **(2017)**
Accounts of China and India, by Abū Zayd al-Sīrāfī **(2017)**
A Hundred and One Nights (2017)
Consorts of the Caliphs: Women and the Court of Baghdad, by Ibn al-Sāʿī **(2017)**
Disagreements of the Jurists: A Manual of Islamic Legal Theory, by al-Qāḍī al-Nuʿmān **(2017)**
What ʿĪsā ibn Hishām Told Us, by Muḥammad al-Muwayliḥī **(2018)**
War Songs, by ʿAntarah ibn Shaddād **(2018)**
The Life and Times of Abū Tammām, by Abū Bakr Muḥammad ibn Yaḥyā al-Ṣūlī **(2018)**
The Sword of Ambition, by ʿUthmān ibn Ibrāhīm al-Nābulusī **(2019)**

Brains Confounded by the Ode of Abū Shādūf Expounded: Volume One, by Yūsuf al-Shirbīnī (2019)

Brains Confounded by the Ode of Abū Shādūf Expounded: Volume Two, by Yūsuf al-Shirbīnī and **Risible Rhymes**, by Muḥammad ibn Maḥfūẓ al-Sanhūrī (2019)

The Excellence of the Arabs, by Ibn Qutaybah (2019)

Light in the Heavens: Sayings of the Prophet Muḥammad, by al-Qāḍī al-Quḍāʿī (2019)

Scents and Flavors: A Syrian Cookbook (2020)

Arabian Satire: Poetry from 18th-Century Najd, by Ḥmēdān al-Shwēʿir (2020)

In Darfur: An Account of the Sultanate and Its People, by Muḥammad al-Tūnisī (2020)

Arabian Romantic: Poems on Bedouin Life and Love, by ʿAbdallāh ibn Sbayyil (2020)

The Philosopher Responds, by Abū Ḥayyān al-Tawḥīdī and Abū ʿAlī Miskawayh (2021)

Impostures, by al-Ḥarīrī (2021)

The Discourses: Reflections on History, Sufism, Theology, and Literature—Volume One, by al-Ḥasan al-Yūsī (2021)

The Book of Charlatans, by Jamāl al-Dīn ʿAbd al-Raḥīm al-Jawbarī (2022)

The Yoga Sutras of Patañjali, by Abū Rayḥān al-Bīrūnī (2022)

About the Editor–Translator

Mohammed Rustom is Professor of Islamic Thought at Carleton University. A specialist in Sufism, Islamic philosophy, and Qur'anic exegesis, he is author of the award-winning book *The Triumph of Mercy: Philosophy and Scripture in Mullā Ṣadrā* (2012), co-editor of *The Study Quran: A New Translation and Commentary* (2015), translator of Abū Ḥāmid al-Ghazālī, *The Condemnation of Pride and Self-Admiration* (2018), and author of *Inrushes of the Heart: The Sufi Philosophy of ʿAyn al-Quḍāt* (2022).

Lightning Source UK Ltd.
Milton Keynes UK
UKHW012006230222
399139UK00003B/98/J

9 781479 816590